*Eschatological Relationships
and Jesus in Ben F. Meyer,
N. T. Wright and
Progressive Dispensationalism*

Eschatological Relationships and Jesus in Ben F. Meyer, N. T. Wright and Progressive Dispensationalism

J. Richard Fountain

WIPF & STOCK · Eugene, Oregon

ESCHATOLOGICAL RELATIONSHIPS AND JESUS IN BEN F. MEYER, N. T. WRIGHT, AND PROGRESSIVE DISPENSATIONALISM

Copyright © 2016 J. Richard Fountain. All rights reserved. Except for brief quotations in critical publications or reviews, no part of this book may be reproduced in any manner without prior written permission from the publisher. Write: Permissions, Wipf and Stock Publishers, 199 W. 8th Ave., Suite 3, Eugene, OR 97401.

Wipf & Stock
An Imprint of Wipf and Stock Publishers
199 W. 8th Ave., Suite 3
Eugene, OR 97401

www.wipfandstock.com

PAPERBACK ISBN: 978-1-62564-001-7
HARDCOVER ISBN: 978-1-4982-8594-0

Manufactured in the U.S.A.   JULY 28, 2016

Contents

Preface | vii
Acknowledgments | ix
Abbreviations | x

1. Introduction | 1
2. How Apocalyptic Literature Is Read in Relation to Eschatology | 18
3. Antecedents and Apocalyptic Literature in Ben F. Meyer's Theological Construct | 66
4. Antecedents and Apocalyptic Literature in N. T. Wright's Theological Construct | 104
5. The Approach of Progressive Dispensationalism to Eschatological Relationships | 143
6. Hermeneutics and Exegesis of Mark 13:1–2 and 13:24–27 | 171
7. Summary and Conclusion | 201

Appendices
1. Establishing a Synoptic Framework | 209
2. Sequence and Literary Relationships in the Synoptic Gospels for Prophetic and Apocalyptic Sayings with Priority Given to Mark's Content and Order | 216
3. Biblical Historical Pattern | 220

Bibliography | 223
Index of Scripture and Other Jewish Literature | 241

Preface

This book began as a doctoral dissertation by the same title. I invite you to consider the explanations about the restoration of Israel and eschatology in apocalyptic literature provided by both Ben Meyer, N.T. Wright, and Progressive Dispensationalism. I enter this conversation as a Progressive Dispensationalist and the Gospel of Mark is my starting point.

Mark combines the Jesus tradition with the Hebrew Scriptures. It is his innovative work I find interesting. He serves to show how Jesus' teaching is different to Judaism broadly speaking while Matthew and Luke, make fascinating connections with Mark. There is enough difference between Mark and the Jewish Apocalyptic Tradition to warrant a separate strand of apocalyptic tradition. The Jesus tradition has a unique sequence of eschatology in apocalyptic literature, which is what we see transferred from Mark to Matthew and Luke. I give examples where the eschatological settings are different in Matthew and in Luke from those in Mark's gospel. Apocalyptic Eschatology, the transfer of the tradition that Mark understand as a whole stratum--is everywhere in the other Synoptic Gospels. It is helpful in a way because Matthew and Luke don't need to start from scratch, yet it is so pervasive that as linguistic baggage, it colours everything they do with their eschatology. Often the synoptic writers go beyond Mark by developing their own oral traditions about Jesus, yet the fact they are stuck with Mark's sequence for preserving their eschatology is confirmed in detail again and again. These passages can be some of the toughest passages to interpret, but despite all the challenges, these literary relationships are worth exploring.

I so appreciate those who have made this work possible. I would like to thank Peter Lineham, Yve Cruickshank, and Mikel Del Rosario for reading early drafts of my manuscript and providing editorial assistance. I am grateful to Wipf and Stock Publishers who accepted the proposal for this book. Finally, I hope this work continues to bring to people's attention the hermeneutical issues surrounding Israel and eschatology.

Acknowledgments

IN ADDITION TO THE wonderful support from my family I am deeply indebted to many for the ideas contained in this study. Two teachers at the forefront are Dr. Darrell Bock and Dr. Elliot Johnson, who taught me hermeneutics in my first class in the doctoral program at DTS. The tone they set in our class discussion and their attention to the issues at hand were an inspiration to me and encouraged me to examine the relevance of hermeneutics to biblical and theological studies. Thanks must go also to Drs. Jay Smith, Dan Wallace, Joe Fantin, and Buist Fanning for their insights in the seminar on the Apocalyptic Literature. My hope is that this study will contribute to a greater appreciation for Jesus and Christian hope, and to a better understanding apocalyptic eschatology in the Gospels.

Abbreviations

ABRL	Anchor Bible Reference Library
AE	Apocalyptic Eschatology
Abot R. Nat.	Abot de Rabbi Nathan
Aland	Aland, Kurt. *Synopsis of the Four Gospels: Greek-English Edition of the Synopsis Quattuor Evangeliorum.* 10th ed. Stuttgart: German Bible Society, 1993.
Ant.	Josephus, *Antiquities of the Jews*
Apoc. Ab.	Apocalypse of Abraham
Bar	Baruch
BDAG	Bauer, W., F. W. Danker, W. F. Arndt, and F. W. Gingrich. *Greek-English Lexicon of the New Testament and Other Early Christian Literature.* 3rd ed. Chicago: University of Chicago Press, 1999.
BDF	Blass, F., A. Debrunner, and R. Funk. *A Greek Grammar of the New Testament and Other Early Christian Literature.* Chicago: University of Chicago Press, 1961.
BFCT	Beiträge zur Förderung christlicher Theologie
BJRL	*Bulletin of the John Rylands University Library of Manchester*
BR	*Biblical Research*
BZ	*Biblische Zeitschrift*
CD	Cairo Genizah Copy of the Damascus Document

Abbreviations

CBQ	*Catholic Biblical Quarterly*
CurTM	*Currents in Theology and Mission*
DRev	*Downside Review*
ExpTim	*Expository Times*
EvQ	*Evangelical Quarterly*
FF	*Foundations and Facets Forum*
Greg	*Gregorianum*
ICC	*International Critical Commentary*
Int	*Interpretation*
JAT	*Jewish Apocalyptic Tradition*
JETS	*Journal of the Evangelical Theological Society*
JBL	*Journal of Biblical Literature*
JSHJSup	*Journal for the Study of the Historical Jesus: Supplement Series*
JQR	*Jewish Quarterly Review*
JSJ	*Journal for the Study of Judaism in the Persian, Hellenistic, and Roman Periods*
JSPSup	*Journal for the Study of the Pseudepigrapha: Supplement Series*
JSOT	*Journal for the Study of the Old Testament*
JSNT	*Journal for the Study of the New Testament*
JTC	*Journal for Theology and the Church*
JTS	*Journal of Theological Studies*
Jud	*Judaica*
L.A.E.	*Life of Adam and Eve*
LSJ	Liddell, Henry George, and Robert Scott, comps. *A Greek-English Lexicon*. Rev. and augmented by Henry Stuart Jones and Roderick McKenzie. 9th ed. with a revised supplement 1996, ed. P. G. W. Glare and A. A. Thompson. Oxford: Clarendon, 1940.

Abbreviations

1–2 Macc	1–2 Maccabees
Mart. Ascen. Isa.	Martyrdom and Ascension of Isaiah
MSJ	*The Master's Seminary Journal*
NA^{27}	*Novum Testamentum Graece*, ed. E. Nestle and K. Aland et al., 27th rev. ed.
NET	New English Translation
NJB	New Jerusalem Bible
NLH	*New Literary History*
Neot	*Neotestamentica*
NICNT	New International Commentary on the New Testament
NIDNT	*New International Dictionary of New Testament Theology*
NIGTC	New International Greek Testament Commentary
NIV	New International Version
NKJV	New King James Version
NTS	*New Testament Studies*
NTT	*Norsk Teologisk Tidsskrift*
OAA	Oxford Annotated Apocrypha
OTP	*Old Testament Pseudepigrapha*. Edited by J. H. Charlesworth. 2 vols. Anchor Bible Reference Library. Garden City: Doubleday, 1983.
PD	Progressive Dispensationalism
PE	Prophetic Eschatology
QR	*Quarterly Review*
RB	*Revue biblique*
RHR	*Revue de l'histoire des religions*
RSR	*Recherches de science religieuse*
Sg Three	Song of the Three Young Men
SBL	Society of Biblical Literature

Abbreviations

SBLEJL	Society of Biblical Literature Early Judaism and Its Literature
SBLSymS	Society of Biblical Literature Symposium Series
SBT	Studies in Biblical Theology
SEÅ	*Svensk exegetisk årsbok*
Sir	Sirach/Ecclesiasticus
SJT	*Scottish Journal of Theology*

I

Introduction

The Scope and Intent for the Study on Jesus and Theological Constructs

THIS STUDY IS AN examination of how the theological constructs of Ben F. Meyer and N. T. Wright, in comparison to that of progressive dispensationalism (PD), present the relationship between eschatology and apocalyptic. Specifically, it examines their interpretation of a number of eschatological relationships and Jesus.

Both Meyer and Wright, representatives of the third quest, have written extensively on the historical Jesus and have developed theological constructs.[1] Both Meyer and Wright agree that Jesus was Israel's Messiah and that the goal of Jesus' career was the restoration of Israel.[2] This forms

---

1. Scholars sometimes use the term "model" synonymously with the term "construct," but *theological construct* is the preferred term for this study as it clarifies the nature of the work.

2. By affirming these two statements Meyer and Wright show they have thought through two fundamental questions of historical criticism related to the third quest: the situation in Judaism and Jesus' aims. Wright, *Jesus and the Victory of God*, 90–105; Meyer, *Aims of Jesus*, 175, 202. Though the idea of Jesus' messianic claims is debated in historical Jesus study both Meyer and Wright make this theological presupposition from placing Jesus into the context of historical first-century Judaism and from their reading of the Gospels. Wright's survey of Jewish hope centers on liberation, renewal of the world (which he calls the return from exile), and salvation. There was no uniform messianic expectation, yet Jesus is understood as the Davidic Messiah. Wright, *New Testament and*

the basis for the study of these scholars from the third quest perspective.[3] Where they differ is in how Jesus envisaged this restoration, and how he intended to realize it.[4] Both Meyer and Wright find fulfillment in AD 70. Progressive Dispensationalism sees ultimate fulfillment in the end time.

A broad overview of the constructs reveals that differences exist for reading apocalyptic language within a theological narrative. Ben Meyer is sympathetic to J. Weiss's reading of apocalyptic texts such as Mark 13 and Luke 17:21. Like Weiss, Meyer rejects the "sterility of liberal theology" and seeks to address issues pertinent to the milieu of early Christianity so aligning himself with the *religionsgeschichtlich Schule*.[5] Yet Meyer's understanding of apocalyptic is more complex than Weiss's as he highlights the theme of the restoration of Israel. Meyer draws on Second Temple Jewish traditions about rebuilding the temple and Jesus' temple actions and their meaning.[6] Wright's theory is that Jesus saw himself as ending Israel's continuing exile. He examines Second Temple Jewish traditions on the temple like Meyer but also "enthronement" texts in 1 Enoch which speak about exaltation.[7] PD has developed independently of Meyer and Wright, and has two fundamental differences with Meyer's and Wright's view theologically. These points of difference are (1) the events of AD 70 as presented in the Synoptic Gospels, and (2) the relationship between Israel and the Church.[8] Wright's rejection of a closure in earthly history in the Synoptic Gospels is a significant difference from the progressive dispensational interpretation and understanding of the actual function of the language in Mark 13.[9]

---

the People of God, 307–20; Wright, *Victory of God*, 12, 612, 477–539.

3. Meyer and Wright, along with E. P. Sanders, J. Gnilka and B. Witherington (in contrast to D. Crossan and P. Meier) tend to downplay the importance of noncanonical gospels for their contributing to the historical Jesus tradition. Powell, *Introducing the New Testament*, 11.

4. Meyer, *Aims*, 202.

5. Meyer, *Aims*, 40. See also Buchanan, "Meyer's Support."

6. Meyer, *Aims*, 168–70, 174–202.

7. Wright, *Victory of God*, 615–45, especially 642.

8. See Blaising and Bock, *Dispensationalism, Israel and the Church*.

9. Others question whether or not Wright's thesis about Jesus is too simplistic. See Rowland and Barton, *Apocalyptic in History and Tradition*, 4. Another commentator who questions N. T. Wright's interpretation of figurative language in Mark 13 in terms of its intentionality is R. T. France. France notes Wright among interpreters who find no place in Mark for the traditional doctrine of the Parousia or for "any closure to earthly history." France, *Gospel of Mark*, 32. France makes several points in response. First, the author of Mark lived in a time when an imminent expectation of the Parousia was real. Second,

Introduction

However, Wright and PD agree to use traditional Jewish writings from the Intertestamental period while distinguishing them from Scripture.

The benefits for comparing these constructs with PD for their similarities and dissimilarities are threefold. First, it allows a comparison of how they explore a historical investigation into apocalyptic language, its background, and its potential understanding in a first-century Jewish context. Furthermore comparisons in Christology are possible, specifically, what is the role of Jesus in the OD and what is the function of the Son of Man?

Second, it assists an examination of hermeneutics. Both Meyer and Wright make a serious attempt to address fundamental issues of method in their interpretation of theological narrative (e.g., the author's horizon; see below).[10] In Wright's estimation, Meyer is responsible for introducing sophisticated methods to the third quest movement.[11] As an understudy

---

the Gospel of Mark includes a passage resembling the Parousia language of the other Synoptic Gospels. Third, interpretation must start with an OT perspective and attempt to summarize how the events cohere in Mark's narrative: "In the 'Old Testament' sense of the word, Mark's gospel is full of eschatology" and the OT is about the "fulfillment of God's promises within history." The good news of the fulfillment of the Scriptures, which is signaled in Mark's opening salvo of prophetic testimony (1:2–3), is a recurrent theme throughout the story, not only with reference to Jesus' proclamation and demonstration of God's kingship, leading up to his "Davidic" approach to Jerusalem, but also and especially in the apparent disaster which follows as the Son of Man "goes as it is written of him" (14:21; cf. 9:12; 14:49), so that eventually the stone rejected by the builders may be elevated to become the cornerstone (12:10–11). Through Jesus' death on behalf of many a new covenant is established and the people of God reconstituted (14:22–25). Fourth, this is eschatological language, but it is not the language of the end of the world but rather of a new beginning of the world restored under God's kingship. Mark uses the enthronement language of Dan 7:13–14 to describe the imminent vindication of the rejected Son of Man and his authority at the "right hand of power" (14:62). Fifth, the historical horizon dominating Mark's gospel is bounded by the coming destruction of the temple and all that it stands for and the indefinite period during which the newly regathered people of God will then continue to live under the authority of the enthroned Son of Man (13:24–27). This is a period during which the good news will continue to be proclaimed throughout the world (13:10; 14:9). Sixth, while the language about the "coming of the Son of Man" in 8:38, 13:26, 14:62 (and 13:24–31 overall) does not refer to a Parousia which will mark the end of earthly history, the subject changes to the Parousia in 13:32. Seventh, Jesus' authority, though located in heaven, is "operative within earthly history." See France, *Mark*, 33.

10. Meyer, *Aims*, 76–110; Wright, *People of God*, 31–144. Wright questions our perception of the worldview of first-century Jews, and argues that Israel's apocalyptic hope has been grossly misunderstood by many scholars. What Israel hoped for was not an end to this space-time universe, but the end of her exile under foreign domination. Wright, *People of God*, 284–85.

11. In one of his early books, Wright identifies Meyer as one of the key people in the

Eschatological Relationships and Jesus

of Bernard Lonergan, Meyer was conscious of some missing dimensions of hermeneutics and addressed this extensively in his writings.[12] The hermeneutical similarities and differences between Meyer and Wright are also important for their interpretation of apocalyptic language. Examining Wright's interpretation in light of key antecedents like G. B. Caird is therefore helpful.[13] Tracing this application of hermeneutical theory to understanding Jesus, via the Meyer–Wright connection, is therefore warranted.

Third, a study which draws comparison of theological constructs, by noting continuities and discontinuities at a variety of levels, can help to develop discussion about how the OT relates to the NT[14] and how the Synoptic Gospels relate together.

With this in mind, the study is structured to examine two kinds of questions about eschatological relationships and how apocalyptic is read. First, the questions of formulation: (1) What is apocalyptic eschatology,

---

third quest movement. Wright, *Who Was Jesus?*, 14. See also acknowledgments by Dunn, *Jesus Remembered*, 123.

12. Meyer, *Aims*. This work was followed by a more in-depth look at hermeneutical issues in Meyer, *Critical Realism and the New Testament*. See particularly Meyer, "Relevance of 'Horizon.'" Cf. Hawkin, "Markan Horizon of Meaning." His final major work before his death in 1995 was Meyer, *Reality and Illusion in New Testament Scholarship*.

13. Cf. Ellis, *Making of the New Testament Documents*, 13. Here it is said the tradition with Caird, in claiming that Mark 13 identifies Jesus' Parousia with the destruction of Jerusalem in AD 70, really follows after B. H. Streeter and C. H. Dodd. This was part of the "realized eschatology" which readers then gave an "end-of-time-space-universe" reference in Matt 24–25. Streeter, "Synoptic Criticism and the Eschatological Problem," 425–36; Dodd, *Parables of the Kingdom*, 154–74; Caird (with Hurst), *New Testament Theology*, 243–78, 365; Wright, *Victory of God*, 425–36. For Streeter, first-century Jewish apocalyptic was "the expression," determined by local and temporal conditions, of certain essential "elements of religion." There is a "residuum" of apocalyptic eschatology in the authentic teaching of Jesus, yet Jesus "endorsed with reservations" the details of contemporary Jewish expression. Dodd denies that Jesus foretold a period of waiting between his death and resurrection and his coming glory. The "Parables of Crisis" (i.e., the Faithful and Unfaithful Servants, the waiting Servants, the thief at night, and the Ten Virgins) do not refer to the Second Advent, but represent the paraenesis of the early church. Instead, these parables are set in the context of the "exhortations to be ready," found in 1 Thess 5:2–8 and Eph 5:8–14.

14. Of special interest for this discussion of eschatology is the varying discussion on the kind of "theological presuppositions" which a Jewish audience brought to the text. For an example of greater fulfillment expected from Dan 11:40—12:3 among Qumran readers, see Schultz, *Conquering the World*, 92. In general, see Barrett, "Interpretation of the Old Testament in the New," 380–87; Bock, "Scripture Citing Scripture," 256-62. Meyer adopts a *sensus plenior* ("fuller sense") approach to understanding the limitations of Jesus' prophecy. Meyer, *Aims*, 246.

Introduction

and how exactly does apocalyptic relate to eschatology and to history? (2) How is apocalyptic understood in the history of NT interpretation, and in the study of the historical Jesus? The second set of questions concern the theological constructs and themes which are correlated:[15] (1) What are the components in the various features of history, hermeneutics, and language in each; and (2) How do Meyer and Wright read apocalyptic and correlate it with the theme of the restoration of Israel? So what is the character of the discourse? Is it "early restored Israel" or a "little apocalypse" with apocalyptic Jewish Christian sequence? Specifically, how do they understand the connection between history (Mark 13:2; Jesus' prediction of the destruction of the temple) and Mark's transcendent concerns (Mark 13:24–27)? And where should the discourse be placed in the scheme of early Christianity? An analysis of the progressive dispensational approach, its connections and differences, follows this investigation. The thesis of this study is that the historical crisis and the eschatological crisis are not parallel (the same) historical event but two scenarios and that, for Jesus, a pattern relationship existed between AD 70 and the period of the eschaton so that AD 70 is like the end. AD 70 is an eschatological event in the sense that it is a type of the end. It therefore follows that the language of eschatology in the process of fulfillment is not merely metaphorical. Furthermore, Mark's apocalyptic eschatology in 13:24–27 does not describe a transfer of power to the disciples. Rather, it refers to a universal display of heavenly power; the in-breaking of God's rule, with a visible transformation on behalf of the righteous at the end of time.

---

15. John Meier describes how any criticism is reconstruction. The reconstructions of the Jesus of history from the sources through historical-critical research are "modern abstraction and construct" even though their goal is objectivity; see Meier, *Marginal Jew*, 25. The point of departure between a "theoretical construct" and a theological construct (which attempts a broader outlook) will be examined and argued for by comparing Ben F. Meyer with Bultmann and John P. Meier in chapter 3. In addressing "aims" Meyer is significant for understanding theological constructs. This reliance on goals is spelled out in part 3, *Theological Hermeneutics*, in Meyer, *Reality and Illusion*, 145–49. I will argue Meyer has partly developed a new way of doing theology related to historical Jesus study. The central concern is to apply a theological goal to all that the historical Jesus did and said. Cf. Lawrence, *Linguistics and Theology*. Although the study begins with examining constructs in detail, its wider goal remains a better understanding of the canonical text, historical questions that arise, and how passages cohere with one another.

Justification for this Study

There are reasons for a study of this nature. One set of problems revolves around the confusion between the meaning of apocalypticism, apocalyptic eschatology (hereafter AE) and eschatology. Another set of problems involves the different views on eschatological relationships in the Olivet Discourse. The Synoptic Gospels sometimes report major differences in the content to Jesus' sermon, as the parallels show. When the Bible retells its stories, the question arises where does meaning reside in a given statement or saying. For example, a feature of Matthew's gospel that stands out is his narration of Jesus' warning about the fate of disciples (Matt 10:17–25, §100). Meyer does not think this warning from Jesus works in this setting.[16] The result is the relation of Jesus' public to private teaching (in the Olivet Discourse) is read as "performance to theme."[17]

In another example, Luke's account of the desolating sacrilege mentions Jerusalem surrounded by armies (something that happened in AD 70) while Mark's and Matthew's versions do not (Mark 13:14–20 / Matthew 24:14–22 / Luke 21:20–24). This leads to a choice being made in favor either of AD 70 or the final Day of the Lord as the intended focus of prophecy. The majority of critical scholars hold to the first position while traditional dispensationalism takes the second position. It is fair to say that too often traditional dispensationalists have argued the Olivet Discourse (OD) is only about the Second Advent.[18] The question therefore arises, how do we know a pattern exists and where is it found in Mark, and what is the basis for such a reading?[19] What did Jesus teach in the Olivet Discourse? Was a

---

16. Meyer's reading of eschatology mentioned here in Matthew (Matt 10:23; and Matt 24:16, cf. 24:20 both use the term φεύγω, "to flee") is based on his analysis of Jesus' public and private teaching. He holds that Jesus' remark in Matthew 10:19 about the disciples being brought before governors, kings and Gentiles was not included in the original mission of the twelve but originates from the Olivet Discourse and so does not discuss it as such in this setting. Thus the content of this setting is diminished as meaning is seen at the level of the word. This matter of language-referent is a major hermeneutical issue to address. Meyer does not touch on possible additional meaning to the utterance and the disciples' immediate historical situation. On his own proposal and the relevance of Matthean redaction, see Meyer, *Aims*, 44.

17. Ibid., 174.

18. See Stedman, *What on Earth's Going to Happen?*; Walvoord, *Prophecy Knowledge Handbook*; MacArthur, *Second Coming*.

19. A reader-response criticism has been commonly employed to read Mark. But sometimes the emphasis of the impact upon the reader at the discourse level more than the exegetical level has influence on how performance is analyzed. Along similar lines,

Introduction

pattern fulfillment something that Jesus envisaged? Some like Carson hold to a "unifying method" of reading Mark 13 and its parallels yet dismiss a dispensational viewpoint.[20] Others agree that AD 70 mirrors the eschatological end in principle but reject that something as significant as the display of cosmic signs (Mark 13:24–26 / Matt 24:29–31 / Luke 21:25–26) is part of the pattern because context requires this is fulfilled in the short term. This study therefore shows how Mark understood the concept of a pattern in Jesus' discourse and then how the evangelists developed the themes in the discourse in line with Jesus' teaching about the future. Some significant differences between a progressive dispensational interpretation and a unifying method of interpretation are also discussed.

Working on the assumption that Luke and Matthew are dependent on Mark, we also find that Mark's verbal performance (imperative form) of the historical Jesus in Mark 13 has transferred in the rewriting of Luke 17, though the echo of a distant introductory apocalyptic scene (itself much wider than the teaching of the historical Jesus) remains. Luke 17 retells the story, bringing it back, so to speak with a pattern—a repeated phenomenon of the judgment to address the final sequence moving toward the end. And if we observe Luke's material carefully on the Noah and Lot sayings we have to assume that the author had independent access to traditions which go back to the historical Jesus. The distinctions in these two apocalypses should be observed because they are not contradictory but complementary.

Definitions

In 1932, M. Goguel specified that the terms "eschatology" and "apocalypticism" are so closely associated that they seem to be synonymous.[21] Therefore three preliminary definitions are necessary at the outset: (1) Eschatology is commonly described as the doctrine of last things. (2) Apocalyptic is concerned with God's knowledge and the secrets of the "world above." Apocalyptic therefore discloses a "transcendent reality."[22] It is about the revelation of heavenly things behind the scenes. (3) AE is described as a "kind of

---

see Johnston, "Jesus and the Climax of Israel's Story." However, the nature of the Gospels with differences and similarities also means that they are not repeating themselves; the Gospel accounts are not presenting a single performance in terms of eschatology.

20. See Carson, "Matthew," 491.
21. Goguel, "Eschatologie et apocalyptique dans le christianisme primitif," 381–424.
22. Collins, *Apocalyptic Imagination*, 5. Bornkamm, "μυστήριον," 815.

eschatology" that is frequently found in apocalypses.[23] Some scholars today deny the existence of AE. With these issues in mind, enquiry starts with the genre question.

1. Apocalyptic as Genre

The term *apocalypse* (Gk. ἀποκάλυψις, "revelation"), following Revelation 1:1, has been used as a generic term to describe documents with content and structure similar to the book of Revelation.[24] This is called the generic approach. The issue of the genre of apocalyptic is thought to have been first raised by Friedrich Lücke. In 1832, Lücke first suggested the book of Revelation belongs to a distinct literary type.[25] Later in 1895 Hermann Gunkel began the modern search for an agreed definition of apocalyptic which has continued to the present.[26] From this time, two methods, known simply as "genetic" and "generic" (or genre) approaches, have dominated attempts by scholars to understand apocalyptic literature. The genetic approach was primarily concerned with the origin of apocalyptic and led to the study of various historical allusions and to deriving theological doctrines.[27] The genetic approach has been largely abandoned today in NT scholarship. In contrast the genre approach (the study of apocalypses) popular today places its "primary emphasis on the internal coherence of the apocalyptic texts themselves."[28] How Meyer, Wright, and PD handle genre and Synoptic form issues and the matter of symbolism is therefore traced.

23. Collins, *Apocalyptic Imagination*, 11.

24. The noun in Rev 1:1 is not a technical term, but appears in a genitive construction Ἀποκάλυψις Ἰησοῦ Χριστοῦ, and forms the title of the book. This can be either a subjective genitive ("revelation from Jesus Christ") or objective genitive ("revelation about Jesus Christ") or a plenary genitive. See Wallace, *Greek Grammar beyond the Basics*, 120. John affirms the ultimate source of the revelation is God (ἣν ἔδωκεν αὐτῷ ὁ θεός). BDAG, 243, states that the aorist verb ἔδωκεν can relate to "an activity frequently determined by the noun object." But here it describes an action achieved, bounded by a natural end point (i.e., the action to give revelation is completed). The force of the tense does not describe the *period* or *process* in which the action is carried out, but the fact that God gave revelation. ἔδωκεν denotes the action of giving from beginning to end (a whole is in view) and is therefore a constative aorist.

25. Lücke, *Versuch einer vollständigen Einleitung in die Offenbarung Johannis die gesamte apokalyptische Literatur*, 33.

26. See Gunkel, *Schöpfung und Chaos in Urzeit und Endzeit*, 290.

27. Collins, *Apocalyptic Imagination*, 15, 20.

28. Ibid., 21.

Introduction

2. Issues in Mark 13 Relating to the Historical Crisis

A second set of challenges involves interacting with the literary dimensions and the language of Mark 13. What are the OT antecedents? There is the question of how many events are alluded to among the many interwoven themes. How do we explain the ambiguity such as imminence and delay in Jesus' teaching (Mark 13:2, 29; 13:24)? How is Mark 13 correlated to the historical crisis going back to John the Baptist, and to Jesus' urgent mission calling the Nation of Israel to repent (Mark 1:2–11 and par.; Matt 10:5–6; Matt 10:23; Mark 11:15–19; 13:1–2; Luke 21:20–24)? Why is Mark's discourse unlike many Jewish Apocalyptic writings where the reader is located just before the eschaton? These problems alone make the study worthwhile. One example of a problem in interpreting apocalyptic and hyperbolic language is Jesus' prediction of the temple when Jesus says, Βλέπεις ταύτας τὰς μεγάλας οἰκοδομάς; Οὐ μὴ ἀφεθῇ λίθος ἐπὶ λίθῳ, ὃς οὐ μὴ καταλυθῇ (Mark 13:2). This raises the question of referencing in Jesus' language and what exactly Jesus refers to here. Is there a relationship between history and Mark's transcendent concerns expressed here? Is this language relative or absolute in terms of fulfillment? Is it figurative or literal in terms of referent? When does Jesus use hyperbole and when is his referencing more direct? How can this prophecy best be described in terms of its relationship to other eschatological teaching on the kingdom? How flexible are Mark's forms? Could there be a pattern fulfillment here revealing how Mark's eschatological language works with potential match-up challenges in Luke and Matthew, and if so, what is the final awaiting prediction? Such questions are pertinent to understanding Mark's Olivet Discourse. However, the task of coherently integrating the actions, message, and goals of the historical Jesus remains a complex task.[29]

Perhaps there is no powerful example of the ambiguity of apocalyptic than that found in one strand of tradition of Jewish apocalyptic, namely, the temple and its function (Dan 8:13–14; 9:27; 11:31; and 12:11–12). Following another pattern by Daniel, Mark's account starts with the temple in Jerusalem and moves to other related subjects and climaxes with the arrival of the Son of Man to vindicate the elect. This study will in general explore Mark's historical-earth-bound and figurative language. This historical interest is seen in Mark's themes on the destruction of the temple and τὸ βδέλυγμα τῆς ἐρημώσεως ("the abomination of desolation"). Mark's

---

29. Bock, *Studying the Historical Jesus*, 215.

interest is seen in his disclosing of heavenly secrets, God's plan—through the description of cosmic events viewed from an earthly perspective. For example, what is the heavenly perceptive in Mark 13:25 on καὶ οἱ ἀστέρες ἔσονται ἐκ τοῦ οὐρανοῦ πίπτοντες ("and the stars falling from the heaven")?[30] How Mark's AE is different to that of Judaism will be explored.

3. Issues in Apocalyptic and Eschatology

A third major reason for the study is that in addition to the problem of definitions and formulations of AE, little work has been done to study its relevance to the Gospels at a construct level. As mentioned above, the rationale for a study of this nature which compares the work of Meyer, Wright, and PD is therefore warranted. There is only a limited amount of work available on evaluating theological constructs which are based on aims assessment and on how historians and exegetes draw on the insights of others to understand better the historical Jesus and his message. Meyer's book *The Aims of Jesus* has received critical reviews. Wright's reconstruction of Jesus' aims as presented in *Jesus and the Victory of God* has also received extensive assessment.[31] However, no one has examined their views of eschatology together, even though they share similarities.

D. Denton's 2004 work, *Historiography and Hermeneutics in Jesus Studies*, brings together two very different theological constructs.[32] Denton offers an in-depth comparative study of two antithetical models in John Dominic Crossan and Ben F. Meyer. Denton considers Meyer's epistemology and hermeneutics and proceeds to examine historiography and draws conclusions. Denton does summarize N. T. Wright's view of critical realism in an appendix.[33] There is no study, however, which examines Meyer's and Wright's work with the Gospel accounts and explains these in its theological and historical context. It is this angle which this study seeks to investigate.[34]

---

30. Also examined is Mark 13:27, where ἐπισυνάξει describes the "gathering together" of the elect by the angels "from the farthest end of the earth . . ." Cf. 9:1 and 14:25. Cf. a "crowd gathering" in Josephus (*Ant.* 18.37).

31. Book reviews include the following: Dunn, review of *The Aims of Jesus*; Marshall, review of *The Aims of Jesus*; Reumann, review of *The Aims of Jesus*. A major work assessing Wright's treatment of Jesus is Newman, *Jesus and the Restoration of Israel*.

32. Denton, *Historiography and Hermeneutics*.

33. See "Varieties of Critical Realism," in Denton, *Historiography and Hermeneutics*, 211–25.

34. For a reprint of individual writings and essays from each, see Dunn and McKnight,

Introduction

Foundational to this study is the belief that the Synoptic Gospels bring unique content and insights into eschatological relationships in the message of Jesus concerning the future kingdom of God. Such a study must be structured to reflect an interpretive understanding of those relationships.[35]

4. Remaining Issues

For the purposes of this study, there are four antecedent possibilities for describing the semantics of the two entities of apocalyptic and eschatology. These are: (1) the two entities can be discrete and unrelated; (2) they can overlap; (3) they can describe a type of synthesis in which one entity is a subset of the other, where one is encompassed by the other; or (4) the two entities can be identical. These semantic possibilities for apocalyptic and eschatology are important for answering the key questions which this study seeks to answer. The historical question of the study can be posed as, how did Jewish apocalyptic and Christian apocalyptic agree and differ? To bring the question more in line with eschatological relationships discussed so far, the following can be discussed. (1) Is the concept of AE legitimate? (2) Is it part of Mark's eschatology? Bearing in mind the two strands of Jewish apocalyptic, what kind is present in Mark 13:24–27 and why? (3) How is the "little apocalypse"[36] similar and different from the Jewish apocalyptic tradition (hereafter JAT)? What are the resulting implications for reading the Gospels and for understanding Jesus' message about the kingdom of God? (4) Should we assume that Christian apocalyptic is the same as Jewish apocalyptic or should we be open to diversity in the gospel's message regarding how each one presents AE? (5) With Paul writing first, if there are differences between Paul and Mark, how can these be explained? These are the questions that motivate the study.

Historical Jesus in Recent Research; Farmer, *Crisis in Christology*. On a different topic, a helpful study comparing the perspectives of Sanders, Dunn, and Wright is Gathercole, *Where Is Boasting?*

35. At the source critical level, I take Markan priority as a presupposition primarily because the compositional argument from order makes the most sense for redactional studies. See Stein, "Synoptic Problem," 789. On discussions of the relations of the Synoptic Gospels I will also trace selected themes. Cf. the Griesbach (Two-Gospel Hypothesis or 2GH) with McNicol, "Composition of the Synoptic Eschatological Discourse"; Wenham, *Rediscovery of Jesus' Eschatological Discourse*.

36. For a list of the numerable theories presented on Mark's "little apocalypse" over the years, see Beasley-Murray, *Jesus and the Last Days*.

Eschatological Relationships and Jesus

Ulrich H. J. Körtner's 1995 work entitled *Weltangst und Weltende: Eine theologische Interpretation der Apokalyptic* is helpful for the study. In the chapter on "The Ambiguity of Apocalyptic" Körtner introduces the terminology of "negative" and "positive" apocalyptic. About the former, he speaks of an unprecedented historical situation *einer präzedenzlosen geschichtlichen Situation*. Negative apocalyptic, he posits, "is capable only of verbalizing apocalyptic world anxiety."[37] He then proceeds to describe positive apocalyptic. Körtner says that "positive apocalyptic tries to change catastrophe anxiety into crisis anxiety, to interpret the threatening or anticipated catastrophe as crisis, and to understand the end as a passage or transition to a resolution."[38] Although he frames the discussion of apocalyptic as a "contemporary phenomenon, manifest in the public square," he also examines the relation between history and the causes which prompts writing for hope. Körtner's approach of defining negative and positive apocalyptic in relation to each other is helpful for this study in two ways. First, the terms negative and positive apocalyptic can be applied to assess various biblical themes of AE. In Second Temple Judaism, Jewish apocalyptic reveals what takes place "behind the scenes" or what only God knows. Apocalyptic reveals the evil at work under God's sovereign plan and God's sovereign actions including his judgment and salvation.

Finally, it is useful to structure the study to compare theological constructs in a synthetic approach. First, it can present preliminary presuppositions and methodology, which serves to place each person in the context of the third quest. Second, it can view presuppositions worked out in practice by describing what texts are chosen, how they are connected and interpreted together, and why. Third, differences between constructs can surface and guide initial enquiry. These help to clarify the horizon unfolding in Mark.

I argue there is a relationship between the history in Mark 13:2 and Mark's transcendent concerns in Mark 13:24–27. Furthermore, on

---

37. Körtner, *End of the World*, 195.

38. Ibid., 196. The basis of this twofold observation on the phenomenon of apocalyptic is Jewish literature. Citing *1 Enoch* 83:3–10, 84:5 and *2 Apocalypse of Baruch* 25:4 with reference to the messianic woes predicting a time of extreme distress before God's intervening deliverance. These texts illustrate how Jewish apocalyptic tries to overcome catastrophic world anxiety by transforming it into crisis anxiety. He writes: "In Jewish apocalyptic, although hope in redemption does not pass over the catastrophic nature of the present, it does argue against the inescapability of the catastrophe by teaching its readers to understand it as a crisis... In Jewish apocalyptic, so our thesis, there is a transformation of apocalyptic anxiety." Körtner, *End of the World*, 127.

Introduction

examination of 13:24–27 there is evidence that Mark's eschatology has continuity with Second Temple Judaism in that the structure of this passage presents in a simple way the relationship between the historical crisis and the eschatological crisis where vindication or final restoration occurs.[39] I will argue that the historical horizon dominating Mark's gospel is not the destruction of the temple but a second period crisis at the time-of-the-end.[40] One thing is clear: Mark's dualism is a "from above" versus a "from below" kind. It is not focused on the afterlife and does not address aspects of judgment in the way that the Synoptic parallels do.

These issues are not anomalies. They point to how Mark's eschatology is consistent with Judaism in the sense of point 3 above—AE and PE are historically orientated, and apocalyptic is encompassed in Mark's thought. In other words there are two strands or types of eschatology tradition (e.g., PE in Mark 13:2) running through Mark's thought (13:24–27). This does not mean Mark has an aversion for the traditional strand found in Jewish apocalyptic, such as interest in the cosmological or otherworldly journeys or title "Son of Man."[41] Rather, Mark's concern is to show what is behind (apocalyptic) the historical aspects of Jesus' future scenario.[42]

My concern, however, is the historical linkage between Jesus and Mark's apocalyptic teaching in Mark 13 and its parallels. Questions about

---

39. This is not to be confused with Dodd's "most thorough-going" (consistent) "non-eschatological" interpretation. For comment, see Guthrie, *Shorter Life of Christ*, 145. See also Aune, "Significance of the Delay of the Parousia," 94. Aune points out that Dodd's construct of eschatology makes the "question of the delay of the parousia . . . essentially an irrelevant problem, since both its presuppositions and solutions" have nothing to do with Jesus' teaching and therefore is outside the "essential nature of Christianity." Rather, AE and PE are compatible in Jesus and both involve pattern typology where the eschatological structure of Mark's thought is not "wholly temporal" (to borrow Aune's phrase) in its expectation neither is it wholly a crisis.

40. Cf. France, *Mark*, 32. See also n6 above.

41. Mark uses the title "Son of Man" frequently and the source of his Christology is dependent upon the imagery from Dan 7:13. According to the Synoptic Gospels it is also Jesus' favorite title for himself.

42. Cf. Collins, *Apocalyptic Imagination*, 12. Collins has said that AE has been erroneously examined only with the "historical type" of apocalyptic in the past. But in Markan studies the opposite is the case. Apocalyptic is almost exclusively a modified cosmic-spatial version of JAT examined in terms of "imminence" and the Son of Man debate. Focus on one kind of apocalyptic expression in the Christian literature does not justify the denial of AE existing in Christianity or particularly the more non-historical expressions of AE which have their antecedents in Judaism.

the timing of the final kingdom should not interfere with historical questions related to apocalyptic.

Method and Contents of the Study

The study is divided into seven chapters. It begins by examining constructs and concludes with exegesis and evaluation. The first chapter introduces the topic and justifies its need. The second chapter surveys various issues in how apocalyptic literature is read that Meyer, Wright, and PD attempt to address. Questions that arise out of the survey will be addressed in the study.

The third chapter is a description of Ben F. Meyer's theological construct in practice and his interpretation of AE and Mark 13. In placing Meyer in the context of the third quest, the goal of the chapter is to describe and understand his construct in terms of how he reads apocalyptic.

The fourth chapter is a description of N. T. Wright's theological construct which draws on Meyer's insights and develops it further by examining apocalyptic language.[43] The goal of this chapter is the same as in chapter three. The reason why Meyer's work is important to Wright will become evident.

The fifth chapter is a description of the approach of PD to eschatology in general and a description of the importance of pattern typology. The chapter will conclude with a brief summary and evaluation. Key texts in Mark where Meyer and Wright and PD go in different directions will be noted. These are pivotal texts to interpret because they juxtapose two things: prophetic prediction and apocalyptic ideas.

Chapter 6 is an examination of Mark 13:1–2 and 13:24–27 and selected parallel verses in the Synoptic Gospels. The chapter identifies the pattern in Jesus' discourse from a historical and literary perspective, and then lays out a hermeneutic of initial fulfillment of Daniel 9:2 to complement the original meaning. The pattern in Jesus' teaching serves as the basis for identifying the relationship between AD 70 and the time of the end.[44] The development of three themes (suffering, signs and salvation) from Jesus' discourse is traced to show how Luke focuses on the short-term aspect

---

43. Wright has a superb understanding of the history of the quest for the historical Jesus, as shown by his survey, but he does seem to draw from Meyer's hermeneutical and thematic presentation for developing his reconstruction of Jesus' message and aims.

44. The time-of-the-end is not to be confused with the "literal" end of the world.

INTRODUCTION

of the prophecy while Matthew focuses largely on the final awaiting fulfillment. The chapter will conclude by analyzing points where Mark's text correlates with other NT passages. Here Jesus' aims (which form part of his wider vision of the restoration of Israel) can be explored more fully as they relate to the theme of the coming future kingdom.

The seventh chapter will be a review and conclusion to the study as a whole and suggest future direction for study of this kind. The evaluation section will discuss all three constructs and make connections to other texts.

Limitations of the Study

A synthetic study of this kind can explore a variety of topics. A major limitation is the lack of space to devote to an exhaustive survey of the works of these two interpreters.[45] The study does not attempt to prove the Marcan priority hypothesis or to survey the history of the source debate.[46] The analysis in chapters three and four will not chronicle in any extensive discussion how Meyer or Wright formulated their philosophy and hermeneutical ideas. Rather, the focus will be on key features that go into formulating Mark's portrait of Jesus, and his future aims, related to the overall theme of the restoration of Israel. Material is therefore selected as it best relates to the understanding of their perspective of Jesus' view of the future, and especially the relationship between eschatology and apocalyptic.

There is no need for a survey of apocalyptic from the Pseudepigrapha and other Jewish writings. The SBL apocalyptic group has developed a sufficiently detailed investigation of such materials.[47] Similarly, there are numerous studies and monographs on eschatology in Judaism which consider proposals on the origin of apocalyptic which cannot be considered in detail.[48] Summation of these works point to the fact that Judaism is not a

---

45. Wright has authored or coauthored numerous works related to Jesus. His *The New Testament and the People of God* (1992), *Jesus and the Victory of God* (1996), and *The Resurrection and the Son of God* (2003) are the first three volumes of his announced six-volume series entitled Christian Origins and the Question of God (SPCK/Fortress).

46. Cf. McKnight, "Source Criticism," 74–105; Stein, "Synoptic Problem," 74–105; Stein, *Studying the Synoptic Gospels*.

47. For example Murphy, *Structure and Meaning of Second Baruch*; Nir, *Destruction of Jerusalem*; Kulik, *Retroverting Slavonic Pseudepigrapha*; Wills and Wright, *Conflicted Boundaries in Wisdom and Apocalypticism*.

48. Collins, *Seers, Sybils, and Sages*; Millar, *Isaiah 24–27*; Collins, *Apocalypticism in*

monolithic faith when it comes to themes such as the kingdom of God or Israel's Messianic hope.[49] The political and religious influence of the Pharisees and similar groups were not dominant across Second Temple Judaism.

The starting point of assessing the history on apocalyptic for relevance to the Christian apocalyptic text of Mark 13 is the two strands or traditions discerned in the Jewish apocalyptic literature by numerous scholars. These are the "historical" and the cosmic or spatially orientated apocalyptic writings. Jewish background material is therefore incorporated with the exegesis in chapter six in order to show how and where points of contact or divergence with Judaism emerge in Jesus' teaching according to Mark. In doing so, it will indirectly address how first-century Judaism dealt with the tension between prophecy and apocalyptic as well as the tension between historical apocalypses and cosmic apocalypses.

Chapter 14 of Mark, on Jesus' exaltation, is prominent in both Meyer's and Wright's thinking. However, this is not the subject of this thesis.

The question for chapters 3–4 of this study will be more focused on how Jewish background research is used by Meyer and Wright. If it is true that historically much Jewish literature produced, or scriptural reflection during the period of the Second Temple is characterized by midrashic

---

the Dead Sea Scrolls.

49. Extensive work has been done in this area. See Charles, *Apocrypha and Pseudepigrapha of the Old Testament in English*, vii. For others on proposed links between the Pharisees and apocalyptic ideas, see Davies, *Christian Origins and Judaism*, 30. Davies describes the background of Jesus as "the rich complex of Judaism" in which various elements were "constantly coming to terms and mutually modifying one another." Mullen argues that any sense of a "monolithic Judaism" at the time of Jesus led by Pharisaic rabbis should be discarded. Mullen, *Dining with Pharisees*, 61; Chilton et al., *Missing Jesus*. Collins, "Eschatologies of Late Antiquity"; Evans, *Noncanonical Writings and New Testament Interpretation*. See Wright, *People of God*, 307. See also the discussion on "Religion" in Israel in Bock, *Studying the Historical Jesus*, 123–33. On various debates between rabbis and their excluded rival groups, see Instone-Brewer, *Traditions of the Rabbis*, 3–5. On the lack of a "coherent system" of messianic expectations related to the *eschaton*, see Beasley-Murray, "Two Messiahs in the Testaments of the Twelve Patriarchs," Xeravits, *King, Priest, Prophet*, 2. On the contested nature of true prophecy and interest in prophetic authority in Second Temple Judaism, see Floyd and Haak, *Prophets, Prophecy and Prophetic Texts*, 5; Evans, *Ancient Texts for New Testament Studies*. Ben Z. Wacholder, in his recent work *The New Damascus Document*, argues there is evidence of sectarian opposition between Pharisees and the apocalyptic writer of CD. Wacholder's thesis is that the "Just Teacher" and his opponent the "Liar" are presented as figures or personalities of the future. See Wacholder, *New Damascus Document*, xx, 154.

writings,[50] then how does Jesus respond to this, and what is Mark's response in light of the JAT, and Jesus' teaching?

Other limitations relate to the treatment of individual motifs or concepts. For example, a whole monograph could be devoted to the concept of the delay of the Parousia. However, an acquaintance with apocalyptic interpretation in general is important. Before examining the constructs of Meyer and Wright and their interpretations on Mark's gospel, it is essential to examine two areas: first, how apocalyptic is read generally in relation to eschatology, and second, the ways in which NT apocalyptic is historically interpreted in the person of Jesus.

---

50. Wacholder, *New Damascus Document*, xx, 213–15. In summary, Wacholder claims that the rabbinic literature during the period of the Second Temple is characterized by midrashic writings and that even within various apocalyptic orientated groups there is a lack of unity. He makes the following points about rabbinic literature: (1) Some of them are independent while others are diffused with the Talmud; (2) they have their origin in post-exilic times; (3) much of DSS have a language of their own; and (4) the writer of CD is concerned that key "hermeneutical boundaries" have been violated by rival groups. Essentially the Pharisees have departed from the plain meaning of the holy writings.

2

How Apocalyptic Literature Is Read in Relation to Eschatology

THE THESIS OF THIS study is that Jesus' scenario of the future presents a pattern prediction. It was seen that Meyer and Wright see the fulfillment of Jesus' teaching in AD 70. PD sees initial fulfillment in AD 70 and a future fulfillment. This chapter surveys in detail the debate over Jesus' scenario of the future and relates it to the topic of eschatological relationships in Meyer, Wright, and PD. The fundamental problem is what is Jesus' scenario of the future? The debate shows, as Meyer has said, "the incapacity of biblical scholars, and practitioners of research into the historical Jesus, to define the various contexts in which future events signified by the words and acts of Jesus might be convincingly placed."[1] An important question for this chapter then is, do Meyer, Wright, and PD raise issues from the debate and how do they address them? Specifically, what do each say in reference to Jesus, history and apocalyptic, symbolism and the use of the Old Testament in the New? The chapter will conclude by describing a set of problems the remainder of the study will address. The survey with the similarities and differences between Meyer, Wright, and PD will raise a number of theological, textual and hermeneutical questions. These are precise questions to ask in examining again the AD 70 versus tribulation or historical crisis versus the eschatological ordeal question in light of Jesus' future teaching.

---

1. Meyer, "Jesus's Scenario of the Future," 1.

How Apocalyptic Literature Is Read

The Issues of Apocalyptic as Genre and History

Chapter 1 began to outline the issues of apocalyptic as genre and distinguished between the genetic approach and "generic" (or genre) approach. The genetic approach was primarily concerned with the origin of apocalyptic and the study of historical allusions. In brief, the genetic approach, or the quest for sources, produced three solutions to the question of the origin of apocalyptic. In 1913, R. H. Charles with the help of fifteen other scholars composed two massive volumes on *The Apocrypha and Pseudepigrapha of the Old Testament* covering the noncanonical Jewish literature from 200 BC to AD 100.[2] From the abundance of material collated, Charles drew several conclusions. First, apocalyptic and rabbinic Judaism originate from the same source. Furthermore, Charles discerned that apocalyptic Judaism and legalistic Judaism were not essentially antagonistic, but shared the same covenant focus in Torah.[3] Second, the apocalyptic writers recognized the validity of the prophetic writings and saw their writings as the "successor" to them. Third, Charles argued that ultimately (post AD 70), apocalyptic and rabbinic Judaism developed into Christianity and Talmudic Judaism.[4] Four, apocalyptic material discloses the secrets of the beyond.[5]

Others who followed Charles in arguing that apocalyptic is derived from OT prophecy were O. Plöger, W. Schmithals, D. S. Russell, and P. D. Hanson (but Plöger and Hanson denied Persian dualism was influential). On the other hand, W. Bousset and P. Vielhauer expressed a strong aversion to the prophetic school, and argued solely for Persian dualism as the source of apocalyptic. Gustav Hölscher and G. von Rad alternatively argued the source of apocalyptic was wisdom literature.[6] One benefit of the genetic approach overall was recognition of the importance of biblical allusions in apocalyptic literature and the use of mythological motifs.[7] Since chapter 2 explores these and other topics in detail there is no need for further explanation here.

---

2. Charles, *Apocrypha and Pseudepigrapha*.

3. Ibid., vii. He cites *The Testament of the Twelve Patriarchs*: "This Law is the light that lights everyman" (*T. Levi* 14:4; cf. *T. Levi* 19:1). See also *As. Mos.* 9:6.

4. Charles, *Apocrypha and Pseudepigrapha*, vii.

5. Charles and Morfill, *Book of the Secrets of Enoch*.

6. Hölscher, "Die Entstehung des Buches Daniel," 113–38; Rad, *Old Testament Theology*. For a historical review of the approach to understanding NT apocalyptic in Germany in the late 1800s, see Koch, *Rediscovery of Apocalyptic*, 36–48.

7. Collins, *Apocalyptic Imagination*, 18–19.

Eschatological Relationships and Jesus

Charles' contribution to the genetic approach resulted in many textual editions, translations, and textual notes on the OT Apocrypha and Pseudepigrapha. These works provided the literary foundation for defining the apocalypse as a genre (the second approach).[8] A flurry of research seeking to define the genre of apocalypse in the 1970s led to a SBL Genre Project which published its definition of apocalypse in Semeia 14 in 1979. The SBL description is recognized as the standard definition of an apocalypse: An apocalypse is "a genre of revelatory literature with a narrative framework, in which a revelation is mediated by an otherworldly being to a human recipient, disclosing a transcendent reality which is both temporal, insofar as it envisages eschatological salvation, and spatial insofar as it involves another supernatural world."[9]

There are clear benefits to the generic framework. First, it enabled scholars to identify "apocalypse," both Jewish and Christian, as a distinct class of writing.[10] Second, the literary approach has enabled scholars to list the core traits or phenomena related to apocalypses.[11] Third, this project helped in the identification of two types of Jewish apocalypses—the heavenly journey and the historical apocalypse.[12] These two kinds of apocalypse are seen codified together in the book of *1 Enoch* in late Second Temple Judaism. Thus, by defining the form of apocalypse (a narrative of revelation) and the content (revealing eschatological salvation and, in the opinion of some, judgment) this approach provided a generic framework to study.

Many hoped the genetic and generic approaches would clarify the questions surrounding the discussion of apocalyptic, yet some significant problems have surfaced. For example, the Qumran texts showed certain eschatological traits of the apocalypses, yet they did not express these views in the literary form peculiar to apocalypses. According to García Martínez, both the *religionsgeschichtlich* understanding of apocalypticism and the "generic" approach to apocalypse have failed to clarify Jewish apocalyptic.[13]

---

8. Charles' contribution in other published editions include Charles, *Book of Enoch*. Others include works on the *Ascension of Isaiah, 2 Baruch, Jubilees, Testaments of the Twelve Patriarchs, Assumption of Moses*, and *2 Enoch*.

9. Collins, *Apocalypse: Morphology of a Genre*, 3.

10. Collins, *Apocalyptic Imagination*, 14.

11. The SBL Genres Project lists twelve themes present in apocalypses. See Collins, *Apocalyptic Imagination*, 7.

12. Collins, *Apocalyptic Imagination*, 7.

13. Martínez, "Encore l'apocalyptique," 224–32.

How Apocalyptic Literature Is Read

Following this, many of the "unconvinced" entered into dialogue.[14] In his seminal 1979 article Collins sought to clarify the issues.[15] The wider issues related to understanding apocalyptic can readily be grouped under five main topics:

First, there are non-apocalyptic genres, both Jewish and Christian, which also contain apocalyptic themes (Joel 2:1–11, 3–4; Isa 24–27, 56–66; Ezek 38 and 39; Zech 1–6, Mark 10, 13; 1 Thess 4; 2 Thess 2). Recognition of this material enlarges the "pool" of apocalyptic texts to study, complicates its understanding, and suggests that there are other ways to understand apocalyptic. There are also some apocalypses, as Rowland has noted, like *3 Enoch* for example, where eschatology is not prominent.[16] Rowland's observation highlights the non-monolithic nature of eschatology in Judaism, and has led to disagreement over how significant eschatology is at the wider genre level. But the apparent cosmological themes in *3 Enoch*, for example the "first heaven" and "second heaven" reflect the need to discuss the kinds of eschatology expected in original contexts.

Second, while previous research has provided a detailed examination of Jewish apocalyptic literature, there seems to be a need now for a critical examination of how interpreters relate apocalyptic to eschatology. In the quest for a literary definition of apocalyptic, scholars have not focused clearly on the meaning of eschatological relationships and how distinguishing features affect the meaning of apocalyptic (e.g., how AE relates to prophetic eschatology and how their future expectations differ). As seen already, Goguel's understanding of terms "eschatology" and "apocalypticism" as synonymous was not helpful. In the 1970s, Collins recognized the dispute over the names by which the two concepts of future expectation are referred to. He believed that most debates around these relationships were "purely terminological" and made "no real contribution" to the understanding of either phenomenon.[17] Instead, the goal of the genre approach to understanding apocalyptic (and the closely associated question of origins) seemed to focus on identifying "the distinctive" feature or phenomena of apocalyptic.[18] The lack of critical accountability has impacted how scholars

---

14. For their assessment and suggested corrections, see Tigchelaar, "More on Apocalyptic," 138. For a more recent summary, see Collins, *Seers, Sybils, and Sages*, 35–36.
15. Collins, *Apocalypse: Morphology of a Genre*, 3.
16. Rowland, *Open Heaven*, 28.
17. See Collins, "Apocalyptic Eschatology," 22.
18. Ibid.

present their claims to understanding apocalyptic. In the absence of a critical assessment of the relationship of these concepts, some have assumed connections in a piece-meal way.[19] The question must be asked, is this warranted?

Third, the genre approach has not solved some of the perennial problems of apocalyptic. The misinterpretation of the relationship between myth and history and between history and symbolism continues. The dialogue has probably been more confused over this area than anywhere else.[20] Regarding the relationship between history and myth, commentators have commonly stated the problem as follows: that prophetic is historical and that apocalyptic is mythical. This notion has subsequently been corrected with studies which showed that myth is not limited to the Second Temple period.[21] As early as 1976 it was claimed by Roberts that distinguishing AE from prophetic eschatology (hereafter, PE) is a reversion to the "old dichotomy."[22] Jindo, in his "On Myth and History in Prophetic and Apocalyptic Eschatology," seeks to clarify the relationship but assumes Roberts' argument. He understands the oracle of Isaiah 11 as referring to history in "the immediate future" and the concerns of the apocalyptic vision of Daniel 2 as "not history."[23] Rather, these world empires are seen "synchronically, as if all happened at the same time" and in keeping with the cyclical nature of time in myth. Jindo then goes on to cite others in support of the distinction between history and myth, and this perpetuates the confusion.[24]

---

19. For example, the whole question of what is meant by "the relation of prophecy to apocalyptic" needs critical review. In some essays it means the relation of the OT prophets to the NT book of Revelation and the central issue is pseudonymity. See Vawter, "Apocalyptic: Its Relation to Prophecy," 33–46. At another level, G. B. Caird is a good illustration of how interpreters uncritically assume various syntactical relationships about eschatology and apocalyptic without explaining how these are determined. See the following section for this discussion.

20. The literary term "myth" refers to language that evokes or alludes to cosmic realities and does not mean something made up.

21. Clifford, "Roots of Apocalypticism."

22. Roberts, "Myth Versus History." The essay is more an attack on Paul Hanson's definitions than a critique of his construct centered on proto-apocalyptic literature.

23. Jindo, "On Myth and History," 413.

24. Ibid. In this article Jindo cites Collins as if he supports a dichotomy between "myth and history" as it is commonly applied to describing AE. See Hanson, *Dawn*, 10–11. In fact Collins proposes no such idea. Such are the issues of clarity in reading and interpreting terminology.

Similarly, the question of history and apocalyptic is an issue that has generated considerable in-house discussion. The problem relates to the complexity of the nature of apocalyptic language, and how to correctly interpret various phenomena objectively when they do not have chronological tags. Scholars have different literary starting points and so they begin with different source materials. At the level of discussion, these areas are not well integrated, and invariably scholars reach very different understandings of apocalypticism. This phenomenon is illustrated in Paul O'Callaghan's discussion of AE and the Christian interpretation of apocalypse in his 2004 work *The Christological Assimilation of the Apocalypse*. Of particular interest for the discussion is the section on literary style and the interpretation of apocalyptic symbolism.[25] Describing apocalyptic literature as a whole, O'Callaghan, like Barr, recognizes "clusters of features" in Jewish apocalyptic literature and diversity between various groups.[26] His definition of apocalypticism however is centered on one aspect of the late literature, that of symbolism. He states that "apocalypticism may be generally defined as a symbolic universe extrapolated from apocalypse."[27] For O'Callaghan, a "symbolic universe" becomes synonymous with worldview or "apocalypticism." But this is saying too much about the genre and nothing about the kind of historical situation envisaged in Judaism. Not everything in the apocalypse is symbolic, and he confuses imagery and the degree to which symbolism ought to dominate a definition of apocalyptic. Furthermore, even if it were symbolic can imagery have a historical base? Again, O'Callaghan elevates one aspect of the literature while citing Collins in support.[28] Yet this seems to disregard the temporal elements concerning eschatology which the SBL definition on the genre of apocalypse correctly brings out. Not surprisingly then, O'Callaghan says that apocalyptic

---

25. O'Callaghan, *Christological Assimilation of the Apocalypse*.

26. Ibid., 67. According to O'Callaghan, apocalyptic works are a "scribal phenomenon." He lists seven features: (1) the work of apocalyptic literature "as a whole is decidedly symbolic"; (2) symbolic language is used by authors to ensure the integrity of the divine message and "maximum respect for the concrete historical situation they intend to represent"; (3) apocalyptic symbols originate in dreams or visions; (4) visions are explained by an interpreting angel; (5) their content is about "catastrophic cosmic upheavals" to express the powerful action and presence of God; (6) animals are often used as key protagonists; and (7) arithmetic and chromatic symbolism is extensively used (e.g., "red indicates blood"). Cf. Barr, "Jewish Apocalyptic in Recent Scholarly Study," 18.

27. O'Callaghan, *Christological Assimilation*, 67.

28. Collins says, "The worldview or symbolic universe . . . extracted from the apocalypse is what we call apocalypticism." Collins, "Apocalypse and Apocalypticism," 283.

"should be distinguished" from eschatology.[29] This approach does not solve the problem of how to interpret writers, both JAT and NT, that do engage with eschatological themes in Judaism and Christianity and who likewise view as real events the historical events they intend to represent. This raises the issue of how historically rooted this material is. A case in point is the difference between Hanson's source approach with his historical investigation into how and what circumstances generated a change in Jewish worldview outlook. In sum, Hanson's definition of apocalypticism is orientated toward historical expectations while O'Callaghan's definition of apocalypticism is orientated around "symbolic."[30]

Finally, in the absence of clear classification of relationships in eschatology, some reject apocalyptic on hermeneutical and philosophical grounds without any objective assessment. For example, Fuchs claims apocalyptic is opposed to salvation-history (especially that envisaged by O. Cullmann) because it is antithetical to present faith.[31] While a classical definition of "apocalypse" therefore exists, debate on the suitability of apocalyptic as an adjective and the meaning of apocalypticism remains.

Clearly then how scholars approach eschatological relationships is not an innocuous matter. Scholars are beginning to focus more explicitly on the relationship between apocalyptic and eschatology, moving beyond the genre approach.

In 2003, a series of essays by ten scholars from the SBL 2001 meeting appeared under the title *Knowing the End from the Beginning*, in which discussion on the relationship between prophetic and apocalyptic was renewed.[32] Although not a comprehensive treatment of the subject, the study reveals rising interest in apocalyptic eschatology and illustrates how scholars are beginning to nuance discussion in terms of conceptual categories. For example, D. A. Aune closely associates eschatology and apocalyptic and sees the latter as a subset of the former. What Aune means is that everything included in apocalyptic forms part of eschatology, but not all eschatology

---

29. O'Callaghan, *Christological Assimilation*, 68.

30. Ibid., 67. Cf. also Joel 2:2 where the prophetic symbol of "darkness" as a metaphor of distress and suffering describes a devastating locust plague, and is followed by a reverse in fortunes (Joel 1:7, 10, 18; 2:22).

31. Fuchs, *Hermeneutik*. See also Achtemeier's critical response to this understanding of the relationship between faith and history. Achtemeier, *Introduction to the New Hermeneutic*, 109, 134, 142. Caird, *New Testament Theology*, 248–49.

32. Grabbe and Haak, *Knowing the End from the Beginning*. The failure to reach discussion on Mark 13 is one weakness here.

is included in apocalyptic.³³ Such insights are crucial for developing the discussions.

Modern Constructs of Apocalyptic Eschatology

The question "What does the phrase apocalyptic eschatology signify?" has many answers. Debate continues about whether or not apocalyptic eschatology (AE) should be recognized as a significant phenomenon of apocalyptic literature. This section surveys eleven scholars who sought to formulate what AE looks like. Some of the questions that are raised at various levels include: (1) Are there legitimate distinctions? If so, what kind and extent? (2) If there is some sort of unity between apocalyptic and eschatology, what is the extent of the relationship and how do the parts of apocalyptic eschatology relate to each other? And (3) Which dichotomies, inherent in the constructs below, are appropriate and which are false as scholars seek to wrestle with the evidence and come to terms with formulating eschatological relationships?³⁴ The survey will then move to assess them as a group.

Past Research: The Accepted Consensus

R. H. Charles

At the turn of the century, R. H. Charles described eschatology as falling into two divisions. Charles distinguished between prophetic eschatology (PE) and AE in theory. Charles proposed that PE is distinct from apocalyptic in that it devotes itself to the present with the future "rising organically" out of the present, while apocalyptic is "interested in the present as a stage to the final consummation of all things."³⁵ The distinction Charles made was between a "from here" and a "from above" perspective. In practical

---

33. Aune, "Transformations of Apocalypticism," 55. Aune's descriptive term for apocalyptic eschatology is "a system of religious beliefs ... a pattern of religious thought that was widespread in early Judaism and early Christianity." Aune, *Prophecy in Early Christianity*, 107. See also McGinn, "Early Apocalypticism." McGinn holds that "Apocalypticism is a form of eschatology."

34. Wrestling with these issues, Aune says, "In some respects, the dichotomy between prophetic and apocalyptic is a false one, since neither 'prophecy' nor 'apocalypse' designate static types of literature; rather, each represents a spectrum of texts composed over centuries." See Aune, *Revelation 1–5*, ixxv.

35. Charles, *Rise and Development of the Belief in a Future Life*, 5.

terms for Charles, PE focused on the destiny of Israel as a nation and the destiny of the Gentile empires. Moreover, the unique content of AE was the contribution of three beliefs: its teaching on death and the individual in the afterlife, on the new heavens and earth, and on the catastrophic end of the world.[36]

In his works after the nineteenth century Charles focused on the provenance of individual apocalyptic writings.[37] He surveyed vast quantities of apocalyptic writings, translating and publishing the book of *1 Enoch*, Jubilees, and the *Testament of the Twelve Patriarchs* as his primary data.[38] A clear example of Charles' presupposition is that he expected the original documents to exhibit a doctrinal consistency similar to his summary.[39] Works such as *1 Enoch*, with its emphasis on postmortem judgment of the dead, heavily influenced his understanding of apocalyptic literature. On the other hand, works like the *Sibylline Oracles* that viewed eschatology as "confined to this world" and evidenced a "reticence as to the higher doctrines of a future life" had "secondary importance" to him.[40] Thus the approach of Charles tended to assimilate apocalyptic literature to the familiar world of the OT prophets and paid little attention to the issues of mythological symbolism or literary structure.[41]

Charles was emphatic on the eschatology of Israel and the relationship of apocalyptic and prophetic.[42] Charles denied that the prophetic and apocalyptic were opposed to each other. But in his own inconsistent terminology he states that apocalyptic and prophetic each had their own eschatology and they were viewed as inconsistent as they "by no means agree."[43] His view dominated scholarly consensus for most of the twentieth century.

---

36. Charles, *Critical History of the Doctrine of a Future Life*, 173–84.

37. Charles, *Assumption of Moses*; Charles, "Early Source of the Testaments of the Twelve Patriarchs."

38. Charles, *Apocrypha and Pseudepigrapha of the Old Testament*.

39. Collins, *Apocalyptic Imagination*, 15.

40. See Charles, *Critical History*, 176–77.

41. Collins, *Apocalyptic Imagination*, 15.

42. See Charles, *Religious Development*, 16; Charles, *Immortality*, 4–5. He points out that AE and PE are not opposed to each other in terms of being two distinct religions.

43. Charles, *Critical History*, 173. See also Charles, *Religious Development*, 12–46.

How Apocalyptic Literature Is Read

H. H. Rowley

H. H. Rowley devotes considerable attention to the topic of apocalyptic in his work *The Relevance of Apocalyptic*, which went through three editions. He treats apocalyptic as having considerable overlap with prophecy: "apocalyptic is the child of prophecy yet diverse."[44] Rowley does not explore in detail the differences between the Jewish parties in the Second Temple Judaism period. He does, however, make four points about the relation of prophecy to apocalyptic. First, they both share predictive traits. Second, the prophets and apocalyptists share moral concerns and a spiritual message. The differences lie in the prophetic preaching of righteousness and godliness to their own age and the apocalyptic message for a future age. Third, (in contrast to Charles' formulation) PE for Rowley describes the prediction of future events that arise out of the present while AE breaks from the outside into the present.[45] Rowley's method is the first example of tracing the development of "early" prophecy (which he describes as prophecy of a political and religious nature), its interpretation and its predictive element.[46] He concludes that PE was announced by prophets who were devotees of the national God, lovers of political independence, and keen to throw off foreign domination, both political and religious.[47] Fourth, Rowley, like Johannes Lindblom, regards the "marks of apocalyptic" as including transcendentalism, mythology, cosmological orientation, pessimistic treatment of history, dualism, division of time into periods, a doctrine of two ages, playing with numbers, pseudo-ecstasy, artificial claims of inspiration, pseudonymity, and mysteriousness.[48]

S. B. Frost

Stanley B. Frost discusses the relation between eschatology and myth in his *Old Testament Apocalyptic*.[49] He examines apocalyptic in the OT history,

---

44. Rowley, *Relevance of Apocalyptic*, 13.
45. Ibid., 34.
46. Ibid., 12–15, 35.
47. Ibid., 19.
48. Lindblom, *Die Jesaja-apocalypse Jes. 24–27*, 102; Rowley, *Relevance of Apocalyptic*, 23.
49. Frost, *Old Testament Apocalyptic*. Frost is one of a handful of scholars who has studied the relationship of the temple and proto-apocalyptic texts with reference to myth. See Frost, "Eschatology and Myth," 70. Manson et al., *After the Exile*, 149. Avis,

and in his interpretation of Jewish ideas about the future he posits that the Jewish exile marks a line of division between the historical and the metahistorical or eschatological. Frost makes three claims about the differences between apocalyptic and prophecy. First, prophecy and apocalyptic are chronologically distinct; prophecy was preexilic and apocalyptic was from the postexilic era. Second, one was a historical perspective and in the other, expectation was increasingly expressed in mythological terms. Third, it is the fusion of myth and eschatology which produced what is known as apocalyptic. Thus, apocalyptic is defined as the "mythologizing of eschatology."[50]

The issue of myth and this description of how it relates to eschatology are pivotal in the understanding of apocalyptic. Subsequent scholars refer to Frost's idea of the last of the prophets becoming the first apocalyptists as the eschatological perspective *replacing* the historical.[51] Some have questioned whether it is possible to identify a point in time for such a change of thinking.[52] Others claim that eschatological mythology meant a change in time perspective from "linear" to "cyclical."[53] With reference to modern scholarship, K. Koch has noted these kinds of problems and says that all definitions contain stereotypes which get transferred from decade to decade.[54]

God and the Creative Imagination, 196. However, Frost's definition of myth is somewhat controversial. His discussion concerning myth and eschatology states that: (1) myth is static but eschatology is dynamic, (2) myth presents cyclical events and has an eternal thrust whereas eschatology moves to a definite conclusion according to the divine will. Thus, apocalyptic combines eschatology and myth.

50. Frost, *Old Testament Apocalyptic*, 33. Frost forcefully rejects the idea of history in apocalyptic. He claims that because of pessimism, the hope for salvation moved to the transcendent away from the historical. Frost, "Apocalyptic and History." Compare the response by Ladd, "Apocalyptic and New Testament Theology," esp. 292.

51. See Vawter, "Apocalyptic," 36; Jindo, "On Myth and History," 412–15.

52. Vawter, "Apocalyptic," 36.

53. Jindo, "On Myth," 412. Frost himself draws sharp distinctions akin to German scholarship in later writings, when he interprets myth as antithetical to linear history. He claims the apocalyptists abandoned the historical thinking of ancient Israel. Frost defines three features of myth as "aetiology, a supernatural world, and absolute time." See Frost, "Apocalyptic and History," 105–6, 112. Cf. Koch, *Rediscovery of Apocalyptic*, 53.

54. Koch, *Rediscovery of Apocalyptic*, 11. One interesting example by application is the term "linear" when used by Jindo in reference to the oracle in Isa 11 about Hezekiah. Jindo understands it refers only to "the immediate future" (PE). However, the AE ("cyclic") use in Dan 2 which describes world empires the "reverse is the case." Here "history functions as a form of expression" so that the ultimate concern of Daniel's vision is "not

How Apocalyptic Literature Is Read

O. Plöger

In Germany, OT scholars largely ignored apocalyptic. For Otto Plöger, who is credited with the renewal of interest in apocalyptic in Germany, there was an undisputed connection between prophecy and apocalyptic, and that lay in eschatology.[55] His 1959 article traced two traditions of development in Israelite religion. One group, the Hasidim, was thoroughly apocalyptic and represented a dualistic eschatological tradition. The other group according to Plöger's theory was the noneschatological Maccabean group who saw their role as political revolt against Roman oppressors. Thus Plöger recognized continuity in eschatology between prophetic and apocalyptic traditions but also claimed that a different perspective developed among the Hasidim.

G. von Rad

Gerhard von Rad considered the theme of apocalyptic in his *Old Testament Theology* under the title "Daniel and Apocalyptic," but rejected any link with prophecy.[56] Von Rad understood apocalyptic history as largely negative and "incompatible" with the prophetic view of history.[57] Like Frost, von Rad questions whether apocalyptic had any relation with history at all "since it abandoned the approach by way of saving history."[58] He argues the characteristic feature of apocalyptic eschatology is dualism, or the "clear-cut differentiation of two aeons."[59] All this is based on his view that Daniel makes no mention of Israel's history, only her great tribulation (Dan 7:21; 9:26b–27; 11:31), and that the Son of Man is not connected with Israel, but "with the clouds of heaven" (Dan 9:13). Von Rad understands Daniel as only describing the outcome for the Gentile nations whereas the prophetic message is rooted in Israel's saving history. It was von Rad who noted that apocalyptic goes beyond the investigation of the "peculiar

---

history but the predetermined ending of the world" which in the myth pattern is order over chaos. Jindo, "On Myth," 413. It is hard to accept how Dan 2 is exclusively cyclical, however, when the narrative distinguishes the kings and sets out a kind of chronology.

55. Ibid., 39. Plöger, *Theocracy and Eschatology*, 27.
56. Von Rad, *Old Testament Theology*, 303.
57. Ibid., 99.
58. Ibid., 304.
59. Ibid., 301–2.

literary phenomenon" to understanding of theological phenomena of its worldview.[60] Since then others have concurred.[61] Von Rad, therefore, recognized negative apocalyptic in earthly terms, but denied that there was any positive apocalyptic in earthly terms. Looking more broadly at the notion of divine heavenly power, von Rad sees no relation to this and positive apocalyptic.[62]

D. S. Russell

D. S. Russell goes further than H. H. Rowley in advocating two key scholarly streams in late Judaism, one apocalyptic and the other rabbinical.[63] Apocalyptic is not a substitute for prophecy, but by certain respects is a continuation of it as it represents a readaption and development of its message.[64] Russell helped to clarify the nature of PE as the hope to restore the Davidic line pictured in an earthly kingdom. He argues the future hope of restoration in Israel became increasingly transcendent in Deutero-Isaiah.[65]

Russell set out to define a set of typical traits that define apocalypse as a genre.[66] His hope was that by identifying a common, if not universal, set of traits for the literature, he would be able to understand the nature of apocalyptic. Identifying the traits of apocalyptic allowed Russell to separate what he calls four presuppositions of apocalyptic in its theological sense (primordiality, conflict, eschatology, and universalism) from the literary features of apocalyptic (esoteric in character, literary in form, symbolic in

---

60. Ibid., 301.

61. Cancik, "End of the Worlds of History." Dunn, *Unity and Diversity in the New Testament*, 310; Ladd, "Why Not Prophetic-Apocalyptic," 192.

62. Von Rad recognizes that in the OT the term "heaven" is used not only in a cosmological location sense, but also with a theological understanding in which heaven denotes the dimension of the source of God's saving power and salvation. Von Rad, "Ouranoj," 507.

63. Koch, *Rediscovery of Apocalyptic*, 53; Russell, *Method and Message of Jewish Apocalyptic*.

64. Russell, *Method and Message*, 92, 128. Since the work of Charles, Rowley, and Russell, it is commonly held by most historians of Judaism that the apocalyptic views of Daniel and intertestamental Judaism find their roots in prophecy. See also Ehrman, *New Testament*, 247.

65. Russell, *Method and Message*, 265.

66. Ibid.

nature, and pseudonymous in authorship).[67] The emphasis is on the "age-long story" of salvation-history back to creation and the fall, the intervening conflict, as well as to "the end." Based on this Russell concludes that the apocalyptic view of history is "essentially deterministic" and must follow the pattern as "ordained by God."[68]

The problem with the genre approach noted so far is the cardinal question concerning the investigation of history.[69] For Russell, the literature of apocalyptic is central. This writing, it seems, is equated *a priori* with symbolism, and he does not define apocalypticism. Later he uses terms "religious thought" and symbolism almost interchangeably except when the context refers to the coming Messiah.[70] Apocalyptic writing often merges the transcendent and temporal into a synthetic unity.[71] In all other circumstances, AE applies to the afterlife of bliss and coming judgment. His view is a significant contrast then with Frost who saw PE and AE as distinct. If for von Rad, the negative and positive (divine power) aspects of apocalyptic in Daniel 9:21 and 9:22 are irreconcilable in historical terms, Russell saw an indistinguishable synthesis of these two ideas.

P. Hanson

One study that emerged in the mid-1970s which distinguished AE from PE was that by Paul D. Hanson, *The Dawn of Apocalyptic*. Hanson rejects von Rad's theory that apocalyptic derives from wisdom or can be attributed to Persian origin. The social setting of the dawn of AE was the conflict between disenfranchised Levites who were against those in charge of the temple. Like Philipp Vielhauer, Hanson holds that biblical apocalyptic is best understood as a strand of thought within Jewish eschatology.[72]

Hanson highlights the continuity and change in the development associated with AE and PE by way of definition. The material revealed in apocalyptic is called "secrets." Apocalyptic eschatology is "a religious perspective which focuses on the disclosure (usually esoteric in nature) to the elect of the cosmic vision of Yahweh's sovereignty—especially as it

---

67. Ibid., 106.
68. Ibid., 200, 219, 106, 230.
69. See Rowland, *Open Heaven*, 71; Barr, *Reality of Apocalypse*, 74.
70. Russell, *Prophecy and the Apocalyptic Dream*, 12, 26, 32, 101.
71. Russell, *Apocalyptic, Ancient and Modern*, 24.
72. Vielhauer and Strecker, "Apocalypses and Related Subjects," 543.

relates to his acting to deliver his faithful—which disclosure the visionaries have largely ceased to translate into terms of plain history, real politics, and human instrumentality due to a pessimistic view of reality."[73] He emphasizes that AE, with its emphasis on the cosmic realm, can be found "fully developed" as a strand of teaching within Jewish eschatology in early mid-fifth-century writings.[74] Drawing on the early work of Michael Stone, who also emphasized that "secrets" epitomize the revelation of apocalyptic, Hanson concludes that "wisdom was wedded to the tradition of apocalyptic eschatology."[75] For Hanson, the idea that AE is fundamentally about the cosmic realm and Yahweh's future saving act on behalf of his people is influenced by the wisdom tradition. Prophetic eschatology on the other hand focuses on the "prophetic announcement to the nation of the divine plans for Israel and the world . . . which [the prophet] translates into the terms of plain history, real politics, and human instrumentality; that is the prophet interprets for the king and the people how the plans of divine council will be affected within the context of their nation's history and the history of the world."[76] Jewish hope in AE is, therefore, different from PE not primarily for theological reasons, but because the manner of the new deliverance which AE expresses has changed.[77] The type of hope and deliverance envisaged in AE texts is no longer of a nationalistic/materialistic domain prevalent in Jewish prophetic writings but rather from the cosmic and heavenly realm that can only be realized by divine "irruption" into history to overthrow evil.[78] Hanson also calls for new methods of "contextual-typological"

73. Hanson, *Dawn of Apocalyptic*, 11. Hanson, "Jewish Apocalyptic," 35.

74. Hanson, *Dawn of Apocalyptic*, 8–9.

75. Ibid., 9. See Stone, "Lists of Revealed Things," 423. Subsequently, Stone has successfully demonstrated that the link between wisdom and apocalyptic continued in the later apocalypse of *4 Ezra*. See Stone, "Way of the Most High," 351.

76. Hanson, *Dawn of Apocalyptic*, 11. The concept of the kingdom of God in early Judaism is thought to be shaped by two tendencies in thinking. See Caragounis, "Kingdom of God," 418–20.

77. Hanson has received some unfair criticism for his definition. See Roberts, "Myth Versus History," 1–13. Hanson holds that apocalyptic is fundamentally Jewish at its base and not influenced by "outsiders" or Persian dualism. On this point it can be said there is a difference between Persian origin and Persian influence. The claim, however, that AE is unwarranted because of Hanson's misrepresentation of myth and other religions is unsubstantiated. It has been picked up and repeated. Jindo, "On Myth and History," 412–15. In fact, Hanson speaks of classical prophecy utilizing myth for its religious significance. See Hanson, "Zechariah 9," 38.

78. See Rowland, "Apocalyptic," 29.

readings.⁷⁹ Hanson makes two points about the nature of contemporary tools. First, there exists a lack of sensitivity in the historicizing method for the interpretation employed frequently does not apply to the material at hand. This approach tends to limit apocalyptic to writings that simply "conform to literary type."⁸⁰ Second, a new investigation must start with a clarification of the genre and utilize a method that is sensitive to early apocalyptic in the prophetic tradition.⁸¹ In other words, one could not assess the apocalyptic claims, ideas, and phenomena of Jewish writings such as Isaiah 24–27 and Zechariah 9 or the NT Apocalypse (Revelation) without first examining how apocalyptic motifs appear in these other writings with their wide range of contexts. Third, the kind of methodology required is a study of the relationship between early apocalyptic writings and their actual historical significance in contemporary events (e.g., the loss of nationhood for Israel). Philipp Vielhauer has also adopted this outlook search for resemblances in his *Apocalypse and Related Subjects* which he applies to a group of writings written in the Christian era.⁸²

J. J. Collins

The essay that spear-headed discussion of the distinctive character of AE over PE is John J. Collin's "Apocalyptic Eschatology as the Transcendence of Death."⁸³ Collins begins by avoiding "purely terminological discussions" and goes on to describe three unsuccessful formulations to the problem as the idea of a definite end of the world, the distinction of two periods, and apocalyptic as myth. Collins rejects these views and argues that Jewish apocalyptic must be understood at the level of the individual. In practice, Collins, like Charles and Russell, prefers to relate AE to hope in the hereafter and expectation of divine judgment of the dead beyond history.⁸⁴

The concept of AE is also embedded in his 1979 definition of apocalypse as a genre which states that "apocalypse is a genre of revelatory

---

79. Hanson, "Jewish Apocalyptic," 33. Note the change in "instrumentality."

80. Hanson, *Dawn of Apocalyptic*, 7–12. Hanson, *Old Testament Apocalyptic*, 28.

81. Hanson openly critiqued contemporary methods of studying apocalyptic. See Hanson, "Recapitulation of an Ancient Ritual Pattern," 37.

82. Vielhauer and Strecker, "Apocalypses and Related Subjects," 558.

83. Collins, "Apocalyptic Eschatology," 21–43.

84. Ibid. The same argument is made in Collins, *Apocalyptic Imagination*, 10. See also Collins, "From Prophecy to Apocalypticism," xv.

literature with a narrative framework, in which a revelation is mediated by an otherworldly being to a human recipient, disclosing a transcendent reality which is both temporal, insofar as it envisages eschatological salvation, and spatial insofar as it involves another supernatural world.[85] This definition helps scholars to distinguish between two distinct types of material: historical apocalypses and cosmic apocalypses. From his extensive study of apocalyptic, Collins further recognizes that eschatology is consistent in apocalypses and that the noun "apocalypticism" refers to the worldview common to apocalypses, and that the worldview emphasizes the activity of supernatural agents.[86]

S. L. Cook

Another work analyzing apocalyptic eschatology from a sociological view is that of Stephen Cook in *Prophecy and Apocalypticism: The Postexilic Social Setting*.[87] Cook poses one of the key questions for apocalyptic: What do non-apocalyptic genre texts reveal about eschatology? Cook makes three main points about AE. First, "proto-apocalyptic" Jewish texts (Isa 24–27; Ezek 38 and 39; Zech 1–8; and Joel 2:1–11, 3–4) originate within disenfranchised groups.[88] Responding to Hanson's view of the linear development of apocalyptic, Cook denies Persian influence (namely of transcendence and dualism) as the origin of Jewish apocalyptic.[89] Second, the proto-apocalyptic texts are compatible with PE. Proto-apocalyptic texts form a bridge to the distinctive worldview which is later characterized as apocalyptic. A

---

85. Collins, *Imagination*, 5. The genre of apocalypse as literature along with discussion of worldview remains for Collins the focal point of discussing apocalyptic. Collins, "From Prophecy to Apocalypticism," xiv.

86. Collins, *Imagination*, 12–13. Murphy, *Religious World of Jesus*, 163.

87. For a brief review, see Cook, *Prophecy and Apocalypticism*, 5. Cook criticizes Rowley and Russell for not using sociology in their biblical studies of apocalyptic and for merely describing the literary characteristics of apocalyptic texts as distinct from prophecy.

88. The opposition comes from the priestly establishment as inner-Israelite social alienation not external persecution. See Cook, *Prophecy and Apocalypticism*, v. Like Hanson, Cook opposes the thesis of Plöger, that prophecy and apocalyptic were linked, and that of two traditions of development in Israel religion one (the Hasidim) was thoroughly apocalyptic.

89. These are identified as "secondary features" of apocalyptic literature. Cook, *Prophecy and Apocalypticism*, 125–33.

number of scholars follow Cook in this regard.[90] Third, in the line of Plöger and Hanson, Cook argues that the eschatology envisaged in Zechariah 1–8 is despite the "genre question," significantly different from normative PE and distinctive enough to be characterized as AE. Proto-apocalyptic Jewish texts in practice reveal a type of eschatology where "final salvation will be brought about by the intervention of the transcendent (*durch Transzendenten Eingriff*) into history" (Zech 1:13–16).[91] In Zechariah's vision, the "mythical-realistic image" of the four horns (1:18–21) can be identified with the world powers arrayed against Israel (as in Dan 7:7–8, 24; 8:3, 5–9; Rev 13:1; 17:12–13).

Cook emphasizes positive apocalyptic. In contrast to Frost, Cook along with Russell and Collins, emphasizes apocalyptic fits the reality of the historical situation it intends to represent concerning the eschaton and the anticipated presence of Yahweh in the city of Jerusalem. A more recent essay by Cook further emphasizes the importance of earthly and heavenly reality in close connection with the view of reality known as apocalypticism: "Apocalyptic worldviews—held by 'millennial' groups and expressed in writing as apocalyptic texts—expect a heavenly, ontological separate world to intervene imminently in actual history, ending the current era and radically improving the world."[92]

Moving Away from the Consensus

C. Rowland

One study which appeared in 1982 reached conclusions very different from the prophecy school. This is Christopher Rowland, *The Open Heaven*.

---

90. Similarly, Reddish notes that although Isa 24–27 is not thought to belong to the genre of apocalypse, it contains similar eschatological pronouncements to those found in Jewish apocalypses. These include: (1) universal judgment, (2) the eschatological banquet, and (3) destruction of God's enemies. These Hebrew passages are seen by various scholars as probably reflecting the beginning stages of apocalyptic literature in Israel. "They provide the bridge between prophetic and apocalyptic thought." See Reddish, *Apocalyptic Literature*, 29. Since the time of B. Duhm many scholars have interpreted chapters 24–27 as belonging to the apocalyptic genre of literature. Duhm, *Das buch Jesaia*, 172–94. W. Rudolph and J. Lindblom studied this thesis and concluded that these chapters describe an eschatological judgment within history. For example, see Lindblom, *Prophecy in Ancient Israel*, 417.

91. Cook, *Prophecy and Apocalypticism*, 127.

92. See also Cook, "Mythological Discourse in Ezekiel and Daniel," 85.

Rowland's understanding of apocalyptic is controlled by problems he finds with earlier genre studies. He points out that not all apocalypses contain eschatology (e.g., *Slav. Enoch* 39.2 and 65.6f), and that others show "little or no interest in eschatology."[93] His examination of apocalyptic leads to the conclusion that "what we are faced with in apocalyptic, therefore, is a type of religion whose distinguishing feature is a belief in direct revelation of the things of God which is mediated through dream, vision, or divine intermediary."[94] For Rowland, apocalyptic is defined as the revelation of secrets. However, he also views apocalyptic in the NT and in 1 Corinthians like church prophecy and sees it as direct revelation (1 Cor 12–14; 3:16; 6:19). Rowland sees the "religious outlook" of NT prophets as "merged" with a charismatic framework and unlike Jewish apocalyptic writers.[95]

The guiding question in Rowland's study is whether eschatology in the apocalypse is a distinct category in Judaism. He makes four points about OT apocalyptic. First, it cannot be denied that eschatology has a part to play in apocalyptic because there is overlap between the two. Second, apocalyptic and rabbinic eschatology are closely associated and apocalyptic is consistent with the view of God's covenant held to by the rabbis.[96] Third, a work is no less an example of apocalyptic because it lacks eschatology.[97] Here, Rowland is thinking of the kind of eschatology found in the Qumran writing. This eschatology is distinctive. One example he cites of this is the rabbis' "stereotypical" perceptual axis of thought which moved on temporal lines and contrasted the present age with the future age. Among the rabbis this doctrine of the two ages was not "infected" with this pessimistic form of dualistic outlook.[98] On this basis, Rowland identifies the basis of the rabbinic shift to other groups was the apocalyptic enthusiasm and "fervent expectation" seen in certain groups like Qumran. He quotes two texts. A contemporary of Josephus, Rabban Johanan ben Zakkai, says, "If you have a seedling in your hand, and they say to you, look here comes the Messiah, go out and plant your seedling first, and then come out to meet him" (*Abot. R. Nat* 31).[99] Similarly, R. Jose b. Halafta (c. AD 150) forbids any calculation

---

93. Rowland, *Open Heaven*, 28.

94. Ibid., 21.

95. Ibid., 353.

96. Ibid., 29–30. The dichotomy between "law" and a "prophetic view of history" held by G. F. Moore and T. W. Manson cannot be "maintained."

97. Ibid., 28.

98. Ibid., 35.

99. Saldarini, *Fathers according to Rabbi Nathan*, 182.

of the date of the end.[100] Rowland is keenly aware of the problem of boundaries when assessing apocalypse as a genre. Fourth, Rowland seems intent on not defining AE clearly. He claims that "advice from patriarchs (*T. Reu.* 3:11; *1 En* 40:1), oracles and divine mysteries[101] involving "direct revelation" and "heavenly encounters"[102] are important elements in apocalyptic that are passed over. Thus, he argues, it is incorrect to highlight AE as a distinctive form of apocalyptic. On the basis of this context, he in fact equates AE with a sectarian outlook dominated by imminence, pessimism, and an unhealthy dualism which is far from mainstream Judaism.

From this investigation Rowland states, "We do not want to give the impression there . . . is a completely coherent apocalyptic eschatology."[103] He aims to raise questions about other elements in apocalyptic literature yet avoids attempts to construct an apocalyptic eschatology which differs "from the ideas of other writers at the time."[104] Chapter 2 of his book is entitled "Apocalyptic and Eschatology" and in it Rowland effectively argues that eschatology is a subset of apocalyptic. In other words, apocalyptic literature encompasses eschatology, but the degree or kind of eschatology is less relevant to general discussions of worldview. Fifth, he claims the features identified as distinctively apocalyptic demonstrate how eschatology dominated early Christianity.[105]

Rowland's choice of reframing or reformulating of the eschatological restoration is certainly legitimate when Jewish apocalyptic studies are considered in their broadest terms. He is correct to note that the term apocalyptic cannot be used as a synonym of eschatology. But the same conceptual relationship cannot be said to hold true when biblical and like-minded apocalyptic writings are considered, and a definition of AE can effectively be pursued and construed. He goes too far in questioning whether a distinctive type of AE exists. For Rowland, eschatology is a minor subset of apocalyptic. In practice, then, the two have little connection and need to be disassociated. This represents a significant departure from the consensus of scholars.

---

100. Rowland, *Open Heaven*, 31. *Abot R. Nat.* chap. 31.
101. Rowland, *Open Heaven*, 18–20.
102. Ibid., 21–22.
103. Rowland, *Open Heaven*, 37.
104. Ibid., 71, 25–30.
105. See his critique of J. Dunn. Ibid., 355.

Eschatological Relationships and Jesus

L. J. Grabbe and R. D. Haak

A more recent study in 2001 edited by Lester Grabbe and R. D. Haak is *Knowing the End from the Beginning*.[106] Its ten essays aim to renew attention to the subject of the relationship between prophetic and apocalyptic. Grabbe uses "apocalyptic" as a noun (as the equivalent of "apocalypticism") and as an adjective.[107] Predominantly his concern is the noun form as it describes two literary and sociological phenomena.

The various authors explain apocalyptic in terms of its relationship to eschatology. Grabbe's position is that apocalyptic eschatology is not central to the discussion of apocalyptic. Following Roberts' criticism of Hanson's work in 1976 and 1992, he makes two points about apocalyptic. First, myth is important for the apocalyptic worldview. Second, he identifies the problem with Hanson's view as its false supposition that prophecy has a historical worldview but that apocalyptic has a mythical one; this he says is "a false dichotomy."[108] Third, the dichotomy forces a distinction between AE and PE:[109] "These definitions are problematic. They assume a major difference between 'this-worldly' actions and events and 'otherworldly' ones. It is essentially the old dichotomy of history versus myth, a distorted and still widely influential view, does not hinder the discussion."[110]

In an essay in response, Collins affirms that distinctions must not be absolutized but they are necessary to bring clarity to the understanding of apocalyptic.[111] Collins and Grabbe agree that a simple "history versus myth" dichotomy is inaccurate and needs to be addressed. It is more correct to say that myth is present in the worldview of prophecy and apocalyptic ideas. These are not antithetical worldviews, yet the language of myth is the focus and expression in the second worldview. Just because revelation draws on mythical worldview it does not mitigate its historical aspect.

---

106. Grabbe and Haak, eds., *Knowing the End*.
107. Grabbe, "Introduction and Overview," 3.
108. Grabbe, "Prophecy and Apocalyptic," 112.
109. Grabbe, "Introduction and Overview," 18.
110. Grabbe, "Prophecy and Apocalyptic," 112.
111. Collins, "Prophecy, Apocalypse and Eschatology," 51. Horsley, *Revolt of the Scribes*. Horsley downplays eschatology in apocalyptic texts and attempts to explain this literature in terms of scribal resistance to imperial rule.

How Apocalyptic Literature Is Read
Assessment and Conclusion

It is not a simple matter to determine how apocalyptic is to be read in relation to eschatology. The review of the historical discussion has identified key problems; (1) in the formulation or articulation of various relationships and (2) in how modern interpreters read, interpret and assess the works of others. There are some preliminary lessons that can be learned. Also some trends have emerged and a number of questions remain.

Two main lessons emerge from the review. First, a solely genre focused approach can be detrimental for understanding AE. Attempts to define AE will vary depending on the kind of literature in view within a broad ranging JAT. So, comparisons between prophetic and exilic eschatology compared to one between full blown AE from apocalypses such as Daniel and *1 Enoch* has interesting findings. Other factors such as canonical status and progressive revelation are important as well. From the perspective of a large pool of writings (where certain texts make the cut into the apocalyptic genre in the whole scheme of things) eschatology may hold a minor role and AE seemingly insignificant. How this relates to the historical situation of various groups, their popularity in Judaism, and the influence their writings did or did not have is another issue.[112] It is still paramount for the analytical scholar to engage with the text and evaluate the truth claims that the text affirms. Similarly, Charles's idea that PE involves Gentile empires while AE does not seems a false dichotomy. Why is it not possible to have the theme of the defeat of foreign nations as found in the *Sibylline Oracles* central to early Jewish apocalyptic and its literature?

Second, perspective is a key concept for apocalyptic. On this note, attempts to identify a single defining point of AE are counterproductive. Past distinctions made by Collins describe the distinctive phenomena of AE to be either (1) the cataclysmic end of the world, (2) dualism, (3) myth, or (4) individual hope of resurrection. These are choices the interpreter does not need to make. Collins's choice of identifying a hope for "blessed immortality" and belief in the judgment of the dead as uniting themes is an expression of what Jewish hope of reality from the perspective of an apocalyptic worldview looks like. Other elements, whether or not they take place in the world of real history are no less "real" in the Jewish tradition. If there is a complementary core of features, not just one, we should reject the

---

112. See Davies's chap. 2, "Apocalyptic and Pharisaism," in *Christian Origins and Judaism*, 19–30.

idea that apocalyptic writings are dominated by an "urgent expectation of the overthrow of all earthly conditions."[113]

Third, Collins concludes that eschatology is consistent in apocalypses. The significance of this for a text like Mark 13 is that both positive and negative features of apocalyptic would apply. Spatial dualism—a "from above" distinction versus a "from below" description would be appropriate and a description of merging of the transcendent with the temporal would be unlikely unless proven exegetically. Furthermore, Collins notes that the common view of apocalyptic in popular consciousness is expectation of the cataclysmic end of the world. But neither he nor D. E. Aune supports this notion.[114] Rather, it would be more productive if AE shared a conceptual framework that would form a "scenario" as a type of eschatology commonly recognized as "apocalypticism." As Collins says, implicit in that genre is a worldview that people express to "view the problems of life."[115] That apocalypticism may be defined in terms of a social-historical-theological movement in post-exilic Judaism that has a unique perspective on God's activity in the world concerning the time of the end is a fair proposal based on the data.[116] Furthermore, most of its believers share "the conceptual framework of the [apocalyptic] genre, endorsing a worldview in which supernatural revelation, the heavenly world, and eschatological judgment played essential parts."[117] Other distinctive features of this framework include the prominence of supernatural beings, angels and demons, and their involvement in human affairs. So if these themes are expressed in a variety of contexts and movements, a group "can be apocalyptic apart from the production of apocalypses."[118]

Fourth, there is still a trend to marginalize apocalyptic eschatology. The debate centers on issues of terminology, the nature of AE, and overarching categories under which literature can be subsumed and less about

---

113. On the "speedy end of the world," see Koch, *Rediscovery of Apocalyptic*, 28.

114. Cancik, "Greek and Roman Antiquity," 129. Aune, "Apocalypticism," 25.

115. For Collins the worldview expressed in normal life is applied individually to the expectation of death and the hope of afterlife. Collins, *Apocalyptic Imagination*, 8.

116. Cf. Allison, "Apocalyptic," 19.

117. Cancik, "Greek and Roman Antiquity," 13. He reasons that in this sense early Christianity is arguably apocalyptic apart from the production of apocalypse.

118. Ibid. Collins goes on to argue that apocalypticism as worldview was not the "exclusive property" of any one sect, but was typical of different movements from time to time. Cancik, "Greek and Roman Antiquity," 158.

sociology or origins. It is no longer possible to say, as Collins did in 1974, that all scholars admit there are two types of future expectation.[119]

Fifth, in Jewish writings, there is the question of negative and positive apocalyptic. What would these labels mean for a text like Mark 13? The significance of these labels for Mark 13 would be that Daniel presents no resolution to the plight of apocalyptic and that AE is isolated from any real solution for Israel. For Meyer and Wright apocalyptic needed to be reinterpreted to derive any value for Christianity.

Finally, concerns about false dichotomies between "history and myth" and "law and apocalyptic" and the issue of the consistency of eschatology must be clarified. Some formulations of AE assume various Jewish groups were in total opposition to it. This is incorrect. Roberts' idea, recently re-expressed by Grabbe and Haak, that Hanson's definition of AE fosters a "false dichotomy" between the historical and mythical, is incorrect. To speak of AE was to speak of change. Such scholars often implied that an eschatological perspective necessitates the replacement of the historical. Hanson, Aune, and Collins along with other scholars are right in holding to AE, while allowing for a developing definition in the JAT. This development is found in the *emergence* of full-blown apocalypticism or AE within Second Temple Judaism.

Related to this is the question, should we use just one definition of apocalyptic. With regard to the formulations in Jewish apocalyptic and modern scholarship the answer is no. The review illustrates the diverse treatment given to AE. Not all Jewish groups held to an imminent expectation. Not all had the same perspective on the doctrine of two ages.

It also shows the way that *relationships are formulated* reflects what criteria or phenomena one is willing to work with (sociological, literary, theological, or historical). If, like von Rad, the central phenomena are identified as the dualization of the world as history, then all other relationships will be related to this central idea. The most significant attempts to describe the phenomena of AE, however, are those that link history and prophecy. A construct can either cover details about apocalyptic by designating one overarching category or it can work to be descriptive in several areas. These are questions of perspective and hermeneutics in explaining how aspects do and do not relate. Ultimately the questions about the conceptual

---

119. Collins, "Apocalyptic Eschatology," 22. Back then Collins argued "terminological discussion" could be avoided with priority given to discussing the phenomenon of future expectations related to AE.

framework of AE must be tested exegetically so that its nature, scope and related themes may be determined. However, we must first review how NT interpreters understand apocalyptic in the Gospels.

Apocalyptic Literature in the History of New Testament Interpretation and Historical Jesus Study

As the preceding survey has shown, our understanding of apocalyptic eschatology has changed considerably over the past 100 years. AE initially was interpreted in the light of just one trait, then it was linked with worldview as a definition of apocalypticism was developed, and subsequently some have questioned its existence. The motif of imminence has similarly played an inflated role in views of apocalyptic in the history of NT interpretation. Among Jesus scholars, personal titles and paradigms, such as "Jesus was an apocalyptic prophet" or "Jesus was a noneschatological prophet," have overshadowed discussion of apocalyptic eschatology.[120] This survey now seeks to trace the interpretation of apocalyptic from the narrower perspective of historical Jesus studies.[121]

Given the complex debate over the elements of AE and apocalypticism, it is a daunting task to frame categories in the history of NT interpretation on apocalyptic. The impetus for the study of the Historical Jesus has often been the question of the unity and diversity of New Testament doctrine and the need to find an acceptable approach to apocalyptic. Over the modern history of NT Study, there have been at least five broad approaches or basic paradigms to understanding NT apocalyptic.

Apocalyptic as Unimportant in Classic Liberalism

In the modern critical period of New Testament study, when Gospel studies were first critically examined, several scholars articulated views on biblical theology. H. S. Reimarus (1694–1768), the initiator of the quest for the historical Jesus, separated the teaching of Jesus from what the Apostles taught about him. This rationalistic approach focused on political goals, not on apocalyptic. Others, like H. G. Paulus (1761–1851), rejected the miracle

---

120. Rowley, *Relevance of Apocalyptic*, 34.

121. For a summary of the phases of the quest of the historical Jesus, see Theissen and Merz, *Historical Jesus*, 1–14; Bock, *Studying the Historical Jesus*, 141–52.; Bock, *Studying the Historical Jesus*, 141–52.

events in the life of Jesus. The posthumously published work of F. D. E. Schleiermacher, *Leben Jesu* (1864), differentiated between the Jesus of history and the Christ of faith. A choice demanded between the Synoptics and the Johannine account. In 1787, during the period when source criticism was underway in Gospel studies, J. P. Gabler, professor of theology at the University of Altdort, introduced a distinction between biblical theology and dogmatic theology. In his inaugural lecture, Gabler argued that one must emphasize the differences between NT texts. Gabler rejected the idea of "a unity in diversity" in the theology of the New Testament and this influenced subsequent scholars researching NT themes like apocalyptic. As a rationalist, he rejected miracles and instead focused on irreconcilable differences between NT books.

This line of thinking was developed by the founder of Tübingen school, F. C. Baur (1792–1860), and H. J. Holtzman. Baur argued that the Jerusalem church and Pauline mission had different theologies. The school reconstructed the history of the apostolic and subapostolic age by claiming a fundamental antithesis between Peter and Paul. The solution Baur presented was a synthesis that the NT writings were not apostolic documents by eyewitnesses, but second-century works that presented a developing Catholicism. D. F. Strauss (1801–1874) a student of F. C. Baur, rejected the idea of divine intervention in the world, and thus dismissed the doctrine of the incarnation, and held the Jesus of the Gospel narratives as mythological. He also denied Jesus' foreknowledge of the destruction of the temple in Jerusalem (Mark 13:2) and declared that the discourse on the Second Advent was inauthentic.[122]

Others at Tübingen who focused on the moral teachings of Jesus included A. Ritschl who interpreted Christianity as purely an ethical religion. Ritschl attempted to construct a theology that directly related to salvation for the church. Thus he expounded the kingdom of God as the highest

---

122. Strauss, *Life of Jesus Critically Examined*, 597. Strauss acknowledges that in this discourse Jesus begins to speak of the destruction of Jerusalem and then discusses his return at "the end of all things." The two events are "in immediate chronological connexion." Strauss, *Life of Jesus Critically Examined*, 585. Strauss lays out his interpretive options for explaining the relationships: (1) either deny that Jesus spoke in part of something now past and allege that he spoke only of what is still future, (2) or deny part of the discourse relates to something still future so that the entire prediction in the discourse refers to what is already past, (3) or admit the discourse of Jesus does partly refer to something which is still future to us, but either deny that he places the two series of events in immediate chronological succession, or maintain that he has also noticed what is intermediate.

good and task of the Christian community.¹²³ On this basis the *religionsgeschichtliche* school of Tübingen attached less importance to contemporary Jewish influence and faith (imminence and Jewish messiah) and held that the Hellenistic world influenced Christianity. As a result apocalyptic was considered a minimal influence on Jesus and early Christianity. However, its complete avoidance of the topic was unjustified as the Hellenistic world (Baur's reference point) had its own apocalyptic.¹²⁴

Apocalyptic as Central:
The End of the World in Weiss and Schweitzer

Concurrent with Baur's writings in a climate of distrust in the unity of the NT documents and Scripture and developing the work of Gospel criticism, J. Weiss (1863–1914) wrote *Die Predigt Jesu vom Reiche Gottes* (1892) in protest at the widely accepted view of eschatology of his father-in-law Ritschl and Wrede. Weiss made several points. First, Weiss argued for a close continuity with apocalyptic Judaism¹²⁵ in Jesus' teaching. In Jesus, the kingdom of God was viewed as something future and eschatological which only God could bring about (Matt 24:38–39; Luke 17:26–27). Second, Weiss rejected any notion that the kingdom was inward or spiritual.¹²⁶ Jesus recognized no preliminary actualization of the rule of God in the lives of his disciples. He denied there was ever a notion of "two stages"; one preliminary, the other "the kingdom of completion."¹²⁷ Third, this expectation of an imminent kingdom equated to expectation of a catastrophic end of the world. Fourth, the catastrophic end of the world did not come to pass and Jesus and the church got it wrong. Regarding the coming kingdom, Weiss understood that the apocalyptic "in breaking" kingdom meant Jesus did not distinguish between it and his Parousia. Furthermore, he viewed the temple's destruction as an incidental feature with the approaching end of the world.

---

123. Swing, *Theology of Albrecht Ritschl*, 28, 174. Apocalyptic falls "within the goal" of supporting instruction in the Christian religion.

124. Cf. Cancik, "End of the Worlds of History," 84–125. BDAG, 112 (s.v. ἀποκαλύπτω). The literal sense of the term is to "uncover" as of a head (Hdt. 1, 119, 6).

125. For this common view, see also Case, *Evolution of Early Christianity*.

126. Weiss, *Jesus' Proclamation of the Kingdom of God*, 133.

127. Ibid., 129.

How Apocalyptic Literature Is Read

Yet for Weiss, this historical critical interpretation was a methodological first. As Perrin has noted, the relationship between historical critical study and hermeneutics meant the acceptance of consistent eschatology regarding the end of the world. It also raised a problem of relevance which Bultmann was to answer.[128]

Albert Schweitzer (1875–1965) developed and popularized the work already completed by Weiss. He also began a quest for the "historical Jesus." The purpose of the quest was to reconstruct the Gospels, and the sources behind the Gospels, in order to understand and interpret Jesus in strictly historical and human categories.[129] In *The Quest for the Historical Jesus* (1906), originally published as *Von Reimarus zu Wrede: Eine Geschichte der Leben Jesu Forschung*, Schweitzer summarized 250 authors from the late eighteenth century to the beginning of the twentieth who investigated the life of Jesus.[130] Schweitzer opposed Baur's thesis of a monotheistic Judaism represented by a Petrine party out of which Pauline Christianity emerged. He acknowledged the complexity of the contemporary Jewish thought world, and argued that one cannot understand Jesus without appreciating his apocalyptic message in its setting. Consequently, he held that interpreting Jesus is only possible with the aid of the Jewish apocalyptic literature and that John the Baptist, Jesus, and Paul are "culmination manifestations of apocalyptic thought."[131] Since Jesus was a Jew there was no reason why first quest scholars should not give weight to his Jewish context. For Schweitzer, Jesus was an apocalyptist but he denied any rabbinic background for understanding Jesus as he thought rabbinic Judaism and apocalyptic Judaism were essentially antagonistic.[132]

---

128. Perrin, "Eschatology and Hermeneutic," 7. Consistent Eschatology is a phrase associated with Schweitzer. The view emphasized the arrival of kingdom in the future, particularly the near future (Mark 14:25; Matt 8:11 / Luke 13:28). Schweitzer held that the historical Jesus believed the kingdom would arrive when the present evil age ends.

129. Gnilka summarizes the first quest in three points. First, the goal was the separation of Jesus and the Gospels; the historical Jesus could not be discovered in the Gospel. Second, the Gospels were not historical documents but were intentionally written as biased theology. Third, the Gospels reveal a *Kerygma* that reinterpreted Jesus' words for its own purpose and the kingdom of God as an institution synonymous with the church. Gnilka, *Jesus of Nazareth*, 2.

130. Schweitzer, *Von Reimarus zu Wrede*. Some consider the time from Reimarus to 1990 as the first phase of research into New Testament Christology which focused on Jesus' messiahship. See Theissen and Merz, *Historical Jesus*, 514–23.

131. Schweitzer, *Quest of the Historical Jesus*, 365.

132. Ibid.

Eschatological Relationships and Jesus

On the other hand, Schweitzer, who was taught by Weiss, argued that Jesus expected the end to come during his ministry (Matt 10:23), and that the kingdom proclaimed by Jesus should be understood as an objective, messianic kingdom. When it did not arrive, Jesus went to the cross. In his thoroughgoing scheme of eschatology (a term translated by Montgomery) Schweitzer denied the kingdom was wholly transcendent, however, and he saw eschatology divided into two epochs in the ministry of Jesus.[133] The dividing point in Jesus' ministry is the sending out of the disciples (Mark 6:1–13; Matt 10:23) in anticipation of his imminent inauguration as the Son of Man and the arrival of the kingdom. Schweitzer argued that the disciples did return before the appearance of the Son of Man and kingdom (delay of the Parousia) so Jesus initiated a second stage in his ministry. This view denies that the cross was central to Jesus from the beginning of his ministry (Mark 8:31; 9:12; 10:33 and parallels).

W. Bousset in his 1913 book *Kyrios Christos* traced evolving theories of the eschatology of the church.[134] He sharply distinguished between the beliefs of historical Jesus, the faith of primitive Christianity, and the belief of the Hellenistic church and Paul. He expressed the view that the early Christianity shared the existing eschatological form of Jewish messianic hope. According to Bousset, the distinctive feature of the church was the identification of Jesus with the apocalyptic Son of Man. This was developed at Antioch of Syria and expressed in the phrase "Jesus is Lord." Early Christianity departed from being a faith in a coming messiah to develop into the cult of Jesus as Lord. In this view, the historical Jesus was non-apocalyptic.

After the time of Weiss, there was continued debate over Christology and eschatology—especially over Jesus' attachment to apocalyptic. Following the anti-dogmatic vein of the first quest, R. Bultmann emphasized myth over theological coherence of the quest.

Bultmann held that apocalyptic was central to early Christianity and Judaism but needed to be demythologized. Myth for Bultmann was necessary because the nature of historical experience denies the reality of divine

---

133. Schweitzer, *Quest of the Historical Jesus*, 246, 354, 359. Consistent eschatology is the phrase Schweitzer used in 1906 to describe the teaching of the historical Jesus consistently based on the idea of the near arrival of the kingdom of God. Montgomery translates *Konsequente Eschatology* as "thoroughgoing Eschatology." See also Sauter, *What Dare We Hope?*, 32. Though Weiss and Schweitzer's theological position is rightly classified together in their affront against the historical-critical ideas of classical liberalism, their differences are important.

134. Bousset, *Kyrios Christos*.

How Apocalyptic Literature Is Read

intervention.[135] He accepted eschatology as horizontal language (to describe the apparent movement forward in time) whose actual referent is the possibility of moving upwards spiritually into a new level of existence. He interpreted it as Gnosticism in Jewish language.[136] This phase of research in NT Christology and apocalypticism was, therefore, represented by the synthesis of form-critical skepticism (of history) and history-of-religions transference theories concerning Hellenistic worldviews.[137]

Apocalyptic as Reinterpretation of the OT by the Church

A number of scholars fit under this category. They read apocalyptic as a reinterpretation of the OT in the New. Several scholars are considered here: E. Käsemann, C. H. Dodd, N. Perrin, M. Borg, and proponents from the Jesus Seminar.

In his influential essay *The Beginnings of Christian Theology*, first published in German in 1960,[138] an address given at a reunion of Bultmann's students began a new quest (now called the second quest) of the historical Jesus.[139] Ernst Käsemann opposed Bultmann's historical skepticism and advocated a reinterpretation of apocalyptic.[140] Käsemann separated discussion of Jesus' use of apocalyptic in the Gospel of Matthew from the view that Jesus had some apocalyptic ideas.[141] In Matthew 10:41–42; 12:4,

---

135. Ladd, *New Testament and Criticism*, 183.

136. Wright, *Jesus and the Victory of God*, 208.

137. This period in NT interpretation was critical for: (1) the rise of form-critical skepticism, (2) the history-of-religions transference theories of Bultmann, and (3) the transformation of this synthesis in the phase of the new quest of the historical Jesus after 1953.

138. An English edition appeared nine years later. Käsemann, "Beginnings of Christian Theology," 92–98.

139. The third revision of Christology research coincided with the new quest which dated from Oct 20, 1953, and reopened with Bultmann's students J. Robinson and E. Käsemann. They applied new critical methods of form, redaction and tradition criticism to determine the authenticity of Jesus' sayings. The theme of Son of Man and Jesus were accepted. For many in the second quest period, apocalyptic was of minimal importance for Jesus but became important to the early church. Theissen, "Historical Skepticism," 514–23.

140. Käsemann, "Problem of the Historical Jesus."

141. Käsemann argued the *ipsissima verba* of the earthly Jesus are lost on the one hand and accepted that Jesus used apocalyptic on the other. But his reconstruction of the Gospels makes the question of how Jesus used apocalyptic moot. Käsemann, "Beginnings

32 and 13:12, the emphasis is on applied apocalyptic eschatology in the form of prophetic speech. There are two dimensions to Käsemann's claims. First, when one sees apocalyptic themes in Matthew, the reader realizes that what is being highlighted is the apostolic response to local divisions in the church over universal teaching about the time of the end. In other words, apocalyptic expectation (namely "imminence") turns gnomic future sayings into eschatological future sayings. This form-critical approach recreates a history behind the text.

Second, Käsemann understood that the issue was in understanding the relation of the proclamation about Jesus to the message of Jesus, and he sought to clarify the roots of apocalyptic. But where Schweitzer turned the whole question of apocalyptic into a problem of researching the historical Jesus to explain the Gospel narrative in terms of the delay of the Parousia,[142] Käsemann makes the Parousia irrelevant to Jesus.

His understanding of apocalyptic is controlled by several factors. First, he recognized the concept of apocalypticism (worldview) and AE in particular is not in itself a shocking thing. On Matthew 11:23, for example, Käsemann adduces this comparison between Capernaum and Sodom is about an "apocalyptic pattern" which has its antecedent in the OT and is consistent with late apocalyptic thinking in Judaism. Likewise, Matthew's famous warning, "He who speaks a word against the Son of Man will be forgiven. But he who speaks against the Holy Spirit will not be forgiven, either in this age or that which is coming" (Matt 12:32), particularly the reference to the "two ages," is typical of temporal or eschatological dualism from an apocalyptic viewpoint.[143] Yet this "adaptation" by the church of the "two age" schema of history for its own esoteric teaching to "insiders" is not typical of the Jewish apocalyptic scenario. Even in the Qumran tradition, it is not the wandering faithful but the demise of the present world order that is the focus of Satan and his human accomplices.

This said, the more contentious point of Käsemann's thesis was that Matthew's gospel supports an *apocalyptic eschatology* that draws on OT themes and reflects a coherent apocalyptic worldview.[144] The problem in his

---

of Christian Theology," 101–3.

142. Ibid., 101.

143. On this reckoning Luke 17:26 follows the similar pattern of ethical dualism that contrasts the "wicked" and the "wise" or "righteous" and the "unrighteous."

144. His essay invigorated scholars in the 1970s, many of whom spoke of an "apocalyptic renaissance." See Koch, *Ratlos vor der Apokalyptik*. Translated the same year into English as Koch, *Rediscovery of Apocalyptic*, 11–17. Braaten, *Christ and Counter-Christ*.

theory is that Jesus has no synthesis of apocalyptic.[145] Käsemann has been criticized since imminence is not the central feature in Jewish apocalyptic thought, and Käsemann's view gives too much prominence to prophets and apostolic prophecy.[146]

In seeking to avert the dichotomy between proclamation and delay by Schweitzer, Käsemann went the other way in reinterpreting apocalyptic of early Christian prophets. In response, he created a new dichotomy by interpreting the early church in a period of community crisis as a revelation of its apocalyptic mind.[147] Käsemann's thesis was that since "apocalyptic was the mother of all theology" then the historical Jesus cannot be seen in these terms, for "the preaching of Jesus cannot be classified as theology."

C. H. Dodd had been noted for his views on apocalyptic. In focusing on the parables of Jesus, Dodd concluded apocalyptic was not a dominant characteristic feature of Jesus' teaching, but became important to the church as it reinterpreted some of his apocalyptic teaching.[148] Dodd separates discussion of the prophetic words of historical Jesus in Mark 13:2 from the church's reapplication of apocalyptic in the kerygma message in Mark 13:25–28. The role of the NT interpreter is, therefore, to untangle the prophetic words of the historical Jesus from apocalyptic words.

Ladd, "Apocalyptic and New Testament Theology." The links Käsemann drew with Jewish apocalypticism became a sticking point and embarrassment to some scholars. See especially Rollins, "New Testament and Apocalyptic," 454–76. Although originally critiquing Käsemann's thesis, Rollins addresses broader questions and denies the legitimacy of applying the term "apocalyptic" to describe the early church's writings or theology. Instead, Rollins argues the NT is the product of "post-apocalypticism" which from its inception was in its theological orientation in fundamental conflict with Jewish apocalypticism. R. Funk gives four objections about the theology and history with Käsemann's interpretation: (1) themes are "intertwined," (2) the historical basis for the theological construct is doubtful, (3) judgments made about the continuity and discontinuity with Jesus and apocalyptic result in a number of theological "conceptual hostages" and they need to be identified, and (4) a "unilinear development" from Judaism through Jesus to the primitive church does not exist. Funk, however, recognizes the need to examine the "interplay between continuity and discontinuity" for history to be done justice. Funk, "Apocalyptic as an Historical and Theological Problem." See also the criticisms by Marshall, "Is Apocalyptic the Mother of Christian Theology?," 33–42.

145. Jeremias, *Parables of Jesus*, 14.

146. For a critique of the prominence given to prophets in the NT tradition by Käsemann, see Brown, "Prophet," 84–87.

147. Käsemann, "Beginnings of Christian Theology," 102.

148. Dodd, *Parables of the Kingdom*, rev. ed.

Eschatological Relationships and Jesus

There are two points of focus in Dodd's discussion. First, realized eschatology is a reality of the Gospel message. Many of the kingdom of God sayings of Jesus were related to a present reality (e.g., Matt 12:22/ Luke 11:20). Some sayings point to the kingdom of God beyond history (e.g., Mark 9:43–47; 10:17, 24; 12:25). Second, Dodd rejects the notion that apocalyptic imagery has a historical referent. He claims there is no certainty of how literal apocalyptic imagery was interpreted by first-century Jews.[149] Certain sayings in the Olivet Discourse (e.g., the Son of Man) are viewed symbolically without clear referents.[150] Dodd understood as authentic Mark 8:31, 9:31 and 10:31 concerning Jesus' prediction of his death and Mark 14:28 which records Jesus' predicted resurrection. But the relationship between the resurrection and the coming of the Son of Man in Mark 14:62 was shaped by a later church demarcation into two stages in light of its own experience.[151] These are symbols for saying the kingdom of God had come in history or is the ultimate triumph of God.[152] Only later did the church modify them to present a future Parousia in which Jesus' return "on the clouds of heaven" is shaped in apocalyptic terms. Dodd's decision became the precursor for Caird's and Meyer's avoidance of the topic of exaltation in their study of Second Temple Judaism. Wright and PD, however, go in different directions.[153]

J. Jeremias corrected Dodd's exaggerated emphasis on realized eschatology. He argued Jesus' view of the kingdom in its future aspects has more in common with current apocalyptic expectations which saw the kingdom as a supernatural event that was soon to come.[154] The kingdom was not a radical departure from apocalyptic Judaism as Dodd had maintained. Norman Perrin, like Jeremias, sees apocalyptic as essential to Christianity. He makes several points. First, Q like the Synoptic Gospels is an expression of "apocalyptic Christianity."[155] Perrin understands AE as the dominant eschatology in Q and represents an early Jewish apocalyptic Christianity

---

149. Dodd, *Apostolic Preaching and Its Developments*, 87.

150. Dodd, *Parables of the Kingdom*, 29, 73, 80.

151. Ibid., 74–77.

152. Ibid., 68, 82.

153. See Wright, *Victory of God*, 624–45; Bock, *Blasphemy and Exaltation in Judaism*. See Bock's recent updating in Bock, "Blasphemy and the Jewish Examination of Jesus," 53–114.

154. Telford, *Theology of the Gospel of Mark*, 76.

155. Perrin, *New Testament: An Introduction*, 100.

How Apocalyptic Literature Is Read

found in Palestine. Second, its collection of sayings and discourses exclusively attributed to Jesus are inauthentic. Third, the most dominant form of apocalyptic hope is the expectation of Jesus coming from heaven as the Son of Man (Luke 11:30; 12:8–9; 12:40; 17:24; 17:26, 30 and Matthean parallels). The Q community expected the return of Jesus from heaven as the Son of Man with power to execute the eschatological judgment (Luke 12:8–9). The Son of Man would come suddenly and unexpectedly, but he would certainly come (Luke 12:40). Fourth, Perrin along with most scholars sees Daniel 7:13–14 as the origin of the expectation of Jesus coming from heaven.[156]

Perrin, like Käsemann, sees the prophets as central to the form of AE in the Q tradition. Perrin concludes that Jonah's coming to the Ninevites (Luke 11:30) and the lightning striking (Luke 17:24) and the judgmental catastrophes associated with Noah and Lot (Luke 17:26, 30) are images drawn in characteristic fashion from the prophetic and apocalyptic tradition by prophets in need of giving form and content to their expectation of the return of the Son of Man.[157]

M. Borg, like Käsemann and Perrin, defines Jesus in a predominantly non-apocalyptic eschatology paradigm, and like Dodd he excludes texts that require an apocalyptic reading. He believes Jesus did predict some drastic political events if Israel did not repent (Mark 13:2). Yet, for Borg, this and all other which are apocalyptic (e.g., Mark 9:1; 13:25–28), are excluded from the Jesus of history.[158] Borg prefers grand titles for Jesus from "millenarian prophet" or "sage" to "mystic-healer-wisdom teacher-social

---

156. Perrin argues the community is interested in the "earthly ministry" saying of the Son of Man (Luke 7:34; 9:5; 12:10 and parallels) and in "eschatological judgment." Against H. Tödt, who held that Jesus proclaimed the coming of the Son of Man as eschatological judge without identifying himself with that figure leaving the early church to identify the Son of Man, Perrin holds the church formulated its expectation independently. His view has four assumptions of historicity: (1) the resurrection of Jesus was interpreted in light of Ps 110:1 and Dan 7:13–14, (2) Jesus did not speak of the Son of Man as eschatological Judge at all, (3) all the apocalyptic Son of Man sayings fail the criteria test for authenticity, and (4) instead the apocalyptic Son of Man exhibits the typical characteristics of early Christian prophecy.

157. Perrin, *New Testament: An Introduction*, 104. "The community *reached back* into the past history of the Jews and *claimed* that it would be like ... prophets spoke of ... soon to return Jesus."

158. According to Borg, there are only a few Son of Man expressions of imminent apocalyptic eschatology. These few coming of the Son of Man sayings and Matthew's judgment sayings can be ascribed to the post-Easter church. Borg, "Jesus Was Not an Apocalyptic Prophet," 41.

prophet-movement-initiator." Unlike Käsemann, Borg seeks to find other ways to explain apocalyptic themes, including viewing Jesus as a social prophet. Käsemann shows the broader elements of apocalyptic eschatology as a movement "at work," but assigns them to the early church. In rejecting the "imminence" texts, Borg must, however, contend with what he calls "secondary apocalyptic" aspects in Jesus.

A final group of interpreters insist that Jesus was a non-apocalyptic prophet. The Jesus Seminar claims that apocalyptic means the literal end of the world and they reject that Jesus taught it.[159] Crossan, like other Jesus seminar scholars, goes as far as to argue that apocalyptic teaching in Q belongs to a secondary apocalyptic layer in contrast to the original document.[160] Others, like D. Barr, have shifted discussion away from interpreting eschatology and apocalypse to interpretive issues covering the different worlds for readers of apocalyptic.[161]

Apocalyptic as Metaphor for Renewal

G. B. Caird's 1980 work, *The Language and Imagery of the Bible*, has an extended summary of eschatology and language and has been significant in the reading of apocalyptic. Particularly relevant for this discussion is chapter 14, "The Language of Eschatology," in regards to how he treats and defines eschatology and makes various assertions about the different relationships. First, instead of defining AE or mentioning it by name, Caird lists seven different interpretations of eschatology.[162] On the basis of comparing individual eschatology (Eschatology^I) and historical eschatology (Eschatology^H), he affirms the existence of "immortality" in the OT hope, the afterlife and resurrection (Ps 73:25–26), which the NT continues (Acts 24:15) and which Paul further associates with life with Christ (2 Cor 5:6–8;

---

159. Funk and Hoover, *Five Gospels*, 137. See also Meyer and Hughes, "Jesus Seminar and the Quest," 137.

160. Crossan, *Birth of Christianity*, 273–74. For a good defense on the unity of Q and its differences with Thomas, see Horsley, "Kingdom of God and the Renewal of Israel," 310.

161. Barr, *Reality of Apocalypse*, 73.

162. See Caird, *Language and Imagery of the Bible*, 246. For the idea of the transfer of language from one situation to another, see Caird, New Testament Theology, 246–47.

How Apocalyptic Literature Is Read

Phil 1:23). He also asserts that the theme of "immortality" is a distinct feature of AE.[163]

Furthermore, Caird picks one trait of AE (dualism, or the belief in the two ages) and proceeds to make a categorical judgment about how the two are related. For example, Caird concludes from the famous cry of the martyrs to God in Revelation 6:10 saying "how long ... before you judge those who live on the earth," (and the response) "each of them was given a white robe," that "Eschatology^I is firmly dissociated from Eschatology^H."[164] Second, Caird holds Weiss's interpretation of *Konsequente Eschatologie*, which foresaw the imminence of the end of the world, is misleading. Along with Dodd, Caird shows the "incoherences" of Weiss's view, by pointing to texts suggesting delay such as Luke 17:22–37, the beginning of woes preceding the great tribulation in Mark 13:3–13, and the parable of the absent landlord in Mark 13:32–37.[165]

The problem is that he does not investigate the possible alternatives involving AE and real world history. Caird's presupposition is that first-century writers regularly used end-of-the world language metaphorically to refer to events which they knew did not refer to the end of the world.[166] In other words, terms like "the day of the Lord" were used metaphorically for events occurring within history. The language used to describe Jesus' resurrection furnishes him with a prima facie case for saying that this is metaphor. End-of-the-world language refers to something that is literally not the end of the world.[167] Finally, although Caird devotes considerable attention to Weiss's view of apocalyptic, he only partially rejects it. The differences between AE and PE are considered to be one of historical circumstances in the context

---

163. He points out that "[teaching about] immortality came slowly and along two lines of development ... it is not surprising, therefore, to find New Testament writers' speaking of the heavenly life for the 'soul' or 'spirit' (1 Cor 5:5; Heb 12:23; 1 Pet 3:18; 4:6; Rev 6:9-11)." Caird, *Language*, 245.

164. Ibid., 246. On the same passage and cry for vindication 'within earthly history,' see *New Testament Theology*, 244.

165. There are three important points of comparison between Caird and Dodd: (1) he affirms Dodd was right in describing the beliefs of Jesus and the church as realized eschatology, (2) Caird denies the term adequately distinguished events of the Gospels from other events (church creations) as Dodd claimed, and (3) he disliked the fact Dodd spoke of eschatology (albeit church creation eschatology) as concerned with the *eschaton*, or the final event, as if "beyond which" nothing can conceivably happen. Ibid., 271.

166. Caird, *Language*, 256.

167. The category of typological is not denied here either, Caird, *New Testament Theology*, 247.

of Hellenization. The first is the breakdown of national boundaries resulting from the rule of Alexander the Great. The second circumstance is the persecution under Antiochus Epiphanies in 167 BC which Caird believes separated apocalyptic from discussions on Second Temple eschatology. He does not review his sets of eschatological relationships in light of other interpretations because his aim is to elevate the centrality of metaphor for understanding apocalyptic. Caird's overriding claim, therefore, is that apocalyptic cannot be interpreted with "flat-footed" literalness. Caird is right, but equally, everything does not need to go back to the Second Temple context. It is sufficient to describe Caird's overall description of AE, not as aversion for history, but an appeal to a different approach to history.[168] On Caird's theory, then, Mark is stating a single history, but it raises questions about why his Olivet Discourse is so vague and why he address long-term realities elsewhere. Caird's theory also seems to provide no ground for denying details in the language of Mark's metaphors or to ignore discussion about "levels of intent" or "points about ambiguity."[169] Caird should have examined Mark 13:24–27 and compared it with Mark 14:62. Caird has heavily influenced Wright in this regard and this is largely why Wright understands Mark 13 as referring solely to AD 70.

Apocalyptic as Central for Jesus and the Church

Finally, J. C. Beker has written in support of apocalyptic and against the "spiritualizing and excision of apocalyptic eschatology."[170] Beker notes how it was common in the mid-twentieth century to reject apocalyptic as dangerous. He describes the change that came with Dodd and others as a broad movement (neoorthodoxy) within enlightenment thinking that "collapsed apocalyptic eschatology into Christology" and came when eschatology was no longer "an ontic event expected in the future."[171] Beker identifies the

---

168. He treats Revelation this way also: ". . . about an eschaton John has nothing to say." Ibid., 271. For his theological treatment of Revelation, see Caird, *Revelation of St. John the Divine*.

169. See Caird, *Language*, 37–61, 109–21. See the category of language transfer as 'illustration' applied to Mark 6:41. Caird, *New Testament Theology*, 247.

170. Beker, *Paul the Apostle*, 139–40.

171. Ibid., 139. See Schnackenburg, *God's Rule and Kingdom*, 69. See also Dodd, *New Testament Studies*, 67–128.

How Apocalyptic Literature Is Read

imprecise meaning neoorthodoxy assigns to "eschatology" and notes that it is set in *opposition* to "bad term apocalyptic."[172]

D. C. Allison, in agreement with Beker, has offered a defense of Schweitzer's apocalyptic.[173] He treats Jesus' AE and its relationship to PE as important.[174] Allison makes three points about the nature of AE. First, the characteristics of AE and its influence are emphatically present in the Gospels and in Jesus.[175] He gives five characteristics of apocalyptic eschatology as evidence of Jesus' interest in eschatology: (1) he taught the resurrection of the dead (Mark 12:18-27), (2) he looked for a transcendent kingdom of God (Matt 25:31-46), (3) he referred to the eschatological downfall of Satan (Mark 3:20-27; Luke 10:18), (4) he anticipated the eschatological tribulation (Luke 12:49-53), and (5) he warned of a final judgment (Matt 11:20-24).

Second, Jesus adopted much of the language and teaching of apocalyptic eschatology, but he revised certain elements and consciously rejected others. Allison insists that Jesus' interaction with AE fits with Jesus' critique of contemporary beliefs. Yet for Allison, any fulfillment of Jesus as the Son of man is ruled out. Jesus spoke of the Son of Man coming on the clouds of heaven with Daniel 7 in mind.[176] He believes that Jewish apocalyptic writings can be traced in Jesus' teaching. For Allison, Jesus' ideas about "cosmological states" from Jewish apocalyptic are not important, compared to the "radically new world that only God could bring."[177]

Third, Jesus is placed as an apocalyptic prophet who is akin to an "ascetic" or millenarian prophet. Like Weiss and Schweitzer, Allison insists that AE relates to an imminent end and concludes that Jesus was wrong about the final coming because the final generation of Jesus' contemporaries all

---

172. Beker, *Paul the Apostle*, 142. It "signifies the transcendent, ultimate character of the Christ-event as God's new self-revelation." Beker singles out Rudolf Schnackenburg as example of one who has antiapocalyptic sentiment.

173. Allison, "Plea for Thoroughgoing Eschatology," 651-68; Allison, "Jesus and the Victory of Apocalyptic," 128.

174. Allison, "Apocalyptic," 18-19. Allison notes that apocalyptic eschatology is not common in all Jewish apocalypses (e.g., 2 Enoch). Allison defines AE broadly as a "cluster of themes and expectations which developed often in association with belief in a near end, in the altered circumstances of the post-exilic period."

175. Ibid., 19. Cf. G. Ladd who outlines five common characteristics of Apocalyptic Eschatology: (1) dualism, (2) historical perspective, (3) pessimism over the present historical situation, (4) determinism, (5) and ethical passivity. Ladd, *Presence of the Future*.

176. Allison, "Apocalyptic," 19.

177. Allison, "Jesus and the Victory of Apocalyptic," 129.

passed away.[178] Finally, in critiquing Wright's quest for historical metaphor, Allison argues metaphor is recognized when read for, example, the beasts in Daniel.[179]

Summary: The Key Questions for the Remainder of the Study on Eschatological Relationships and Jesus

This above survey has reviewed and catalogued a significant discussion in the debate of how apocalyptic literature is read in relation to eschatology. It is clear that scholars are divided on how Jesus viewed the future. Furthermore, many critical scholars view Mark 13:24–27 as secondary. There is no question that many see patterns both in the concept of AE in general and in Jesus' eschatological teaching in the Gospels. Biblical scholars might well question, therefore, if denying a distinction between AE and PE is helpful. A second observation is that NT scholars pursue common problems in different ways. For example, treatments vary regarding the timing of the kingdom of God, and the tension this theme generates between the OT and NT. Students of biblical studies may well ask, what are the best theological, literary, hermeneutical, and historical lines of investigation to follow? The example cited above of this tension of continuity and discontinuity with the OT raises the question for this study of whether or not a pattern exists in Jesus' teaching that is a solution to the problem of imminence and delay? The remainder of the chapter identifies some precise questions that come out of the survey; questions that are important to ask and answer in examining again the AD 70 and tribulation-end question, since it is the "end" phase that is in view.

Five problems are examined here (the use of the OT in the NT, the question of imminence and delay, historical Jesus, apocalyptic language and symbolism, and history). These categories overlap to some extent in the discussion. The summary begins with explaining how Meyer, Wright, and PD pursue these problems in different ways, and then indicates whether or not the issues and methodology advanced by Meyer, Wright, and PD are pursued in the rest of this study.

---

178. Allison, *Jesus of Nazareth*, 211.
179. Allison, "Jesus and the Victory of Apocalyptic," 130.

How Apocalyptic Literature Is Read
The Use of the Old in the New

The questions that remain: (1) If Mark 14 is the antecedent to Mark 13? (2) If *Sensus Plenior* (i.e., "fuller meaning") is adequate? Or does the OT find direct fulfillment, fuller meaning or typological-pattern in the NT?

1. Meyer and Wright regard Daniel 7:13 on enthronement as a key antecedent to Mark 13 supported by Mark 14. Meyer notes the leading motifs in Jesus' vision of the future were Jesus' coming ordeal (suffering and death) and its resolution by the triumphal enthronement of the Son of Man.[180] Later, he says enthronement is thought of "as a [1] transcendent exaltation conceived as messianic investiture in an eschatological function [2] before the eyes of the whole world."[181] Meyer also notes that Daniel 7:13 does not meet either definition exactly but parts of both seem to be present. Bock recognizes the significance of exaltation in Mark 14. The study will not pursue Meyer's interpretation of enthronement but focus on the role of the Son of Man in the context of Mark 13 instead. If Mark 13 and Mark 14 are distinct literarily, but related in their themes, then what is Mark's Christology from Mark 13, especially the role of the Son of Man in restoration? If there is a biblical connection between AD 70 and the tribulation so that for Jesus AD 70 is like the end time, where is such a pattern in Mark 13?

2. Meyer and Wright hold to *Sensus Plenior* (or "fuller meaning") when understanding prophecy and the interpretation of the OT in the New. God intends more than the prophet [human author]. For Meyer, the lack of determinate knowledge in Jesus' understanding is found in reference to his use of symbols not his aims. Wright finds more direct fulfillment in Jesus' teaching than Meyer (such as a direct fulfillment of Daniel 7 in Mark 13 and other passages related to the eschatological day). Wright takes the passage metaphorically. Bock holds that Jesus did not have complete determinate knowledge of the future (see below) and that Jesus was not mistaken about the future. But his view differs significantly from Meyer and Wright. Bock has written extensively on

---

180. Meyer, *Aims of Jesus*, 206. In accordance with M. Delcor and T. W. Manson, Meyer supports the notion and origin of the 'one like a son of man' to be represented as ascending with the clouds from earth to heaven. The ascension of Israel and its messianic king is "investiture in royal power over the whole world." Meyer, *Aims*, 307.

181. Meyer, *Aims*, 306.

the use of the OT in the New[182] and has received criticisms from other dispensationalists.[183] Bock like Hanson and Stone supports a method that examines contextual-typological readings. More specifically, Bock argues for a complementary hermeneutic in the interpretation of the OT in the New. A complementary hermeneutic allows that God may promise more than he originally promised but never less, and it produces layers of sense and specificity for a NT text.[184] The first point guarantees the emerging meaning in the NT is not at the expense of the original reading and that the emerging meaning, through progressive revelation, is truly allowed for. The second point recognizes the fact that an OT text can be read at different levels; the event itself, and by how others have historically responded to the text. For these main reasons, PD operates with a complementary hermeneutic. The main point is that teaching about God's plan and Jesus' role has continuity with OT hope and promises but "can also contain fresh truth." The Old and New Testaments are placed side by side and "complement each other."[185] For this study, there is no either/or choice therefore between the option of AD 70 or the end time; rather a "both/and" approach is adduced. Unlike Meyer and Wright, PD adopts a *Sensus Plenior* and a historical model for interpreting the Old in the New and to explaining pattern prophecy. PD holds that symbolic or figurative language was an exemplary feature of Jesus' discourse because metaphorical language was part of the Jewish thought world. But Jesus' lack of determinate knowledge is not related to the symbols or symbolism or with the limited horizons of a writer of history (i.e., the Gospels), but with the timing of the end. This study follows the PD model of interpretation of the Old in the New. Finally, Meyer, Wright, and PD recognize that Jesus' symbolic language pointed to a "two-act drama" of crisis and resolution. PD recognizes an inaugurated eschatology but distinguishes between Israel and the church. And so the kingdom of God is presented as present (Matt 12:27 / Luke 11:20; 21–22); present and future for different recipients (Matt 22:1–14); and future (Matt

---

182. Bock, *Proclamation from Prophecy and Pattern*; Bock, "Son of David and the Saints' Task"; Bock, "Use of the Old Testament in the New"; Bock, "Scripture Citing Scripture."

183. Thomas, "Hermeneutics of Progressive Dispensationalism."

184. Bock, "Son of David," 445.

185. Ibid., 447.

19:2 / Luke 22:30). But in contrast to Meyer and Wright the final form of the kingdom is preceded by another two-act drama of crisis and resolution. This study will explore the themes which apocalyptic also discloses (behind the scenes) in this period of crisis and resolution known also as the restoration for the righteous.

Jesus' View on Imminence, Delay and the Differentiation of Future Events

The questions that remain: (1) If an imminence reading should dominate when the Synoptic Gospels also have passages on delay? (2) If the standard NT scheme of eschatology had come into existence, totally, after the Easter experience of the disciples? (3) How referents of future sayings fit into Jesus' future scenario?

1. Meyer and Wright hold that Jesus expected the imminent consummation of the present world order[186] for the establishment of the new kingdom of God. This expectation is supported by the historical context: (1) *before* Jesus' ministry in the imminent end-time expectation and preaching of John the Baptist and, (2) *after* Jesus' ministry in the imminent end-time expectation and preaching of Paul. Wright's view of Jesus' ministry supports this idea of a realized view of the kingdom of God with an imminent timeframe. PD holds that the Gospels present passages that reflect a sense of imminence and delay and that these must be held in tension. In other words, AD 70 is part of Jesus' scenario of the future but it does not encompass, in Jesus' mind, the final horizon. Furthermore, neither is the Son of Man's role *in Mark 13* fulfilled at present. This study will pursue the idea that Jesus taught both imminence and delay as part of the pattern, that AD 70 is like the end, and that he did not know when the time of the end would start (Mark 13:32). It also affirms that the passages referring to delay are old.[187]

2. Meyer holds that the cross was for Jesus the sole context for Jesus' words about the historical future (including the eschatological ordeal in Mark 13) and that the church later modified this scenario.[188] Wright

---

186. Note: not the literal end of the world, as Weiss held.
187. See discussion below on the historical Jesus.
188. Meyer is heavily influenced here by Dodd and Jeremias here.

holds that Jesus differentiated between his death and resurrection on the third day and the destruction of the temple. PD holds that Jesus differentiated between his death, resurrection and the eschatological crisis. The church did not change the scenario; it developed themes in the Olivet Discourse after the Easter event according to the pattern in Jesus' teaching. This study will follow this scenario. The discussion of the development of themes (in this case based on Jesus' discourse) by the Synoptic evangelists is crucial for chapter 6. Here the hermeneutics of initial fulfillment for texts based on Jesus' sermon is demonstrated from a literary perspective.

3. Meyer, Wright, and PD, to varying degrees work with large numbers of texts from the Gospels (which are deemed to be authentic to the Jesus tradition) and these texts' referents, and attempt to fit them into Jesus' future scenario. This study will examine these texts in Meyer, Wright, and PD (where appropriate) in light of the thesis and the topic of eschatological relationships, but it will not seek to construct a comparable record only a framework for understanding Jesus' future teaching. It is essential to understand the structure and function of AE but this has been overlooked. Studies on "righteousness," "judgment," "imminence," and "suffering" are profitable. Without a framework, however, there remains little to build the concepts of OT, NT and AE on or to compare and contrast them to.

The Historical Jesus

The questions that remain: (1) If critics are justified in saying the tradition of Mark 13 does not go back to Jesus? (2) If Jesus' revelation on the future is final in terms of content? (3) If Jesus merely repeats his teaching to the disciples in private?

1. Meyer and Wright for the most part reject the liberal position of historical Jesus research, and strongly affirm the data in the NT Gospels as reliable and something Jesus said. This includes some key sayings (Mark 13:2, 7, 14, 32). However, like most critical scholars, Meyer holds that Mark 13:24–27 is secondary in part. He maintains that probably the day of the Son of Man was a "counterpart" in private teaching after Caesarea Philippi.[189] Caird, Wright and PD hold that

---

189. In general Meyer holds that the disciples were privileged witness to Jesus' private

13:24–27 is original but they go in different directions. Bock affirms that the Gospels are reliable in recording the voice of Jesus.[190] The study accepts the authenticity of Mark 13 but touches on the issues of validation. The study advances Caird's treatment of the literary features of Mark 13:24–27 but does not hold to his interpretation.

2. Meyer also holds that Jesus is the unique and *final* revealer of God. PD believes that Jesus is the eternal son of God who came into this world to reveal God to people and redeem lost humanity. On his human side, Jesus became and remained a perfect man and that his earthly life sometimes functioned within the sphere which was human and sometimes within the sphere which was divine (Luke 2:40; John 1:1–2; Phil 2:5–8).[191] PD holds that the dispensations are stewardships by which God administers his purpose on the earth through people, that his kingdom functions in different eras, and that God's plan is revealed in successive stages or by progressive revelation. PD also affirms that God has committed himself to Israel and her faithful people through his promises to Abraham and David. Importantly for this study, fulfillment of the promise is interpreted as happening as revelation progresses through one dispensation to the next. For Bock, AD 70 shows that God's plan is on track. This study supports the idea that Jesus, on his human side, did not know the exact time of the end (Mark 13:32) and that he did not tell his disciples all the details of God's plan in advance (John 16:12). It also advances the idea that, humanly speaking, the evangelists were not able to comprehend the themes of Jesus' teaching apart from examining his career and ministry in light of the whole (Luke 1:1–4; Acts 1:8). It will continue to show that Jesus' future teaching is the sure guarantee that God's promises will be fulfilled. The study will advance the idea that the pattern in Jesus' teaching is seen in progressive revelation and that the prediction of an initial fulfillment in AD 70 is evidence that the final fulfillment awaits. The study distinguishes between adopting a pattern-typology interpretation and an "application" interpretation of a future event. Some dispensational writers may support the view of the prediction of

---

teaching and that the eschatological discourse in Mark 13 contains a pre-Markan topic unit of sayings on the historical crisis. Meyer, *Aims*, 209, 286, 273, 288.

190. Bock, *Studying the Historical Jesus*, 194.

191. See Dallas Theological Seminary, "Doctrinal Statement," in *2006–2007 Catalog* (Dallas Theological Seminary), 183.

AD 70 as a NT application of an OT prophecy instead of a pattern typology.[192] AD 70 as an application of Daniel, however, is inadequate as it suggests possibly many applications, rather than a future scenario, which Jesus intended.

3. Here is the fundamental error of Meyer and to some extent Wright: that Jesus merely repeats his public teaching to the disciples in private. This robs apocalyptic of its essential characteristic that it reveals "secrets." For Meyer, the Mosaic dispensation and Law revealed "God's pleasure, wisdom and will."[193] Apocalyptic does not. In Meyer's scenario, the historical Jesus does not demonstrate wisdom or call for reflection to contemplate his future scenario. There is no tension or issue to solve concerning the problems of the eschaton, and there is no ambiguity. These are big problems for Meyer's scenario. As a result, Jesus' use of apocalyptic is pulled out of the wisdom tradition. PD recognizes Jesus presented a pattern which fundamentally required wisdom that comes through reflection to understand, and assistance from the divine helper according to John's gospel (John 14:17; 26). This is a vital part of apocalyptic and will be developed in this study in regard to Jesus' interpretation of Daniel 9 for the future. Mark's call is telling; may the reader discern and respond to the issues that Jesus presents (Mark 13:14)!

Apocalyptic Language, Symbolism

Questions that remain: (1) If apocalyptic is a symbolic universe, or metaphorical, (2) and if myth (cosmic language) is disconnected to linear time? (3) If future language signified symbolically is necessarily an undifferentiated future scenario?

1. Like Russell, AE for Meyer is a synthetic unity. Unlike Russell, AE eventually finds reality when reinterpreted to apply to AD 70 instead of the afterlife. Meyer does not follow O'Callaghan's definition of apocalyptic as a symbolic universe. But it is referred to as adopted prophetic symbolism like many critical scholars (Weiss, Allison, Käsemann, Dodd, Perrin, Borg etc.) The nature of apocalyptic and the concept of AE in Jesus' teaching (or the church) is associated with "imminence." Jesus

---

192. See Thomas, "Hermeneutics," 93.
193. Meyer has only one reference to wisdom in his discussion. Meyer, *Aims*, 218.

therefore adopts symbolic prophecy for his discourse. Caird holds that apocalyptic language collapsed but contradictorily maintains ideas through parataxis. PD rejects that apocalyptic language is taken metaphorically. Apocalyptic discloses hidden things. Apocalyptic is unique in Daniel because it is prophetic but distinct from the majority of the prophetic writings in that it adopts a perspective of deliverance from above. PD also believes that Jesus did not adopt symbolic prophecy. This study will advance the PD viewpoint. It will advance Caird's use of language, and his observation about parataxis but reaches different conclusions. The feature of parataxis in Mark is further evidence of pattern in Jesus' future teaching.

2. Meyer and Wright dismiss the second quest attempts to make faith irrelevant in the historical Jesus study because of myth. The survey revealed how some commentators still treat myth as replacing the historical. Bock recognizes myth must not be thought as something made up and it is tied to history and describes cosmic events and concepts. The study will examine how Jesus' language in Mark 13:2 and 13:24–27 reflects either the language of war or is cosmic in its scope and universal in its function.

3. Meyer does not differentiate between events in Jesus' future teaching. Like von Rad Meyer interprets AE only in terms of the theme of "negative apocalyptic" in history. Israel is judged. Wright differentiates Jesus' death and AD 70. For him, like Cook, the positive theme in apocalyptic for the believers is empowerment. PD differentiates Jesus' teaching and holds that apocalyptic reveals what occurs behind the scenes. This study argues that Meyer's and Wright's view of a non-differentiation of Jesus' prophecy about his death, resurrection, and AD 70 (in terms of a transfer of power) is inadequate.

Historical Background

Questions that remain: (1) If the prophecies of Daniel were applied to persecution in the Maccabean period in a general sense or exile motif? (2) If apocalyptic is not to be misunderstood as having a historical base? Or if there is a connection in Jesus' discourse to Daniel then what is the historical referent?

1. Meyer and Wright (more explicitly) focus on historical backgrounds to understand Jesus. Wright holds that Daniel's seventieth week is best

understood as a time of extended exile. PD recognizes the importance of Second Temple Judaism studies to understanding Jesus' contemporaries and the thought world of the NT in general and takes Daniel's seventieth week to refer to the end-time-suffering. Like Wright, Bock relates the history of the Maccabean wars to the JAT to understand how Judaism responds to Gentile led oppression and hellenization of the nation. For PD however, progressive revelation in the NT Gospels and from Jesus' teaching in particular, sheds light on Daniel's prophecy. Furthermore, the historian's task of reading the historical interpretations of texts in Judaism is also important for PD's model of reading the OT in the New.[194]

2. Meyer and Wright hold that because Jesus' symbolic prophecy is temple focused the entire discourse is bounded by this horizon. For Wright, Jesus' suffering, death and persecution are in continuity with the theme of Israel's continuing exile. The struggle to be God's covenant people, and the approaching temple crisis, as the object of Jesus' apocalyptic teaching, are one. PD views the history of Second Temple Judaism and events of 167 BC as hermeneutically pivotal to understanding Jesus' future teaching. The study will advance the idea that although some works in the JAT present the seer as depicting the supposed future (but actually well-known past) Judaism saw the relevance of Daniel's prophecies to their situation. The study will explore the relationship between history and Mark's transcendent concerns in order to understand Jesus' apocalyptic eschatology and what he taught about salvation-history and Israel, which according to Jesus, and recorded by Mark, is part of the reflection process. It will explore the antecedents of Mark 13 in Daniel's prophecy (Dan 9:27; 11:31 and 12:11). These texts point to events that can take place in a real world (e.g., 1 Macc 1:54–64) and are central to understand Jesus' aims for Israel's future according to the Marcan discourse.

Conclusion

This chapter has surveyed the debate on how apocalyptic eschatology is treated by Old and New Testament scholars. Having surveyed how apocalyptic has been read, the question for most commentators is which Jewish history

---

194. See n182.

ought to be associated with Jewish apocalypticism? The study now turns to examine Meyer and Wright's view of Jesus' aims and eschatological hope to see how they address this question. This will be done by comparing their theological constructs, to ask how their various features of history, hermeneutics, and the language of texts apply in comparison to the approach of PD.

3

Antecedents and Apocalyptic Literature in Ben F. Meyer's Theological Construct

Introduction

THE THESIS OF THIS study is that the future teaching of Jesus included a pattern-prophecy. For Jesus, AD 70 was a type of the end. This chapter examines the issues raised at the end of chapter 2 in regard to Meyer. Specifically, it seeks to understand Meyer's thesis that apocalyptic is merely the adopted symbolism of prophecy which repeats Jesus' public teaching in private. To evaluate this claim the chapter will consider Meyer's view of prophecy, apocalyptic eschatology, and Jesus' scenario of the historical crisis, which for Meyer culminated in AD 70. The chapter begins with a discussion of those who have heavily influenced Meyer in the areas of the historical critical method and the themes about the historical crisis in Jesus' scenario of the future. This is followed by a description of Meyer's construct and its themes. The chapter concludes by summarizing where Meyer's construct has strengths that advance the discussion and where it has weaknesses that are detrimental to his conclusions from a PD perspective.

Antecedents and Apocalyptic Literature

Introduction to Meyer

The starting point for understanding Ben Meyer's reading of apocalyptic is J. Weiss's thoroughgoing eschatology. Weiss said apocalyptic is important to Jesus because the end-time breaking in of the kingdom of God and the end of the world is imminent (as noted in chap. 2). Particularly relevant for this discussion is the notion that Meyer shared with Weiss, that the cataclysmic end of the world should be understood in absolute terms. Weiss's propensity for adopting a literal interpretation of everything Jesus said is key. Weiss understands that the words of Jesus connected to the situation envisaged in his sermon (on coming wars and the end of the world) did not occur.[1] This study challenges the suitability of using categories like "literal" interpretation as it raises questions about the meaning of figurative language in Mark's Olivet Discourse. We need to understand how Meyer follows Weiss in expecting an imminent end. Meyer's construct of Jesus' scenario of the future (including apocalyptic) must be traced in the light of his exegesis and its historical background.[2] The conservative German historical Jesus scholar Joachim Jeremias and the Jesuit philosopher and theologian Bernard J. F. Lonergan are other writers who shape Meyer's critique of the second quest.[3] These three scholars are Meyer's antecedents because they have contributed significantly to historical Jesus studies. Meyer interacts with them frequently in his writings.

In order to describe Meyer's theological construct, the first section predominantly examines the similarities and the points of departure of his writing from those of Weiss and Jeremias, as well as the concept of "horizon" which Meyer developed from Lonergan and Hans Georg Gadamer. A description of the construct themes follows and then the chapter concludes with an evaluation of Meyer's reading of apocalyptic.

---

1. JWeiss, *Die Schriften des Neuen Testaments*, 513. Meyer states the question in the following way: Did Jesus envision and predict the end of the world in absolute terms? See Meyer, "Jesus's Scenario of the Future," 6.

2. This dissertation does not discuss how Meyer determines the historicity of individual passages. On the historicity of Jesus' use of *Abba* and *amen*, see Meyer, *Aims of Jesus*, 86–87. For a helpful summary of Meyer's application of the criteria of authenticity in his analysis of the data, see Denton, *Historiography and Hermeneutics in Jesus Studies*.

3. Meyer was born in Chicago in 1927, and spent most of his teaching career at McMaster University in Hamilton, Ontario. He died in 1995. For a biographical sketch of Meyer, including his education at the Pontifical Biblical Institute and at the Gregorian University in Rome (where B. Lonergan taught) and his early career as a Catholic priest, see Meyer, *Aims*, 11–15.

Part one of the *Aims of Jesus* covers "hermeneutical issues." Meyer's chapter 1 introduces the subject of historical Jesus research and features the work of Lonergan. Chapter 2 presents a "review of the quest" to 1979.[4] In his discussion, Meyer begins to formulate what constitutes a historical construct of Jesus, the questions, the errors, and the principles that matter for validation. These in turn shape Meyer's reading of apocalyptic and the data he selects and analyzes. The term "theological construct" in this chapter means the historical reconstruction of Jesus and the themes present in his proclamation as it relates to Jesus' scenario of the future.

Antecedents of Meyer

Bernard J. F. Lonergan

Bernard Lonergan's work, *Method in Theology*, is important for several reasons. First, it sets out an important critique of the Enlightenment and principles of hermeneutics. These ideas were developed in Meyer's subsequent work on critical realism.[5] Lonergan's work in cognitional theory and methodological principles is a "breakthrough" against many "reductionistic philosophies" which scholars assume in their historical Jesus work.[6] Lonergan argued effectively against two prevailing views of post-Enlightenment scholarship. First, the idea that the universe is a "closed system" is simplistic—as is the statement that judgments of the past are limited by present experience (Troeltsch's principle of analogy).[7] Instead, it was Lonergan who insisted that the key to historical interpretation involves engagement by the interpreter in "extrapolation" and "critical reflection" deliberately relating to events and people at different places and points of

---

4. In recent years it has become accepted to categorize the modern quest for the historical Jesus into three stages: the first quest instigated in the eighteenth century by Reimarus, the post-Bultmannian "new" quest (hereafter called the second quest), and the current "third" quest. Meyer is considered to be among the founders of the "third" quest. When Meyer wrote he distinguished the three periods of time. Categorizing the "first" quest, Meyer classified two blocks of time: (1) from Reimarus to Strauss, and (2) from Holtzmann to the first world war. He separated these from the "the new quest" representing the period "from Bultmann to the present day" Meyer, *Aims*, 25–54.

5. Lonergan, *Method in Theology*. See Meyer, *Critical Realism and the New Testament*.

6. Meyer, *Aims*, 16.

7. See Troeltsch, "Was heisst 'Wesen des Christentums'?," 386–451; Troeltsch, "Historiography," esp. 716–18.

time.⁸ Lonergan sees critical reflection (or some insightful flow of experience) as important because it allows for meaning to vary at different stages of human development. He states that "there can be invoked a merging of the clear and distinct into the obscure and undifferentiated. Because all stages of development are linked genetically and dialectically, it should be possible to retrace the steps that lead from the past to the present."⁹ Meyer's construct uses critical reflection to trace the modern developments in the "quest" for the historical Jesus by NT interpreters.¹⁰

Second, Lonergan argued that historical study does not require a choice to be made between the individual and the community.¹¹ This is important for Meyer's critique of Bultmann's individual eschatology. Bultmann consciously transposed eschatology and AE into new categories of existential self-understanding.¹² Meyer does not follow Bultmann's understanding of a transition in the history of Israel's religion from the salvation of the nation to the salvation of the individual.¹³ Related to this is Lonergan's use of the concept of "horizon." A horizon is simply "the boundary of one's field of vision."¹⁴ Metaphorically, it is the limit of what one knows and cares about, but its interest is with its reference.¹⁵ Meyer applies this concept of horizon to Jesus' teaching.

Meyer also drew on the importance of horizon when he points out that John P. Meier's approach is not the way forward.¹⁶ Meier's work reveals the

8. Lonergan, *Insight*, 589. For Meyer's discussion, see Meyer, *Aims*, 17.

9. Lonergan, *Insight*, 589.

10. Lonergan's theory on recognizing knowledge at different stages is important for developing one's hypothesis questions at different stages; see Lonergan, *Insight*, 82, 271–74. Meyer calls the anterior phase of meaning "what" and "why" questions. Meyer points these questions to faith. See Meyer, *Aims*, 104.

11. Lonergan, *Method in Theology*, 130; Meyer, *Aims*, 212.

12. Meyer, *Aims*, 245.

13. Ibid., 212. Meyer notes that, in the apocalyptic view of Bultmann "the individual is responsible for himself only." See Bultmann, *History and Eschatology*, 31. Cf. Meyer on Israel as "house," Meyer, *Aims*, 224.

14. Lonergan, *Method in Theology*, 235. Lonergan follows Gadamer here. See below and Lonergan, *Method in Theology*, 152, 161–64, 169.

15. Coelho, *Hermeneutics and Method*. Lonergan argued that human anticipation of universal viewpoint is part of hermeneutical method and that universal hermeneutic involves working with the speaker's horizon. This is like Gadamer's notion of horizon as a "range of vision" which entails meaning from within the speaker's present perspective. See Gadamer, *Truth and Method*, 302.

16. Meyer, "Relevance of 'Horizon.'"

influence of Bultmann in American studies. Meier separates the study of "the historical Jesus" from any hope of discovering "the real Jesus."[17] Such a claim, Meyer argues, is "simplistic" and an adoption of the Bultmannian definition of the second quest. It is "counterproductive" to what is already a complex issue.[18]

Ben Meyer seeks to avoid this error. His construct has an extensive horizon as it seeks to explore a number of important contemporary questions related to Jesus. It is seen in the thread of his argument which he outlines in *The Aims of Jesus*, and which reveals his disparate discussion of history, hermeneutics, language, and faith. Chapter 3, "The Gospel Literature: Data on Jesus?," discusses early faith-formulations (1 Cor 15:3-5) as evidence of the primitive kerygma.[19] Meyer also has an important section on the development of the Gospel tradition. He affirms the historical reliability of the Gospel tradition, and does so by asking and answering the question "Do the Gospels intend the past [are they history] and intend to supply data on Jesus?"[20] His answer is affirmative. Meyer makes three points about why critics do not need to be skeptical about historicity. First, the Gospel accounts evidence an underlying "global expectation" of faith. Second, a positive expectation of the data is seen in 1 Corinthians 7, where Paul differentiates his words from those of Jesus, and in the catechetical motivation to meet the needs of the changing church.[21] Third, when Meyer reads 2 Corinthians 5:16, he argues that, contra Bultmann, Paul is not saying he

---

17. See Meier, *Marginal Jew*.

18. Meyer, "Relevance of 'Horizon,'" 5-6. Meyer says, "There is no solid reason whatever to define 'the real Jesus' by the conditions of the possibility of a full bibliography." See also his critique of Meier's suggestion to find "reasonable ground" among four different people as "hermeneutically simplistic." Cf. also Gadamer's work on *understanding as participation* and the problem of prejudice and tradition, summarized by Warnke, *Gadamer*, 64-91.

19. Several NT passages included here are Rom 8:34; 1 Cor 11:22-25; Phil 2:6-11; Acts 2:14-36; etc.

20. Meyer, *Aims*, 72.

21. He adds it is unproved there was ever a "class of Christians" who spoke in the name of the risen Christ (contra Käsemann). The evidence for the early church demonstrating a positive "expectation" of Jesus' words (the data) is the evangelist ensuring the *ipsissima vox Jesu* is retained because "the word of Jesus was authoritative." Meyer, *Aims*, 74. Taken together these are reasons why the Gospel narratives are not a creative retrojection onto Jesus by those with independent religious concerns.

cares little for historical details about Jesus of Nazareth beyond the "bare factuality" of the death of Jesus.²²

Several observations are in order. First, Meyer holds to Marcan priority, and Mark 13 contains a pre-Marcan unit of oral sayings on the topic of the eschatological crisis.²³ Second, he holds that "it is not the order of the gospels that counts for historical enquiry but their nature" [i.e., claim to historicity].²⁴ Meyer's principles for historical enquiry are: (1) history is knowledge, (2) historical knowledge is inferential, (3) the technique of history is the testing of hypothesis, and (4) verification of the hypothesis.²⁵ Step 4 is the subject of chapter 9, "Confirmation and Reflection." Third, on the basis of the goal of establishing historicity, Meyer attempts to use traditional criticism to discuss some of the themes of "restoration" but not necessarily all aspects of his construct. Chapters 4 and 5 outline the strategy, principles, and overall subject of the construct. Chapter 4, "Jesus and Critical History," outlines his strategy for doing a critical history of Jesus and elucidates it in the steps of (1) interpretation and explanation, (2) controlling the data, and (3) establishing the facts. The step of establishing the facts contains four principles for working with history critically.²⁶ In chapter 5, "History and Faith," Meyer makes clear that *die Sache*, "the subject" or "thing" as he calls it, is faith and its relation to history.²⁷ Section 1 is called *Relationship to 'the thing' (die Sache)*. In identifying the "subject" as the gospel or "salvation" (Matt 11:5), Meyer identifies one element of Christian tradition that

---

22. Meyer, *Aims*, 75. The question becomes, in what sense did he work independently of the Gospel tradition? Meyer notes that Paul offers literary testimony to the Gospel tradition prior to Marcan narrative redaction. Bultmann based his thesis on the perceived relationship between Paul's comments in 1 Cor 3 and 2 Cor 5:16. He claimed Paul's use of σάρξ is purely evaluative in both texts and so 1 Cor 5:16 contrasts the Jesus of history and the Christ of faith. Bultmann, *Primitive Christianity*, 197. For discussion on language structure, the logic of an evaluation versus descriptive use of σάρξ and the need to take into account the context when understanding the relationship between these two passages, see Thiselton, *Thiselton on Hermeneutics*, 168–69. For a descriptive interpretation, highlighting the arrival of the new order with its new attributes and new life secured by Christ and mediated by the Spirit, see Harris, *Second Epistle to the Corinthians*, 458.

23. Meyer, *Aims*, 71.

24. Ibid., 72.

25. Ibid., 76–94.

26. Meyer's overall scheme of approach is similar to A. Scholes's three steps in critical understanding as "reading," "interpretation," and "assessment." See Scholes, *Textual Power*.

27. Meyer, *Aims*, 96.

enlightenment presuppositions would not see in the historical Jesus.[28] This helps us to assess how Meyer treats these two concerns in his interpretation of the data related to AE (see below). Believing Matthew is not historical, Bultmann argued that a number of heuristic categories[29] represent the level of concern and questions appropriate to the reading of the NT texts. Meyer rejected this and with his questions of history posed,[30] and by employing Lonergan's principle of "thematizing," he developed his construct on historical grounds with the data he finds relevant.[31] Section two raises three questions, which confirm the overall subject of his construct. In light of the prejudices of the second quest against faith and dogma, Meyer addresses the relevance of history to faith.[32]

Johannes Weiss

Turning from hermeneutical interests to biblical interpretation we need to study Johannes Weiss. Weiss and Meyer have a number of important similarities and differences. For Meyer, the scenario of "imminence" is justified for two reasons. First, Jesus' vision and predictions align with that of the prophets of Israel who recognized no distant end to history.[33] Meyer posits that Jesus' eschatology was "absolute" and without any evidence of ambiguity.[34] This means Jesus literally advised his disciples of the end of

---

28. For a hermeneutical critique of Bultmann's closed approach to miracles as a sign of salvation, and for a discussion of his strategy in absence of history, see Meyer, *Aims*, 103.

29. See Heidegger, *On Time and Being*. Heidegger argued that true understanding of being can only proceed by referring to others and the best method of pursuing such understanding involves a hermeneutical circle. The field of hermeneutics and understanding must rely on repetitive yet progressive acts of interpretation. Heidegger's wider existential philosophy was adopted by Bultmann to read the text for what is true of human nature.

30. See n32 below.

31. Lonergan, "Metaphysics as Horizon," 307–18.

32. For a summary, see Meyer, *Aims*, 104. The combinations of questions meant to solve the problem are: (1) what is the integrity of faith, (2) how is the integrity of faith secured in the face of history, (3) what are the purposes of history with reference to faith? Cf. n8 above.

33. Cf. Russell, who argues that the predictive side of OT prophecy to a distant future is clear in passages like Isa 7:14; 9:1; 11:1; 32:1; and Mic 5:1–5. These often relate to the promised coming deliverer or "shoot of David's line," who will come to establish the messianic kingdom, Russell, *Method and Message*, 96–97.

34. Meyer, *Aims*, 250.

the world in his discourse. Second, he adduces from Daniel 12:2 that antecedents in the OT point to human life beyond history. Meyer therefore thinks that Jesus predicted an imminent consummation of history and the restoration of Israel, based on an OT prophetic scenario.

However, in spite of their agreement regarding the notion of "imminence," there are several differences between the views of Weiss and Meyer. Meyer rejects many philosophical arguments made in the period of 1860–1914 that were characteristic of the early methodologies of liberal theology and its exegesis, and the correcting *religionsgeschichtliche Schule*.[35] As noted above, the issue for Meyer in this context is the *a priori* dismissal of the prophetic and miraculous as unhistorical by both these schools.[36] The psychological reconstructions of Weiss and others which Meyer rejects include: (1) speculation about Jesus' self-understanding of his messiahship at his baptism, (2) that the kingdom of God remained a matter of personal faith, (3) that Peter's confession of Jesus was only meant in a proleptic sense,[37] (4) that the turning point of Jesus' career is the change from buoyant optimism to pessimism expressed in the notion that many are "called but few

35. Meyer argues that in seeking to bring correction, the constructs of the *religionsgeschichtliche Schule* gave too much consideration to texts such as Rom 1:3–4 and Acts 2:36. This, plus the exclusion of data in the Gospels deemed unhistorical, if identified as supernatural, further separated discussion of the messianic claims of the historical Jesus from the Gospel tradition. See Meyer, *Aims*, 42, 46, 177. Significantly, Meyer notes Kähler and Troeltsch as founders of these insufficiently tested assumptions about critical history. Kähler and Troeltsch are antecedents to Strauss and the period Meyer summarizes as "From Holzmann to the First World War." For an important critique of Kähler's and Troeltsch's attack on supernaturalism and their advocacy for a "closed system," see ibid., 17, 32.

36. Ibid., 58. On the one hand, the liberal approach (F. C. Baur, H. J. Holtzmann, A. Ritschl) was more a reflection of the liberal's own philosophical interests and recognized dogmatic conceptions instead of history. Exemplified in Holtzmann's *Lebensbild Jesu*, the key was sources in opposition to Strauss. See Holtzmann, "Lebensbild Jesu nach der Quelle A." Holtzmann's understanding of the Gospels is driven by *Traditionsgeschichte* or the transmission of tradition or "source question." He assumed the evangelists (except the early *Urmarcus*) were dogmatic, and that Jesus presented a new timeless moral ethic of the kingdom "within you" (Luke 17:21). On the other hand, the *religionsgeschichtliche Schule* of the 1890s (A. Eichhorn, H. Gunkel, W. Bousset, J. Weiss, and W. Wrede), which attempted in part to situate early Christianity in the religious milieu of Judaism and non-Judaic Hellenism, approached Christianity as a purely historical phenomenon. Meyer, *Aims*, 36–40.

37. Following the position of Wellhausen, in which he reads Rom 1:4 and Acts 2:36 as the starting point of NT Christology, Weiss claims Jesus is considered the messiah only from his resurrection. Wellhausen, *Israelitische und jüdische Geschichte*, 315, 318; Weiss, *Die Nachfolge Christi*, 59–61.

chosen,"[38] (5) that messiahship is "retrojected" into Jesus' public ministry in John's gospel, and (6) Wrede's view that Jesus did not know his passion in advance.[39] With regard to the *religionsgeschichtliche Schule* view Meyer says that such an understanding fails to come to terms with the historicity of the text because of the skepticism of enlightenment philosophy.

Having critiqued assumptions in historical Jesus research, Meyer compares two of Weiss's contemporaries, A. Schweitzer and W. Wrede. Meyer calls the technique of critical history a continuum. Critical method of interpretation starts with the hypothesis and an emphasis on one set of texts; a position that has a hypothesis but without control on the interpreters "presupposed knowns."[40] He also considers Schweitzer's theory of crisis. Meyer suggests views on the continuum progress from little control on the data to not enough data to support the hypothesis. From here the progression moves to understanding the Gospel literature specifically in terms of Markan redaction; the position of Wrede.[41]

First, in critique of Schweitzer, Meyer notes the failure to grasp Matthean placement and redaction. Meyer points to the work of Heinz Schürmann, who argued the original context of the saying on "persecution" in Matthew 10:23 is not the discourse of Jesus prior to the sending out of the disciples but rather the Olivet Discourse.[42] Meyer relates the image of "flight" of the disciples to Matthew 24:16–27 and understands it reveals its character as a "word of consolation" in the climatic eschatological crisis.[43] For Meyer, this

---

38. Meyer takes exception here beginning with Reimarus, Wrede and especially Weiss for their psychological reconstruction on Jesus' discernment for the cross (Mark 10:45) which Schweitzer builds on (Matt 10:23). Meyer, *Aims*, 42.

39. The flaw in Wrede's approach according to Meyer is that there is a lack of evidence for it and the improbability of a pre-dogmatic version of the life of Jesus. Meyer, *Aims*, 47.

40. Meyer, *Aims*, 91, see also 43.

41. Ibid., 45, 91. Meyer notes that Wrede, like Strauss sought to undertake a study of the nature of the Gospel literature. Meyer, *Aims*, 13, 44. Here Meyer focuses on Strusse's *Leben Jesu*. See Strauss, *Life of Jesus Critically Examined*. The problem lay not in the method but in the skepticism shown toward the Gospels and a determination to find a viable alternative to traditional Christian belief. See Meyer, *Aims*, 14.

42 Schürmann, "Zur Traditions-und Redaktionsgeschichte von Mt. 10:23." This is valid for three reasons. The saying is prophetic. It is an "apocalyptic word of consolation," Hübner points out Matthew understood 23b (the coming of the Son of Man) from the perspective of 23a (disciples ministry). See Hübner, "τελέω," *EDNT*, 347. Note also the negative and positive aspects of apocalyptic here.

43. Meyer, *Aims*, 44. Cf. Aland, *Synopsis of the Four Gospels*, 256–58. One has to make an assessment in relationship to the original meaning of Matt 24 in relation to the

is the time that will be shortened for the sake of the elect (Matt 24:22) by the coming of the Son of Man[44] (Matt 24:30; cf. Aland, §292).

Meyer extrapolates two principles related to history from his analysis of Schweitzer's error. First, these redactional changes or new placement of material necessitate a reconstructive activity by the historian if he or she wishes to control the data. Second, Meyer's corrective principle is that critical history controls the data by focusing on the "historian's own questions," and these are not limited to the thematic concerns of the sources. It proceeds by the "projecting of hypotheses" in order to realize a construct.[45] These principles are important when it comes to assessing Meyer's and Wright's AE in regard to history. Two criticisms of Meyer are due here. First, this takes historical method down a non-helpful deconstructive path. Exegesis or historical enquiry cannot proceed without theology. Second, Meyer countered Schweitzer and any thought of delay in the eschatological day by basing his construct completely on the theme of imminence.

A second theological construct which goes in a different direction from Meyer's is the "messianic secret" of William Wrede. Meyer explains the reason why Wrede's construct was created and what it reveals about the influence of the enlightenment. Wrede could not accept (1) the historicity of Jesus' prohibitions of the revelation about his messiahship, or (2) the supposition that Jesus knew his passion in advance.[46] Nevertheless, Meyer recognizes the themes in Wrede's redaction of Mark in its "total conception." The construct of the "messianic secret" highlights five correlated themes from Mark's gospel. These are (1) the recognition of Jesus by the demons, (2) the commands to silence, (3) the riddle character of the parables, (4) Jesus' private teaching of the

---

circumstances/context in which the text appears in Matt 10. Assessment of the Synoptic relationships is made possible by laying the units side by side. The pericope on Matt 10:17–22a (§289, "Persecutions Foretold"), can be compared, identified and assessed as belonging in its original context with Mark 13:9–13, Luke 21:12–19 and John 16:2; 15:21 and 14:26, (§290 "The Desolating Sacrilege"), Aland, *Greek-English Synopsis*, 258–59. Matt 10:23 has no parallel. Furthermore, if Meyer's selection of verses for the original context (Matt 24:16–27) is compared with Aland it is represented by 24:15–28 which would include §291 "False Christs' and False Prophets." Also note the parallel εἰς τέλος in Mark 13:16b; Matt 10:22b and 24:13 not at 24:30. Cf. Gadamer's appeal to take account of the change in circumstances and define afresh a law's meaning. See Gadamer et al., *Truth and Method*, 323.

44. Meyer, *Aims*, 44.
45. Ibid. See n11 and n16 above.
46. Ibid., 46.

disciples, and (5) the disciples' chronic misunderstanding of Jesus.[47] These converge to produce a survey like Wrede's construct of the secret but are built on inadequate Christology. Two outcomes emerge here; one beneficial and the other problematic. First, Meyer does not accept Wrede's Christology. Nor does he adduce the secret as a Marcan creation in the sense that Jesus was not Israel's Messiah but was later identified by the church as such. Meyer holds that a trait of Jesus' historical career is that Jesus avoided giving an explicit messianic claim before Israel (cf. John 4).[48] Second, he pursues a completely different approach which bypasses the need for wisdom and the problem of the disciples' understanding by making a distinction between Jesus' public and private teaching. This move away from wisdom distances Meyer from an important issue in understanding apocalyptic as the disclosure of divine secrets.

Finally, turning to Bultmann's work, Meyer is critical of Bultmann's historical theory and rejects his dismissal of the usefulness of Jesus' history and general disinterest in Jewish background. In Meyer's view, Bultmann erroneously separates questions of Jesus' claims as Messiah and his conceptions of eschatology (as totally present with no future events) from the questions of personal encounter or what the reign of God might mean. Bultmann's existential interpretation leads him to his exclusive interest in what can be "actual now."[49]

But adducing the authentic sayings of Jesus is also important to Meyer and others in the third quest. The similarities and differences between Bultmann and Meyer regarding the history of the Synoptic tradition can be seen by comparing their treatments of two sayings in Mark 13. These are Jesus' saying that only God knows the time (Mark 13:32) and the descent of the Son of Man (Mark 13:26).

Mark 13:32 and the Son

Bultmann sees Mark 13:32 predominantly as Jewish apocalyptic sayings up to the last seven words which had been preserved as a unit before it was worked into Mark. The supposed JAT component of the text is shown

---

47. Ibid., 45–46.
48. Ibid., 309.
49. Ibid., 50; Bultmann, *Jesus Christ and Mythology*, 17.

below in italics. In his view the last Greek clause οὐδὲ ὁ υἱός, εἰ μὴ ὁ πατήρ ("neither the Son only the Father") is a Christian (= church) ending.[50]

Table 1. Historicity of Mark 13:32 in Bultmann and Meyer

Mark 13:32	
Bultmann	Meyer
Περὶ δὲ τῆς ἡμέρας ἐκείνης ἢ τῆς ὥρας οὐδεὶς οἶδεν, οὐδὲ οἱ ἄγγελοι ἐν οὐρανῷ **οὐδὲ ὁ υἱός, εἰ μὴ ὁ πατήρ**	Περὶ δὲ τῆς ἡμέρας ἐκείνης ἢ τῆς ὥρας οὐδεὶς οἶδεν, οὐδὲ οἱ ἄγγελοι ἐν οὐρανῷ οὐδὲ ὁ υἱός, εἰ μὴ ὁ πατήρ

Meyer sees this saying as early and coming entirely from the Jesus tradition and that οὐδὲ ὁ υἱός, εἰ μὴ ὁ πατήρ is what Jesus said, according to Mark. The explanation is that it is entirely plausible according to the prophetic tradition that God alone knows the final time and that the historical Jesus did not have access to such knowledge.

Mark 13:24-27 and the Son of Man

Meyer handles the saying about the "Son" in Mark 13:32 differently to the one about the "Son of Man" in Mark 13:26. Bultmann identifies Mark 13:24-26 as a unit of Jewish apocalyptic sayings that have been preserved.[51] Meyer holds that vv. 24b-25 is old. He adduces that the original form of the Son of Man saying on "coming" (v. 26) is from early Jesus tradition about the vindication of the Son on Man (Mark 14). In Mark's discussion of restoration in Mark 14:62, however, the focus is not only on transcendent exaltation but also on the way it is "conceived as a messianic investiture."[52] Verses 26-27 are authentic Jesus tradition. Extracted from its original form, vv. 26-27 is an example of Markan redaction where the saying retains its meaning. Meyer holds that the motif of "gathering" should be clarified and can be traced though Jesus' ministry (Matt 13:24-30, 44-46).[53] The "signs" introduced in v. 24a, however, is a church formulation after the parousia is

50. Bultmann, *History of the Synoptic Tradition*, 123.
51. Ibid., 122.
52. Meyer, *Aims*, 306.
53. Ibid., 214.

delayed and it contradicts Jesus' teaching in Luke 17:21 where he repudiates the giving of signs. Thus, Meyer sees Marcan redaction both at the front end of the pericope and the back end. In making this literary move Meyer recognizes the authenticity of the Son of Man sayings, but misreads the history of the tradition and overlooks a further role of the Son of Man in Mark 13.

Table 2. Historicity of Mark 13:24-27 in Bultmann and Meyer

Mark 13:24-27	
Bultmann	Meyer
²⁴ Ἀλλὰ ἐν ἐκείναις ταῖς ἡμέραις μετὰ τὴν θλῖψιν ἐκείνην ὁ ἥλιος σκοτισθήσεται, καὶ ἡ σελήνη οὐ δώσει τὸ φέγγος αὐτῆς, ²⁵ καὶ οἱ ἀστέρες ἔσονται ἐκ τοῦ οὐρανοῦ πίπτοντες, καὶ αἱ δυνάμεις αἱ ἐν τοῖς οὐρανοῖς σαλευθήσονται. ²⁶ καὶ τότε ὄψονται τὸν υἱὸν τοῦ ἀνθρώπου ἐρχόμενον ἐν νεφέλαις μετὰ δυνάμεως πολλῆς καὶ δόξης. ²⁷ καὶ τότε ἀποστελεῖ τοὺς ἀγγέλους καὶ ἐπισυνάξει τοὺς ἐκλεκτοὺς [αὐτοῦ] ἐκ τῶν τεσσάρων ἀνέμων ἀπ' ἄκρου γῆς ἕως ἄκρου οὐρανοῦ.	²⁴ **Ἀλλὰ ἐν ἐκείναις ταῖς ἡμέραις μετὰ τὴν θλῖψιν ἐκείνην** ὁ ἥλιος σκοτισθήσεται, καὶ ἡ σελήνη οὐ δώσει τὸ φέγγος αὐτῆς, ²⁵ καὶ οἱ ἀστέρες ἔσονται ἐκ τοῦ οὐρανοῦ πίπτοντες, καὶ αἱ δυνάμεις αἱ ἐν τοῖς οὐρανοῖς σαλευθήσονται. ²⁶ καὶ τότε ὄψονται τὸν υἱὸν τοῦ ἀνθρώπου ἐρχόμενον ἐν νεφέλαις μετὰ δυνάμεως πολλῆς καὶ δόξης. ²⁷ καὶ τότε ἀποστελεῖ τοὺς ἀγγέλους καὶ ἐπισυνάξει τοὺς ἐκλεκτοὺς [αὐτοῦ] ἐκ τῶν τεσσάρων ἀνέμων ἀπ' ἄκρου γῆς ἕως ἄκρου οὐρανοῦ.

These influences on Meyer highlight how issues such as theology, exegesis, the use of the OT in the New, and the history of the tradition are essential for understanding Jesus' scenario of the future and the pattern in his teaching.

The Variety and Scope of Jesus' Teaching: An Alternative View of the Tradition

Meyer's treatment of the tradition, like many critics, assumes a few passages (especially on the role of the Son of Man) determine the direction and meaning of the tradition at large. It is only a short step to see the delay of the parousia as a theological explanation for the redaction in the Synoptic Gospels. This understanding falls under a *Sensus Plenior* reading of prophecy in Scripture. However, this view treats the tradition as monolithic and has major problems. First, it overlooks the fact that as an itinerant teacher Jesus spoke on a variety of occasions, and his teachings would vary in length and substance on a particular topic. Second, not all sayings can be assumed *a priori* to be equal in form, subject and theological content (i.e., the role of the Son of Man). Each saying must be assessed in light of its original form. This is important for understanding Matthew's varied account of the OD in Matthew 10. Second, it overlooks key characteristics of the oral tradition which influenced the form of sayings, and assumes that a cavalier movement of sayings occurred through the history of the tradition. Third, it overlooks the fact that historical events and historical reflection are necessary to reading the Gospels, and that relationships need to be assessed not assumed.

Comparison of how the critics handle relationships in the Synoptic Gospels is important. It is recognized that the Synoptic Gospels present both short-term and long-term accounts. How the passages are handled and how the issues are adduced and critical methods employed is debated. The issues for exploring the OT in the New are: (1) the nature of prophecy, (2) historical understanding of Daniel's prophecy (3) tradition history, and (4) definition of apocalyptic. An analysis shows how form criticism is a poor historical tool when it is adduced that the movement in the tradition is a result of the delay of the Parousia instead of the development of the themes in Jesus' sermon. The above analysis of the issues presents a case that Jesus did not signify symbolically future events without differentiation in his prophecy. This understanding leads to confusion in understanding the redaction in the Gospels because it distorts understanding of the basis for how events historically played out into separate events. It leaves the burden to the church to unfold prophecy as it "writes" a realized eschatology. Comprehension of the process of actual realization of events must proceed with some realistic consideration of how Jesus' future scenario touched on these events in his predictions.

Joachim Jeremias

For Jeremias, the immediate background and concern was the faulty modern critical theology of the second quest. He recognized the failure of the old quest because of the historical gaps in the synoptic tradition offered by Holtzmann, Weiss, Schweitzer, and Wrede, in its "theology of the kerygma" and its continued rejection of history in Bultmann's second quest "endorsement" of Martin Kähler.[54] On this view the historical Jesus and his message have no "decisive significance" for the Christian faith.[55] Jeremias argued that the gospel Jesus proclaimed antedates the kerygma of the primitive community.[56] In order to demonstrate this, his main body of work focused on translations of the sayings of Jesus from Greek into Aramaic.[57] He also asked a number of important historical questions. Along this line, Jeremias opposed G. Ebeling's view that revelation in the Gospels is "not historical datum" (*kein historisches Faktum*) "or a historic event" (*ein geschichtliches Geschehen*).[58] The Aramaic background was the theme for Jeremias which Meyer follows. The goal of historical research for Jeremias was, if not the *ipsissima verba*, then the *ipsissima vox* or "very voice" of Jesus.

There are five main points of interest from Jeremias's work that are influential for understanding Meyer. Because the themes of Jesus' eschatology and the kingdom of God are the backbone of Meyer's construct, they are summarized below. Meyer does not interact directly with many writers in the second quest perhaps because of his reliance upon Jeremias in these areas.[59]

---

54. Kähler, *So-Called Historical Jesus*, 18–23, 46–71.

55. Jeremias, *Problem of the Historical Jesus*, 2.

56. Ibid., 12. See also his 1971 work, *Neutestamentliche Theologie I. Teil: Die Verkündigung Jesu*. The English translation implies Jeremias wished to equate "New Testament Theology" with Jesus' message, whereas the German title made it clear that "Jesus' Proclamation" is part 1. The English translation is, Jeremias, *New Testament Theology: The Proclamation of Jesus*, trans. John Bowden. Bowden was a Bultmannian who had no such interest for Jesus' teaching.

57. That is, he attempted to work back from the Greek accounts to the original Aramaic Jesus might have spoken. He wrote extensively on the theological implications of God as Abba/Father and Jesus' understanding of Abba, especially in the Lord's prayer. See Jeremias, *Abba*; Jeremias, *Prayers of Jesus*. Jeremias' treatment of Jesus' speech includes: (1) fields of meaning, (2) rhetorical range, (3) style, (4) rhythm, (5) variety of tone, (6) conscious allusions, (7) omissions, (8) ambiguities, (9) new coinages, and (10) distinctive idiom.

58. Ebeling, *Die Geschichtlichkeit der Kirche*, 59. Jeremias, *Problem of the Historical Jesus*, 10. Ebeling's view held that revelation was not accomplished and completed in Jesus' lifetime but continues to take place whenever the kerygma is preached. Jeremias saw in this the danger of surrendering the affirmation of the incarnation ("the Word become flesh") and dissolving "salvation history."

59. Meyer does not interact directly with E. Käsemann, except by footnotes in

Antecedents and Apocalyptic Literature

History. In applying his interest in history, Jeremias has some strong views on the relation between the supernatural, historical, and temporal issues in Jesus' message. First, in his work "Eine neue Schau der Zukunftsaussagen Jesu" Jeremias responded to Dodd's original (1935) version of realized eschatology and criticizes the distinction between historical events presented in the prophetic manner and supernatural events presented in the apocalyptic manner.[60] For example, Jeremias rejects Dodd's position to separate a group of judgment "woe" texts to various cities (Matt 10:15 / Luke 10:12;[61] Matt 11:20-24 / Luke 10:13-15; Matt 12:41-42 / Luke 11:31-32) from a second group of sayings considered "outside the historical order" (including "the Day of the Son of Man" in Q: Matt 24:37-39 / Luke 26:26-27 and 17:22-37) and instead argues that all events whether historical or post-historical describe a supernatural sequence reflecting divine initiative.[62]

Second, not only does Jeremias object to the supernatural myth/history distinction in Jesus' proclamation, but also to the temporal distinction between the two groupings of texts which Dodd proposed.[63] Dodd's

---

relation to the protest or development of the Bultmann school or to articles on faith and Christology. Meyer, *Aims*, 54, 74, 107. Käsemann is discussed briefly for protesting the separation of the kerygma theology from "'cosmos', 'history' and 'society.'" Meyer, *Aims*, 54. Meyer does however interact with Günther Bornkamm and his *Jesus of Nazareth* which takes account of the intervening parable research of Dodd (*Parables of the Kingdom*) and Jeremias, *Parables of Jesus*. Farmer, "Reflections upon 'The Historical Perimeters for Understanding *The Aims of Jesus*.'" Meyer sees Bornkamm's new quest as an improvement on Bultmann for abandoning his views on the commissioning of the twelve disciples (Matt 10:1-16; Mark 6:7-11; 3:13-19; Luke 9:1-5; 6:12-16; 10:3) in the ministry of Jesus. See Bornkamm, *Jesus of Nazareth*. But in the tradition of Wrede and Bultmann, Bornkamm nowhere attributes messianic titles and prophetic knowledge to Jesus. Meyer, *Aims*, 51.

60. Dodd, *Parables of the Kingdom*; Jeremias, "Eine neue Schau der zukunftsaussagen Jesu," 216-22.

61. The overlap in material is seen by the change in context from Luke's commissioning of the seventy to the commissioning of the twelve disciples in Matt 10:1-16.

62. Jeremias, "Eine neue Schau der zukunftsaussagen Jesu." Cf. Dodd, *Parables of the Kingdom*, 60-62. Dodd distinguished between texts referring to "the last judgment" ("woes" to the cities) from "supernatural events" that are of "universal significance." About the latter Dodd says: "This day is not like any event in known history but is compared to lightning visible everywhere!" Cf. comment by Meyer, *Aims*, 204. For a comparison of Gressmann's view which influenced Dodd, see Gressmann, *Der Ursprung der israelitisch-jüdischer Eschatolgie*.

63. Dodd notes forthcoming events in Jesus' death, death for some of his followers, disaster for the Jewish people, the capital Jerusalem, and finally disaster for the temple.

interpretation placed some texts without an "absolute" framework which Jeremias sought. Texts like Mark 13:14–25 are separated by "a long series of signs" from Mark 13:2.

The Beginning of a New Age. Second, Jeremias argued that Jesus signaled the reign of God at the beginning of his ministry. In his *Jesus als Weltvollender*, on Jesus' symbolic imagery, Jeremias stressed that the Hebrew verb בשׂר recalled the ancient near eastern announcement of the new age of a new king and that associations with kingship already belonged to the prophecy, including the phrase to "announce to the poor" (לְבַשֵּׂר עֲנָוִים) LXX: εὐαγγελίσασθαι πτωχοῖς in Isa 61:1. He held that this prophecy was quoted by Jesus at the beginning of his ministry to declare the opening of a new age (Luke 4:18–19).

Meyer views the transition from the "days of John the Baptist" (Matt 11:12a) to Jesus' independent career as announcing the priority of the reign of God over the wrath to come. He posits that the kingdom of God in Jesus' proclamation was a distinct term coined to describe "God's final and climatic saving act."[64] The miraculous signs of healing and exorcism Jesus performed, "imaged and actualized" the advent of the kingdom and provided evidence for Israel to believe (Mark 3:24–26; Matt 12:27 / Luke 11:19).[65] The presence of the kingdom is evidenced by forgiveness of sins and table fellowship with sinners (Mark 2:16; Matt 11:19; Luke 15:1; 19:5).[66]

The New Community. Third, and perhaps most importantly for Meyer, along with his emphasis on the beginning of the new age, Jeremias opposed the widespread rejection of the idea that Jesus intended shortly to establish a community. In Matthew 16:18; 18:17 the emphasis is on Jesus' intention to gather together a messianic remnant or ἐκκλησία as the "community of salvation."[67] While the "building of a congregation" at Qumran (4QpPs 37.3.16) is sometimes compared to this, Jesus' movement is by means of

---

These he labeled *Unheilseschatologie*. Dodd singled out Mark 13:14–25 as an event set before a long series of signs which did not fit the forthcoming historical events he arranged with the temple. Dodd recognized an apocalyptic framework in Mark. How Dodd interpreted these texts is a separate question.

64. Meyer, *Aims*, 129.
65. Ibid., 157.
66. Ibid., 159.
67. Compare the saying about earthly relationships in Mark 10:29. See also use of νηπίοις in Matt 11:25, 23:9, and ἀδελφοί in 25:40. See also Meyer's comments on the "unimpressiveness of Jesus' following" as an issue behind Jesus' parables, ibid., 164.

grace (Luke 19:1-10) and not by human striving or separation (contra K. L. Schmidt).[68]

Jesus' Death as a Vicarious Sacrifice. Fourth, Jeremiah's work *The Eucharistic Words of Jesus* addressed the historical question, did Jesus conceive of his death as uniquely salvific and if so how? The answer for Jeremias is as a vicarious sacrifice.[69] Jeremias devoted some attention to the subject of the passion of Jesus. His understanding of Jesus' passion is influenced by three factors. First, he recognizes the meaning of Jesus' last supper words and the vow of abstinence in Mark 14:25 and Luke 22:15-18 as his prediction that he would not eat the Passover meal and drink wine again until in the kingdom of God. Second, this was not to be understood merely as a prediction of his death, but is eschatological and looks *beyond* it (note the oath).[70] Third, Jeremias believed Dodd had erred in conceiving of an apocalyptic eschatology of bliss (*Heilseschatologie*) only in terms of Jesus' career around the vindication of the Son of Man *without* including the resurrection of the dead, the pilgrimage of the nations, and the enthronement of the disciples.[71] Jeremias argued that there is an eschatology of bliss on a historical or temporal plane that corresponds to the eschatology of woe in the Gospels, and that the rewards of Matt 19:28-30 / Luke 22:28-30 are not for another time.[72] For Dodd, the temporal blessings are either supplemented or replaced in the apocalypses by the "age to come."[73] In Jeremias's view, Dodd did not integrate the motif of the restoration of Israel well into Jesus' proclamation. Denying any restoration on the earth Dodd's construct is not unlike the philosophical idealism and dualism of Plato.[74] His choice of Luke 12:49-53 / Matt 10:34-36 (a reference to Jesus' own career

---

68. Jeremias, *NTT*, 160-78. Note on 177 that Jesus' rejection of the Pharisaic and Essene special claims to be realizing the holy remnant was offensive.

69. Jeremias, *Eucharistic Words of Jesus*. Jeremias compares four texts of the words of the institution (1 Cor 11:23-5 and Synoptic accounts, Mark 14:22-25 / Matt 26:26-9 / Luke 22:15-20) in order to determine the earliest form (106). He concludes that Mark is the earliest (115).

70. Ibid., 165.

71. Meyer, *Aims*, 205.

72. Dodd thought the OT prophets balance their eschatology (*Heilseschatologie*) in predicting a time of prosperity in historical terms, but Jesus declared the kingdom had come.

73. Dodd, *Parables of the Kingdom*, rev. ed., 52-54.

74. On transposing the reign of God into "spiritual categories," see Meyer, *Aims*, 243.

causing "division" διαμερισμόν) as the text which unified Jesus' view of the future did not marry with the theme of restoration. Jeremias corrected this interpretation.

Imminence. Fifth, on this basis of Jesus' passion prediction, Jeremias agreed with Weiss about the coming kingdom "being at hand." From Mark 10:45, Jeremias argued that Jesus taught the eschaton comes by the ransom of his life for the world.[75] The passion of Jesus was the *beginning* of the last great hour of temptation for the whole earth and will usher in "the dawn of the day of salvation" (Mark 14:58).[76] He goes on to say that Jesus' use of the symbolic Passover meal and his prayer (Luke 22:16: πληρωθῇ) is for the speedy fulfillment of the Passover in the certainty that the kingdom of God is at hand. Jeremias concludes on this evidence that the eschatological pilgrimage of the Gentiles to the "Temple of the New Age" can take place after three days when the new eschatological sanctuary is erected (cf. Mark 14:58).[77]

Meyer will take these themes and place them with a short-term horizon to develop Jesus' future scenario. Furthermore, by dismissing Mark 13:24–27 he will maintain that there is no justifiable reason for seeing delay in Jesus' teaching.

Summary

Meyer highlights the deficiencies of the second quest. The second quest is skeptical of five things: miraculous events, messiah, prophecy, Jesus' expectation of suffering, and the understanding that eschatology as the cross is the "end." Meyer's break from these interpretive deficiencies was not unprecedented. Bernard Lonergan's insights also provided the impetus for Meyer to wrestle with philosophical views of those involved in the second quest. Jeremias's goal to criticize the effort to separate the gospel of Jesus from the Kerygma of the early church was the opposite of the second quest. Where the second quest assumed discontinuity between Jesus and the early church, Jeremiah explored the link between critical history and faith and described this as a "discerning continuity." The result substituted a historical construct of the early church for the quest for the message of Jesus himself.

75. Jeremias, "Das Lösegeld für Viele (Mk.10:45)," 249–64.
76. Jeremias, *Eucharistic Words of Jesus*, 171.
77. On this theme, see also Jeremias, *Jesus' Promise to the Nations*, 4.

Antecedents and Apocalyptic Literature

The predominant issue that Jeremias and Meyer face is that of historicity. For Meyer, a-historical constructs linking themes are not bad in themselves, but the excesses need to be avoided. Wrede's creative construct of a "messianic secret" was a consequence of Enlightenment ideas and psychological interpretation. Schweitzer engaged in speculation without recognizing redactional changes within the sources. Bultmann's error lay in separating the question of Jesus' role as Messiah from eschatology. What Meyer calls the "kerygmatically conditioned nature of the sources" characteristic of the second quest (especially of Käsemann's approach to apocalyptic) was unnecessarily skeptical.[78] There are two, not one, perspectives possible in the Jesus tradition and the Easter kerygma. In essence the gospel was both historical tradition and pneumatic kerygma.[79] The *Sitz im Leben* of the sayings was the ministry of the historical Jesus and his followers.

The problem with Jeremias's work is that he has avoided historical background questions related to the themes discussed, or aspects of themes he discusses in Jesus' future scenario. These include questions related to Jesus' future view of three things: first, the temple; second, Jewish perspectives on apocalyptic, and third, the Gentiles. Instead Jeremias makes several assumptions about the timing of the kingdom based on conclusions found in chapter 2. First, following Weiffenbach and Dodd, Jeremias denies any differentiation between resurrection and Parousia in Jesus' vision of the future. Second, one's view of fulfillment of prophetic events associated with OT themes rests on appreciating symbolic meaning. Like Dodd, Jeremias rejects the notion that apocalyptic imagery has a historical referent. The impact of Jeremias's hermeneutical method on prophecy, however, is mixed. On the one hand Jeremias analyses considerable amounts of data associated with the theme of vindication in order to discern a coherent pattern in Synoptic Gospels. On the other hand, this analysis fails to consider referents or the breadth of development of meaning in Jesus' teaching that results in different meaning in the Gospels. Furthermore, Jeremias presents only a favorable picture of the Gentiles in Jesus' message.

---

78. Meyer, *Aims*, 51.

79. See also Goppelt for this correction of the second quest. Note Goppelt's examples especially how 1 Cor 15 is "interpreted kerygmatically" by Paul. Goppelt, *Theology of the New Testament*, 41.

Eschatological Relationships and Jesus

Description of the Construct and Themes

The last section noted developments from the second quest, highlighted the problem passages where eschatological relationships are debated, and introduced some assumptions in Meyer's understanding of eschatology. In this section, key themes related to the absolute eschatology presented by Meyer in his exegesis and examination of the historical context are summarized. These are the themes which are subsumed under the predominant metaphor of the restoration of Israel.[80] This is followed by a final description of how Meyer reads apocalyptic as a whole in Jesus' ministry.

1. The Portrait of Jesus

Drawing off the historical evidence provided by Dodd, Meyer holds that Jesus is an authentic prophet.[81] Jesus understood himself to be the unique revealer of the full, final measure of God's will.[82] Jesus' prediction of the destruction of the temple (Mark 13:2) is not *ex eventu*. Meyer follows Jeremias also in two further matters. First, both Matthew and Mark unambiguously define the Elijah-role as one of preparation for the Messiah (Matt 11:10; Mark 1:2).[83] The whole point of John the Baptist was *"preparationist"* in an appeal for Israel's imminent consummation of history.[84]

Second, Jesus' cleansing of the temple and even his "harsh" response is messianic action, not social-political revolutionary action.[85] Jesus' teaching

---

80. Cf. Perrin, *Kingdom of God*; Just, *Ongoing Feast*.

81. See Dodd, "Jesus as Teacher and Prophet." The evidence for Jesus being a prophet is seen by the populace (Mark 6:4, par.; 6:15), by his critics (Mark 14:65; Luke 7:39), by his authoritative teaching (Mark 1:27) and poetic utterances set apart from the rabbis, by his link with the Spirit (Luke 10:18), by his appeal to Isaiah (Mark 7:6), by predictions uttered typical of the OT prophets, including lament ("over Jerusalem" Matt 23:37-39 / Luke 13:34-35), forecast of destruction of the temple (Mark 13:2 / Matt 24:1-2 / Luke 21:5-6; Mark 14:53-65), forecasting his own death at Jerusalem (Mark 10:39). For Dodd, the short-term nature of prophecies is in harmony with the OT prophets. Meyer, *Aims*, 70, 147-151, 242-47.

82. Meyer, *Aims*, 151.

83. Jeremias, "Ηλ(ε)ίας," TWNT, 2:930-43; Meyer, *Aims*, 126.

84. Meyer, *Aims*, 234. For Jeremias' comments on "grace" and a comparison, see the work from n18 above.

85. Jeremias, "Jesus als weltvollender," 35-44. Cf. Schrenk, "ἱερὸν," TWNT, 3:243-47, who denied it was messianic or revolutionary. Cf. also Hengel's view that at the heart of Jesus' message lies a conscious rejection of violence, Hengel, *Was Jesus a Revolutionist?*,

leads to a showdown with religious authorities. Jesus' self-understanding was that he was the "messianic builder of the house of God"[86] and that he presented himself publicly as the messianic builder and restorer of Israel.[87] Although Meyer does not develop the theme of the Son of Man extensively, he acknowledged Jesus has a transcendent role in keeping with his future vindication and enthronement.[88]

For Meyer, Jesus' public proclamation and teaching was about the reign of God (Matt 11:5 / Luke 7:22) and the eschatological Torah (Matt 5:3–48 par.). Jesus' public actions converge around the idea that the kingdom of God is at hand.[89] He asks the question: what had God prepared for Israel and the nations? "The reign of God signified the *kairos* of eschatological fulfillment, the moment at which God would fulfill his age-old and often iterated promises to his people."[90] For Israel, this meant the climactic and definitive restoration; for the nations, "participation in the salvation of Israel" (Matt 8:11).[91] Furthermore, Jesus' victory over Satan shows that Satan is coming to an end. The exorcisms of Jesus are absolutely decisive for the life of humanity, and Jesus' conflict with Satan is "not the endless seesaw of history's long haul, but the apocalyptic turning-point (Mark 1:24–26; 4:39; 5:13)."[92] Five themes from Meyer's construct are discussed here.

2. The Prediction of a New Community

Meyer affirmed that Jesus predicted a new community beyond the cross.

Meyer argues for the historicity of Peter's declaration of Jesus at Caesarea Philippi and Jesus' prediction of the ἐκκλησία (Matt 16:17–19).[93] Particularly damaging to the validity of this theme was Bultmann's demy-

---

26–29; Meyer, *Aims*, 181–84, 199–200.

86. Meyer, *Aims*, 221.
87. Ibid., 217.
88. Ibid., 209.
89. These include: (1) the call of the disciples, (2) the sending out of the disciples to Israel, (3) the miraculous signs of salvation, (4) table fellowship with sinners, (5) public debate and, (6) public formulation of mission, and (7) the final entry into Jerusalem to cleanse the temple.
90. Meyer, *Aims*, 134.
91. Ibid., 171.
92. Ibid., 156.
93. Ibid., 185.

thologizing interpretation of eschatology. Meyer rejected the notion that the conceptual thought of the Gospels supports the "present time" (cross, resurrection) as "the end" because the Jewish apocalyptic conception of the kingdom of God as an eschatological unfolding account in history is mythological.[94] Instead, Jesus would build a new temple belonging to the eschaton.[95] This eschatological temple would be the new community of which Peter is the foundational rock (cf. Mark 14:58).[96] Meyer goes on to interpret John 2:19a not as a prediction of Jesus' resurrection, but as a saying of Jesus about the Jerusalem temple, while the second half of 2:19b ("I will build it in three days") is the evangelist's interpretation which applies only to the second utterance. Thus, John can speak symbolically about the new temple being raised before the old one is destroyed.[97] Meyer treats the saying about three days in a punctiliar sense (expressing a point in time) which corresponds to the "apocalyptic conception of the new temple miraculously raised and revealed." This therefore is the eschatological scheme of Jesus which is characteristic of Jesus' words on the imminent future.[98]

3. Israel

Given his focus on the new community, Israel as a nation receives less treatment by Meyer; he does not explain the judgment on Israel clearly (Matt 23:34-36 / Luke 11:49-57). His interpretation of this passage in Matthew 23 is focused on Jesus as a prophet. The ordeal for Israel which envisaged that God would abandon the temple was near (cf. Ezek 11:23; 14:17; Matt 10:32; 23:37). Meyer develops the notion of the "eschatological scheme" and discerns that aspects of "crisis/crisis resolution" are evident in Jesus' sayings about "three days."[99] First, using Jeremias's evidence that the three day motif derives from Semitic idiom, he shows the phrase does not necessarily refer to "three calendar days."[100] Rather it can mean "shortly," and context dictates the intended duration (e.g., Josh 2:16; 2 Kgs 20:5, 8). Second, drawing on Gray's work on symbolic language, he argues that Jesus' saying about

---

94. See Throckmorton, *New Testament and Mythology*, 134.
95. Meyer, *Aims*, 209.
96. Ibid., 189.
97. Ibid., 181-82.
98. Ibid., 182.
99. Ibid.
100. Ibid.

three days carries a "symbolic sense" because like OT language the third day "brought salvation because God did not leave the righteous in need for more than three days (Gen 42:17; Exod 19:16; Josh 2:16; Hos 6:2; Jonah 1:17)."[101] The resultant eschatological scheme understands Jesus' proclamation as a coherent and thematically linked series of themes interpreting a pattern in events. When the language referring to time is viewed as symbolic, the scheme subsumes a short-term framework. On Jesus' "three days saying" Meyer writes: "The sense does call for an accent on the limitation and shortness of time. The imminent crisis epitomized in the destruction of the temple would swiftly yield to the salvation epitomized in the new temple to be built by Jesus."[102] It is questionable however, whether the resulting construct on the eschatology of the tribulation is consistent with the notion that Jesus did not accurately differentiate substantial events describing the destruction of the temple apart from the fact the temple is included. In other words, Jesus could predict a scenario for the temple which Daniel predicted and which history indicates is clearly plausible.

Meyer understands that Jesus' teaching reserved for his disciples relates to Jesus' public career to Israel as "theme to performance."[103] This is important for Jesus' identity as messiah. Jesus' public actions show who he is and this leads to discussion among his disciples in private. The central category Meyer presents for Jesus' role as messiah is the "builder of the house of God."[104] Meyer draws this category through Jesus' private teaching to discuss the relationship of Israel to her Messiah. Thus Jesus' theme of the coming of the Son of Man in his private teaching to the disciples (Mark 13; par.) is in his view equivalent to his public theme of God's approaching reign. The problem is that Meyer does not take into account the details of Israel's rejection or the ambiguity in the language of the Olivet Discourse itself.[105]

The restored Israel becomes the focus. Restoration is not absolute (or comprehensive) because of the lack of faith (Matt 23:37).[106] Judgment, how-

---

101. Gray, "Day of Yahweh," 5–37. Meyer, *Aims*, 182.

102. Meyer, *Aims*, 182.

103. See chaps. 7 and 8 of *Aims*.

104. Meyer, *Aims*, 201, 221.

105. On the contrary, he claims there is no ambiguity in Jesus' teaching. By his judgment the apocalyptic texts are straight forward in their symbolic interpretation and support imminent restoration of messianic Israel. Ibid., 250.

106. Ibid., 185, 242.

ever, is absolute. The restored Israel is a subset of Israel. As in the parables (Mark 4), Jesus treats unbelieving Israel as "outsiders" in absolute terms. Jesus' words epitomize an awesome event: "the division of Israel and the coming into being of the messianic 'remnant.'"[107]

Jesus' urgent mission is to press Israel to a decision and win them over to the reign of God.[108] Describing Jesus' entry into Jerusalem Meyer says that "Jesus, the disciples, and the pilgrim crowds combined to make the entry a messianic event, so investing the cleansing of the temple with a messianic dimension."[109] The final ransom of Israel depends on faith (Isa 28:16) and it is the messianic remnant that is at stake."[110] He writes: "The fate of the nation would hinge on its response to [the] message" brought by Jesus and his disciples. The nation's destiny was crucial because those who rejected the messiah (Matt 23:37) would be rejected (Luke 13:3) in "absolute," not relative, terms.[111]

4. The Jerusalem Temple

In Meyer's construct, Jesus' public actions and worldview about the temple are central. The temple cleansing signaled the dawn of a new era and is the trigger for his enemies to do away with Jesus (Mark 11:18 / Luke 19:47).[112] Jesus' temple riddle saying cited by his enemies (Mark 14:58; 15:29; Matt 26:61; 27:40) is to be taken literally. Meyer sees the temple as symbolic of messianic Israel in the glory of its restoration.[113] Meyer draws on the terminology of J. Gray to describe the temple's destruction.[114] This destruction and related themes are to be understood in a wide sense; that is in "absolute" terms rather than in "relative" terms. For example, καταλύσω (Mark 14:58; 15:29 / Matt 26:61), is taken as a complete destruction not a cleansing. Meyer thinks that 13:26 supports his interpretation, for he views it as an expansion of the phrase "build again" coinciding with the in-breaking of God's rule and restoration rather than a separate incident for Israel at

---

107. Ibid., 210.
108. Ibid., 199.
109. Ibid.
110. Ibid., 154, 183.
111. Ibid., 210. See also Meyer, "Jesus and the Remnant of Israel."
112. Meyer, *Aims*, 184.
113. Ibid., 200.
114. See Gray, "Day of Yahweh," 8.

the time of the end as others suggest. Thus, the terms θλῖψιν (Mark 13:24), πίπτοντες and σαλευθήσονται (Mark 13:25), and ἐρχόμενον (Mark 13:26) are taken in a passive sense as equivalent either to Jesus' suffering or to the fall of Israel's old establishment on the one hand, or resurrection and vindication for himself and his followers, on the other hand. Meyer therefore treats words like suffering and coming as references to the content of the messianic building of the house of God. The coming of the Son of Man is virtually equivalent to the public theme of God's reign.[115]

Furthermore, the reconstructed temple provides the master image of Jesus' message and career (Mark 14:58 par.; John 2:19; cf. Matt 16:18).[116] Jesus draws upon apocalyptic, but Meyer rejects the idea that there is any "stilted" apocalyptic symbolism in Jesus' prophecy. Rather, the master category that defines all apocalyptic symbolism is the "image of the temple."[117] Jesus intended a reform of the temple practice and his actions were symbolically charged and signified the "imminent eschaton."[118] Jesus disdained to date the future and repudiated apocalyptic calendars (Luke 17:20-21; Mark 13:32).

5. The Gentiles

Most references Meyer makes to Gentiles are positive. The parable of the mustard seed (Mark 4:30–32; par., cf. Matt 8:11; 12:41; 25:31–46) presents the eschatological assimilation of the Gentiles.[119] Central OT texts on the last time such as Isaiah 11:12; 56:8 and 60:3 are described as the time when the Messiah and the messianic people will draw the dispersed Israel from the corners of the earth and stream to Zion.[120] The Davidic king would be a signal for the nations (Isa 11:10). Meyer understands that the promise of entering into salvation and the pilgrimage of the Gentiles is realized in Christian world mission.[121] The public formula of Jesus going only to Israel (Matt 15:24) is primarily for the purpose of the Gentiles being "assimilated"

---

115. See also Wright's comments in his introduction to the Aims of Jesus. Meyer, *Aims*, 9i.

116. Ibid., 249.

117. Ibid.

118. Ibid., 170.

119. Ibid., 164.

120. Ibid., 184.

121. Ibid., 247.

and taking refuge with Israel.¹²² Luke 10:25–37 and 17:11–19 present Jesus' positive outlook to Samaritans and Gentiles. Furthermore, according to Meyer the traditional theme of eschatological vengeance on the Gentiles as a polemical technique in Luke 4:22 and Matt 11:5 is deliberately omitted by Jesus.¹²³ The only negative reference in Meyer's construct is Luke's record of the Gentile army attack on Jerusalem. The timing factor attributed to this event, which Meyer relates to the spectrum that includes Jesus' own suffering, is described as the last attack.¹²⁴ The benefit of Jesus' death is not restricted to Israel. Jesus' death is a ransom for all (Isa 52:15; 53:4–6; 10–12).

6. Suffering, Crisis, Distress

A central focal point of Meyer's construct is Jesus' career and the theme of crisis or suffering. Meyer understands Jesus to predict his own suffering and that of his disciples in four ways. First, Jesus' passion is at hand. Second, this suffering will certainly spill over to his disciples. Third, the theme of imminence or "shortness of time" dominated Jesus' perspective of his own death and the suffering for the disciples and Israel. For example, Meyer extrapolates Jesus' prayer in Matthew 6:9–13 and Luke 11:2–4, such that to lead not "into temptation" (εἰς πειρασμόν, Matt 6:13) refers specifically to the coming distress for disciples with the fall of the temple.¹²⁵ Fourth, these predictions are compatible with the prophetic forecasts of the OT prophets who predicted an "eschatology of woe" (*Unheilseschatologie*). Meyer tends to be non-specific, however, on this theme. Thus, following Dodd, Meyer holds that Jesus made three kinds of predictions of forthcoming events: sufferings for himself, persecution for his followers, and disaster for the Jewish people, their city, and temple. The significance here is how these events are construed in his absolute eschatology.¹²⁶ Although Meyer treats

---

122. Ibid., 167.

123. Ibid.

124. Ibid., 209.

125. Cf. BDAG, 793 (πειρασμός, §2b) relates to *being tempted* or temptation from without or within, that can be "an occasion of sin to a person." This does not necessarily suggest a specific ordeal. Meyer's "full field of meaning" is too broad here (see also Mark 14:38; Matt 26:41; Luke 4:13; 8:13; though cf. "trials" in Luke 22:28 with 22:40, 46). Certainly most references by Jesus relate to moral and ethical qualities (sin, guilt, and wrong doing) of the disciples and such related behavior.

126. Wright, *Who Was Jesus?*, 203; Dodd, *Parables of the Kingdom*, 40–55. Meyer, *Aims*, 249.

these themes and texts in light of their relationships (i.e., how they fit into the crisis-resolution motif) the centered texts (Matt 16:18; John 2:19 and Mark 14:58) dominate his reading and he relates the statement of the inauguration of God's kingdom with the time of the end.

7. Vindication and Restoration

Meyer has retained the key element of Dodd's hypothesis that Jesus did not differentiate between his resurrection and Parousia.[127] Thus vindication "now" means resurrection, Parousia, and vindication for Jesus and final restoration for the new Israel. Overall Meyer concurs with Jeremias when he says the "'Now' was originally defined by Jesus' career. Beyond this 'now' stood a future dominated first by the eschatological crisis to be opened by the repudiation, suffering, and death of Jesus himself (Luke 23:28–32) and destined to engulf his disciples and all Israel. Dreadful but short, it would be brought to an end by the Son of man whose appearance would open the last act of the eschatological drama: resurrection, judgment, the banquet of the saved."[128] When vindication comes, it comes quickly. As already mentioned from Jesus' temple riddle (Mark 15:29; John 2:19) the new temple is rebuilt in three days. The three days motif is taken as "soon" and the Gentiles stream to Zion, the place of restoration.

Confirmation in the OT and Second Temple Judaism

Meyer's final chapter is devoted to confirmation and reflection. First, he offers confirmation from the OT prophets concerning the predicted remnant of Israel. Numerous biblical citations which support the theme of restoration that Meyer argues for are presented (Isa 4:3–5; 6:1–13;7:9; 10:20; 37:31 Amos 3:1; Mic 2:12; 4:6; 7:18; Jer 23:3; 30:8; 31:10; Ezek 34:15; Zeph 2:3; Zech 3:11–13). He provides evidence of a "thematic constellation" of covenant righteousness, poverty, and flock by the prophet Isaiah about the returned exiles. The theme of *God's covenant* is traced from several passages ("people," Isa 57:14; 58:1; 60:21; 62:12; 63:8; 65:10–22; "eternal covenant," 61:8; "blessed race of Yahweh," 65:9, 23; "holy people," 62:12; "elect of Yahweh," 65:9, 15, 22; "redeemed of Yahweh," 62:12). Similarly, the category of

---

127. Meyer, *Aims*, 205.
128. Ibid., 204.

the *righteousness* takes various titles and is contrasted with the wicked (the "just" or "righteous" as opposed to the wicked, the skeptical, the idolaters, thieves, and the hard-hearted). Other groups associated with the righteous include those in poverty (the "humble" and the "broken-hearted," 61:1; the "contrite and lowly," 57:15) and also of the *flock* (65:10).

Second, in his survey of life in Second Temple Judaism, Meyer makes five points about the nature of Jewish religion and Jewish convictions in general. First, the returning exiles understood themselves to be the remnant of Israel and their obedience took shape in the task of rebuilding the temple (Ezra 1:2–4; 3:1–6:22) in order to recreate the religious ideal (Ezra 10:2–5).[129] Furthermore, indispensable to renewal was the priest who became a central figure in the post-exilic community. Second, the rise of various competing religious groups traces the efforts toward restoration in the exile and the post-exilic period. The central question these groups were responsible to settle is, what was Israel to become as a people of God? Third, the economy of Torah was sufficient and highly important. Fourth, strict observance by Pharisaical *halakah* had an important role in the scheme of things as did Torah piety. Torah piety is defined as the cardinal importance of observance of the Torah, and has a structural and historical component. Structurally, it follows the stipulations of the Mosaic covenant and corresponding election of grace. Historically, it is found in the permanent *religious reaction* to national crisis of exile and condemnation for non-observance.[130] Fifth, observance of *halakah* or Torah was radicalized by the emergence of apocalyptic and its absolute eschatology. In short, the horizon that generates Torah piety in the national crisis historically is the problem of non-observance, and absolute eschatology (with its own historical crises) only raised the degree of significance of Torah piety further.

Confirmation from the NT and Reflection

Meyer seeks confirmation of his understanding of Jesus' goal of eschatological restoration of Israel from early Christianity. He engages with numerous NT texts that he seeks to correlate with his reading of the historical Jesus in the Gospels. For the purposes of this discussion, the focus is mainly on Paul, and Meyer's treatment of Romans 9–11. The backing for Meyer's construct has two essential points. First, early Christianity had an "ecclesial

---

129. Ibid., 229.
130. Ibid., 236.

self-understanding" comparable to Jesus' career that saw themselves as the community of the outpoured Spirit of the "last day."[131] Second, in Romans 9–11, the emphasis is on "remnant theology" where Paul argues God has not rejected his people Israel (11:1). There are four aspects of Meyer's understanding of Paul. First, Paul's intention is to explain the "non-entry" of the bulk of Israel into messianic salvation. Second, like the remnant in Elijah's day (1 Kgs 19), so too at the present time there is a remnant chosen by grace (Rom 11:5). Third, Paul's answer is that Isaiah 10:20–23 has been fulfilled in the church: "the Isaian threat/promise that a remnant would be saved ... [has] historic realization."[132] Finally, with regard to the promise that God will save all Israel,[133] phrases like "the Israel of God" (Gal 6:16) and the link to the historical encounter of Christ with Israel (Rom 16:8), one realizes that what is being highlighted are themes that can be correlated under the category of the "salvation of the remnant."

In his final section entitled "reflections," Meyer asks the question, was Jesus mistaken in his prophecy? The answer is no. He then presents his summary scenario in the context of the non-advent of the Parousia.[134] The intention of Jesus' prophecy and its relation to the actual course of events (the temple destruction) is explained as a "symbol-charged two-act drama of crisis and resolution."[135] By following and adopting Weiffenbach's hypothesis, Dodd, Jeremias (with corrections to Dodd) and Meyer hold that Jesus did not distinguish between his resurrection, exaltation, and Parousia.[136] Meyer calls this the "original conception globally" and draws his thesis on prophecy from it. Having listed his assumptions, presented his master symbol (the image of the destruction/building of the temple and Jesus as messianic builder), identified and exegeted particular prophetic texts which are central to the construct (Matt 16; John 2) and explored their

---

131. Ibid., 239.

132. Ibid.

133. Rom 11:27; cf. "full inclusion" in 11:12.

134. Meyer actually lists and critiques nine strategies to solving the problem of delay. Most telling is his quick dismissal that "explanations of delay" in Rom 11:25–32 and Acts 3:19–21 are *ad hoc* and that the solution was persevering watchfulness and persevering hope. Meyer, *Aims*, 243.

135. Meyer, *Aims*, 246.

136. Weiffenbach, *Der Weiderkunftsgedanke Jesu nach den Synoptikern kritisch untersucht und dargestellt*; Dodd, *Parables of the Kingdom*, 76. Jeremias, "Eine neue Schau der zukunftsaussagen Jesu," 216–22; Meyer, *Aims*, 249.

scope (formation of the new community) and eschatological relationships, Meyer turns to explain, how Jesus' prophecy is fulfilled in actual events.

First, in Jesus' prophecy what the symbol intends is identical with what God, for whom the prophet speaks, intends.[137] Second, people and events in the vision may enter the prophet's own horizon only partially and imperfectly. Third, Meyer explores whether Jesus had "determinate knowledge of what God intended by the symbolic scheme of things which Jesus himself was commissioned to announce?" Meyer answers no. He views prophetic knowledge as limited knowledge distinct from empirical knowledge. Thus, Jesus' prophecy of the salvation of the Gentiles (Matt 6:11) was realized through the movement of early Christian world mission (Acts 1:8).

This summary is built on the two premises: (1) the claim to a "holistic approach to the data" and (2) the pervasiveness of the theme of "imminence."[138] Regarding the latter, Meyer does not view sayings with a time limit (Mark 9:1; 13:30 and Matt 10:23) as a major problem in Jesus' eschatology. A major premise of Jesus' proclamation is that there is an implicit time limit which pervades all of Jesus' public statements whether or not these are taken as secondary. When one sees references to "signs" (Mark 8:12; Matt 16:4), "numbers," "three days" (Matt 12:40; Mark 14:58; 15:29) one realizes that what is being highlighted is the "imminence of the eschaton and consummation in symbolic form." In Luke 13:32, the emphasis is on what Jesus does "today and tomorrow" (drives out demons and performs cures) and on the third day "I complete my course."[139]

Meyer's Concept of Apocalyptic Eschatology

What was Jesus' apocalyptic eschatology according to Meyer? Meyer makes several points about the nature of the apocalyptic that Jesus drew on. First, as mentioned Jesus only adopts symbolic prophecy. Apocalyptic reveals anything new. In this sense, it is geared to actual history. Second, Meyer compares the later apocalypse of 4 Ezra 4:33, 37 as evidence that Jesus' apocalyptic was not a presumptuous calendar of the future with unchanged dates. In this regard he finds no evidence of any "human or religious

---

137. Meyer's symbol of "destroying/building the temple" encompasses the motifs of suffering, resurrection, exaltation and Parousia.

138. Meyer, *Aims*, 245. Others will dispute Meyer's selection of data.

139. Ibid., 154.

ambiguity in Jesus."[140] For Meyer, Jesus was certain of the temporal nature of his apocalyptic prediction so that he had no "misleading impressions" or information about the final cataclysmic end.[141] However, one verse problematic for Meyer's argument is Mark 13:32 for it shows that the historical Jesus had limitations to his knowledge. Third, Jesus' apocalyptic drew upon OT motifs of "distress" found in Jeremiah 30:5, 7 and Daniel 12:1 in its "remote background." These motifs of apocalyptic distress worked to heighten the distress and salvation message of Jesus and became final and climatic in Jesus.[142] Fourth, Jesus linked the "distress" (Dan 12:1) in his warning to the "last generation" who stood in unique danger leading to the irreducible "post-historical judgment of the world" (Luke 11:49–51; Matt 23:33–36; Luke 23:28–31).[143] In sum, Meyer understands the relation between AE and PE as sufficiently compatible historically so that they are practically identical. AE and PE function in the same way in describing the absolute end point of the temple and rebuilding of the new community in "three days" through Jesus' resurrection and role as builder of the house of God.

Summary and Evaluation

Cultural Background and Construct Themes

In his analysis of the Jewish Intertestamental or Second Temple period, Meyer separates historical religious discussion from political discussion and indicates that the drive to full observance of the law according to Pharisaic *halakah* was "radicalized by emergence of apocalyptic absolute eschatology."[144] Yet he does not explain how the themes in such movements are discussed or what they suggest about how Second Temple Judaism approached apocalyptic texts and their relationships.[145] Did they see it as absolute or is this merely logical in Meyer's construct? Second, he discusses

---

140. Ibid., 250.

141. Meyer, *Aims*, 250.

142. Meyer, *Aims*, 206.

143. Ibid., 207.

144. Ibid., 236. Cf. the comment that "Jesus was not absorbed by political oppression (Mark 12:16)." Meyer, *Aims*, 249.

145. For example, Meyer's biblical citations from Daniel (Dan 7:13, 14, 27 and 12:1), do not reference the political background or efforts toward restoration. There is a tacit reference to the book of Daniel, associating the expectation of salvation from foreign masters by "divine miracle alone." Meyer, *Aims*, 236.

various reactions to religious failure (by groups like the Hasidim, Sadducees, and Essenes who looked to the restoration of Israel), but not how such a reaction was stimulated by other factors in the intertestamental period, such as the oppression by the Gentile nations like Syria and Egypt.[146] Nor does he discuss how religious failure or "non-observance" in relation to the temple played out in connection to the political reality of Gentile oppression, or what Jewish apocalyptic literature alludes to this struggle. As a result, Meyer is unable to trace key themes and their relationship to Gentile oppression. Meyer's approach seems to have two goals: (1) to trace the theme of restoration, and (2) to overview the general religious context noting the contemporary religious issues in various groups in Judaism. While he notes that Amos 3:11 states that God's word to Israel was judgment, not salvation, on the "day of Yahweh" (Amos 3:1), the majority of texts offers a single themed horizon of investigation: the condemnation of present Israel and a picture of a future remnant in Israel that survives a major catastrophe (Isa 6:1–13; Amos 3:12; Micah 4:6; 7:18–20; Zech 3:11–13; Zeph 2:3).[147] If this horizon that Meyer highlights in the texts he presents is a survey of PE, then he says little or nothing about AE especially in regard to future salvation.[148] Regarding the second goal, Meyer's reading supports the general notion of the importance of Torah observance in Israel without examining how observance is framed in individual books and with apocalyptic

---

146. The Hasidim were a pious group mentioned in 1 Macc 7:12–14; (cf. "soldiers" in 2:42), who received religious guidance from the scribes. Pharisees were leaders of transformation to observance of Torah piety, goals extended to all Israel to possibility of meeting God's demand for a holy people (Exod 19:6; Lev 11:44; 19:2; 20:7). Ibid., 232.

147. Ibid., 225–28. Cf. also in Amos 3:7 the word "secret scheme" סוֹד (*HALOT*, 745, is the plan or scheme "of God towards people, [made known via] the prophets"; also Jer 23:18–22; Ps 25:14). סוֹד denotes God's revelation about coming judgment. "Revealing his plan" גָּלָה סוֹדוֹ) LXX: ἐὰν μὴ ἀποκαλύψῃ παιδείαν "without first clearly showing his instruction") is the prerequisite for the Sovereign God to act in judgment. The semantic force of the divine prerequisite regarding judgment is indicated by the third class condition. Protasis: ἐὰν μὴ ἀποκαλύψῃ παιδείαν αὐτοῦ πρὸς τοὺς δούλους αὐτοῦ τοὺς προφήτας, apodosis: διότι οὐ μὴ ποιήσῃ κύριος ὁ θεὸς πρᾶγμα. It is possible the Jews read this relationship of apodosis to protasis in the intertestamental period as one of "evidence to inference." If the condition can be seen (evidence) then the implication is that God is judging us still. Revealing a plan does not cause judgment to occur. But the question for Second Temple Jews is that there is evidence for judgment at this time. The question becomes why powerful nation after powerful nation occupies Israel without Israel realizing independence. If there is evidence that God has spoken then it shows judgment is permissible. See also Davies, *Territorial Dimension of Judaism*; Halpern-Amaru, *Rewriting the Bible*; Scott, *Exile*.

148. See n136.

themes. Thus, Meyer has evidently overlooked the details of Jewish apocalyptic in this section, and his theological construct does not cover all the data available from Second Temple Judaism. Finally, Meyer is consistent in addressing the issue of the failure of Israel's faith that he raised in chapter 5 on "History and Faith" concerning the horizon of the second quest. However, a good question might be, what generates Torah piety?

Meyer's Reading of Apocalyptic

A similar pattern emerges in Meyer's analysis. Three points are in order. First, Meyer does not define apocalyptic. There is nothing disclosed in Jesus' teaching that has been secret. No wisdom is required to understand the time of the end. In contrast, Amos 3:7 affirms that apocalyptic reveals God's secret plans—what is happening behind the scenes. Yet for Meyer, apocalyptic in Mark 13 says nothing new. It merely refers to the concept of vindication coming out of Daniel 7:13 and affirmed in Mark 14. Second, the classic assumption that absolute eschatology "arose with the emergence of apocalyptic in the intertestamental period" is merely repeated by Meyer.[149] Meyer does not state what he means by Jewish apocalyptic tradition. Which one? Also, he does not clarify what *Sitz im Leben* in particular. Yet as C. Rowland has noted, later Jewish apocalypses not closely linked to the historical events of AD 70 tend to be "more encyclopaedic."[150] In other words, apocalyptic can be more or less specific depending on the historical situation. Apocalyptic can reveal new things. Without any account for progressive revelation there is no progression in the promise. There is evidence, however, that Jesus' use of apocalyptic is focused on the temple and future suffering (themes from Daniel) and is not "encyclopedic" or idealistic as Meyer's treatment would suggest.

Second, there is evidence that the theological concept of "determinism," which is a feature of Jewish apocalyptic, is far from absolute. Charles argues that "determinism becomes a characteristic of the Jewish apocalyptic" and so as a result, "its concept of history, as opposed to the understanding typical of prophecy, was often more mechanistic than organic."[151] While some themes like judgment are predetermined others like suffering and

---

149. Meyer, *Aims*, 183, 236. See his conclusion: "the cosmic rock .. was Zion." *Aims*, 186.

150. Rowland, *Open Heaven*, 28.

151. Charles, *Critical History*, 206.

defilement associated with the temple are undecided but clearly historical. Charles notes this when he says the common Jewish idea of determinism found in 1 *En.* 47:3; 81:1, *T. Levi* 5:5, and *T. Ash.* 2:10; 7:2 is an idea that wavers between "absolute determinism and prediction pure and simple."[152] In other words, because of the pattern in apocalyptic in Daniel, Jewish readers would not be clear if the temple would be defiled on one or many occasions. The Enoch texts refer to the books of the living which are written on "heavenly tablets" and have a sense of absolute determinism. Later on, 1 Enoch 53:2 says, "And their hands commit lawless deeds, and the sinners devour all whom they lawlessly oppress: Yet the sinners shall be destroyed before the face of the Lord of Spirits, and they shall be banished from off the face of His earth, and they shall perish for ever and ever." The text from the *Testament of Asher*, in contrast, discusses wickedness in the context of three themes (the land being desolate, deliverance into the hands of the enemies, and destruction of the holy place) seems determinative (understood as God's plan) but not absolute in the sense of permanent end versus a major disruption.

Third, Meyer introduces the relevance of horizon as a hermeneutical tool for understanding the Gospels. This horizon is to be understood in a wide sense as an "eschatological horizons." It is seen in texts like Mal 3:24 (LXX) and Sir 48:10 and includes the idea that Jesus' work should be interpreted in accordance with the task of Elijah and the fulfillment of God's will in the proclamation to outsiders such as the ignorant, the sinners, the sick and all other groups represented in the "depressed elements in Israel." They were types of Israel to be saved who would experience the καταστῆσαι φυλὰς Ιακωβ ("the restoring of Jacob").[153] Yet Meyer's construct does not recognize the diversity in the Gospels. His thesis over-extenuates a realized eschatology. He lacks close exegesis of Mark's Olivet Discourse and fails to compare and contrast the Synoptic parallels. For Meyer, the coming "crisis" has its roots in Jewish apocalyptic and is reapplied to Jesus and the community of disciples. Gone are the temporal distinctions which Dodd identified in texts like Mark 13:14–25. Furthermore, while apocalyptic is historically grounded (consistent with PE) in its referents, as indicated above, there is little content to Jesus' apocalyptic in Meyer's construct.

---

152. Charles, "Book of Jubilees," 8, 16 for note on 3:10 heavenly tablets.

153. Meyer, *Aims*, 171–73. Cf. BDAG, καθίστημι; the word means "to assign someone a position of authority, *appoint, put in charge*" (cf. Dan 2:48; 3:12; Matt 24:45; 25:21; Heb 2:7).

Meyer's comments about the predictions of Jesus therefore require comparison with wider evidence from Second Temple Judaism and the Synoptic Gospels. Meyer's argument for an absolute eschatology in the whole scheme of things is severely weakened by his discussion being limited to Mark 13:2. An appropriate historical question regarding determinism in apocalyptic is, therefore, did Jewish apocalyptic make a distinction between relative and absolute events? A second is, what scope did Judaism attribute to texts about temple desecration in terms of its likely fulfillment, and why were they impacted by these texts? There is evidence that Judaism interpreted Daniel's prophecy in Daniel 9:2 as fulfilled in the events of 156 BC by Antiochus Epiphanies.

Conclusion

Meyer's view of the messianic builder is influenced by the insights of Lonergan, Weiiternbrog, Dodd, and Jeremias. For Meyer the eschatological aim of Jesus is unlike apocalyptic Judaism because it is realized in the context of the formation of a new community. His passive view of the Olivet Discourse in general treats the word ἐρχόμενον (Mark 3:26) and associated themes as a reference to the content of Jesus' public ministry. Meyer's construct does not help to address the historical question of whether Jesus thought of apocalyptic in historical terms. Several problem issues present themselves from Meyer's construct. These observations relate to hermeneutical assumptions, Christology and method and affect his reading of the historical Jesus:

1. His use of *Sensus Plenior* interpretation and the use of the OT. Jesus' prophecy is characterized by a lack of knowledge—Jesus lacks significant knowledge about concrete events in the scenario.

2. A lack of attention to Christology and specifically the role of the Son of Man in Mark 13. This requires renewed focus because the roles of the Son of Man described in Mark 13 and 14 are similar but distinct. Similarly, Meyer's observations and critique of Schweitzer failure to grasp Matthean placement are appropriate but overlooks the problem of attempting to ask historical questions and exegete texts *without* theology. Furthermore, Meyer attempts to fit his themes within a short-term timeframe (theory of imminence, as Weiss, Dodd and Jeremias)

while dismissing a crucial "delay" text. In short, Jesus' future lacks a long-term horizon.

3. His heavy reliance on personal faith categories, avoidance of progressive revelation (or even relating to others/events or later texts) and no reflection on a text (Gadamer) in other historical contexts for the sake of clarity of meaning. At every stage of the construct, Meyer consistently explores a religious or faith "horizon" without a historical-political dimension. But the two are not necessarily mutually exclusive.

4. Meyer's approach to the historical Jesus affirms historical knowledge and that a Bultmannian approach to the tradition is simplistic. Biblical scholars have access to the tradition of Jesus. For Meyer, Jesus' horizon is AD 70. Here he is Bultmannian over the delay passages such as our Mark 13:23–27 which is classified secondary. His own critique applies. This is a complex issue. It is better to explore the data in light of the presence of imminence and delay and to highlight the pattern Jesus held to.

Themes to Pursue: A Future for Israel

The study will continue to examine the future restoration of righteous Israel. Jesus' knowledge of the future is not indeterminate, neither is it exhaustive and it is not based on an adoption of symbolic prophecy as Meyer holds. Jesus' teaching affects how one views the future restoration of the righteous. but neither is it exhaustive. The view that Jesus differentiated between two periods of time can be defended exegetically. Future attention will focus on "salvation of the remnant" and a future for righteous Israel which is true of God's plan in the future, too.

An Alternative Scenario

Meyer's view of Jesus' vision for the future is deficient for three reasons. First, arguing from a *Sensus Plenior* model only Jesus' vision of the future lacked determinative knowledge and so Jesus could not differentiate between future events. PD agrees that Jesus was not mistaken about the future. Others may well ask, if what God intends did not in fact enter the horizon and perspective of Jesus? The question is stated this way with this caveat: that Jesus as the

Son of God did not know the time when the end would start. No one knows "except the Father alone" (Mark 13:32 / Matt 24:36).

An alternative scenario of the future contains the following categories that will be pursued in the remainder of the study:

1. Present in Jesus' Mind

First, there is additional teaching about end-time events that has continuity with Daniel's prophecy (e.g., Matt 10:23). Second, the differentiation of events in Jesus' own earthly career and ministry. Third, the differentiation of his career from the events foretold about AD 70. Fourth, these events are distinct from specific events in the tribulation-end and distinct from the resolution for the righteous elect. In addition to this, Jesus expected a pattern typological scenario which he revealed to explain how the short-term crisis is *like* the end.

2. Absent in Jesus' Knowledge

There were two concepts that were absent from Jesus' knowledge. The first relates to any determinate knowledge of the hour of the final end-time crisis (Mark 13:32). The second relates to a fixed way of presenting his teaching and its pattern in writing.

4

Antecedents and Apocalyptic Literature in N. T. Wright's Theological Construct

Introduction

THE QUESTION THIS STUDY began by asking is, what is the relation between the historical crisis and eschatological day? This chapter explores in greater detail this connection between Mark 13:2 and Mark 13:24–27 and the nature of AE. Chapter 2 presented Caird's hypothesis that myth and eschatology are used in the OT and NT as "metaphor systems for the theological interpretation of historical events."[1] This chapter will evaluate the implication of this thesis first by exploring Caird's discussion of language. The goal of this section is to show that how knowledge of language functions is essential to read the conceptual thought of NT apocalyptic. Furthermore, eschatology defines understanding of figurative language and its function in an apocalyptic context. The figurative language of Mark 13 is complex and worthy of careful consideration. The goal of this section is to identify the problems in clarifying the Gospel's approach to history and apocalyptic. The next section discusses Wright's construct. A similar approach to that of chapter 3 is taken. The goal of this section is to clarify Wright's understanding of the eschatological relationship in Jesus'

---

1. Caird, *Language and Imagery of the Bible*, 219. What "historical event" can mean in Second Temple Judaism writings and what Caird means by it will be discussed.

teaching. A comparison is made between Wright and his antecedents in order to show that Wright borrows from Caird in his understanding and theological interpretation of the events of AD 70. The chapter concludes with an evaluation and discussion placing Wright in the context of the third quest. Similarities and differences between Meyer and Wright are noted.

Antecedents of Wright

G. B. Caird

George B. Caird (d. 1984) was professor of biblical exegesis at the University of Oxford. Caird studied theology at Mansfield College, Oxford, and graduated from Oxford with a dissertation entitled "The New Testament Conception of Doxa." Caird is considered a premier British scholar of the Bible who has influenced many interpreters, including N. T. Wright, who studied under Caird for a DPhil.

Contribution of Language and Method

Caird was known for his straightforward approach to exegesis. He believed that the interpreter's goal is to find the author's intended meaning. He also believed that twentieth-century philosophical hermeneutics were too abstract and discussion of methodology could hinder the task of doing pure exegesis. Caird also opposed the German historical skepticism at a time when Bultmannian form criticism was becoming popular in Great Britain. In *Language and Imagery of the Bible* Caird devoted some attention to the function and the limitations of language. Caird's concern was to explore how biblical writers use a variety of imagery, idiom, metaphor, and myth in their historical context. In particular he sought to challenge the notion of literal interpretation and denounced a tendency to "flat-footed literalness" especially as it related to NT eschatology.[2]

On the one hand, Caird made an important contribution to biblical studies by highlighting the various kinds of language functions.[3] On the other hand, one of the major objections to Caird's work concerns his interpretive method. Critics have labeled it a common sense descriptive approach, and have noted that it offers little "methodological, theoreti-

---

2. Ibid., 248. See also p. 56 for a tight summary of his thesis.
3. Collins, review of *Language and Imagery of the Bible*, 183.

cal or philosophical sophistication."[4] Concerning the meaning of "literal" interpretation, John Collins noted that Caird does better at illustrating a variety of nonliteral uses, than in giving "precision to the commonsense notion of 'literal' which he uses as a foil."[5] Another criticism by Collins is that Caird dogmatically insists on authorial intention without discussion of methodology.[6]

Of particular interest, however, is Caird's discussion on "Opacity, Vagueness and Ambiguity" (chap. 4), "Hebrew Idiom and Hebrew Thought" (chap. 5), "Literal and Non-Literal" (chap. 7), and "Linguistic Awareness" (chap. 11). The application of these language categories is particularly contentious for the theme of this subject of this study. Several issues arise in the study of Mark 13. These include the signs, functions of language, and the relationship between signs. Other issues include the identity of the referents, and the question of how directly the biblical author describes the referent given in the figurative language.

Functions and Limitations of Language

Caird holds that language is transparent "insofar as its meaning is open to investigation" and opaque "insofar as it has to be learned."[7] This suggestion can be seen to include two key points here: first, language has content to be explored by reading, and second, the various elements of meaning have to be learned if someone is to become an instructed observer.

The language of metaphor is complex but it is capable of describing reality. In discussing metaphorical transparency, Caird analyses the metaphorical meaning of words and how metaphorical language is misunderstood. Metaphorical meaning is intelligible when the reader recognizes the parallel between the literal and metaphorical referents.[8] Caird makes three important points. First, the terms literal and figurative describe types of

---

4. See Pearson, review of *Language and Imagery of the Bible*, 116. Cf. Rhodes, review of *Language and Imagery of the Bible*, 136.

5. Collins, review of *Language*, 183. Collin's comments refer to part 2 which is devoted to metaphor. He says Caird's concern is to show the "nonliteral character of much biblical language."

6. Ibid., 184. Here he calls it a "flawed book."

7. Caird, *Language*, 85.

8. Ibid., 85, 90.

language that can be used in sayings to refer to reality.[9] In other words, figurative language is no less true or false because it is figurative. The way in which figurative language describes content and reality may be important.[10] Second, while figurative language can have referents, it also adds value because it conveys emotive and evocative ideas beyond statements of information or performance. In Matthew 7:5, the phrase "take the plank out of your own eye" is a typical overstatement which is characteristic of Hebrew style which is "nonliteral" but nevertheless corresponds to reality.[11] Jesus' denunciation of the Scribes and Pharisees as "blind guides" (Matt 23:24; cf. the "rich," Mark 10:25) is an example of the use of figurative language which covers these operations.

Finally, Caird understands these examples to reflect the "absolutist" cast of mind of Semitic people which has the tendency to think in extremes without qualification.[12] In Matthew 10:37 / Luke 14:26, the emphasis is on expressing a preference by the use of words "love" and "hate," as a Hebrew idiom (cf. 1 John 1:15). It is this Hebrew perspective that tends to view life in extremes of black and white both in clarity and apposition (see also Gen 29:30–31).

Several of these and other categories that Caird discusses are pertinent for this study. These are now examined, beginning with discussion of the different kinds of ambiguity.

Lexical Ambiguity. In discussing Mark 8:34–37, where Mark uses the Greek word ψυχή four times in quick succession, Caird notes the presence of a lexical problem. He adduces that Jesus' teaching in the Gospels "strongly suggests that he used this device of deliberate ambiguity to provoke hearers into thought about ultimate questions."[13] Admittedly, Caird gives good examples in his discussion of this point and he cannot cover every piece of detail from the Gospels with respect to this category. But there is a level of ambiguity in Mark's Olivet Discourse which Caird does not explore. Depending on what the phrases of figurative language in Mark 13

---

9. Ibid., 131.

10. Caird shows that J. A. T. Robinson's view that the "body of Christ" cannot be a metaphor because language must correspond literally with the organized entity of Christ's presence in the world is unnecessary. The error of such a view is it treats metaphorical language simply as "optional embroidery" which adds nothing substantial to the meaning of a sentence. Caird, *Language*, 131, 191.

11. Caird, *Language*, 133.

12. Ibid., 110.

13. Ibid., 106.

mean, Caird's judgment here may or may not reflect the use of ambiguous language in the biblical text. A contender for this category of lexical ambiguity is Mark's use of the terms τέλος (Mark 13:7 / Matt 24:6 / Luke 21:9) and ἀρχή (Mark 13:8 / Matt 24:8) in adjacent verses. Both terms have the same semantic domain indicating a point in time and here indicate either an end or a beginning of duration of time. This is their sense, but what did Jesus mean to refer to by "end": (a) the temple, (b) the world, or (c) a metaphor for crisis referring to the time of the end period of suffering? Furthermore, when specific synoptic relationships are examined, it is clear that some ambiguity is addressed. This raises the question of the cause of Mark's ambiguity. An example is Mark 13:14. Here Mark has the phrase τὸ βδέλυγμα τῆς ἐρημώσεως, "desolating sacrilege." This is considered an allusion to the Greek Jewish Scriptures (OG) of Daniel 9:27 as the text of Mark does not preserve generally the categories defined by Daniel 9:27.[14] Matthew 25:15 identifies the prophet Daniel as the original speaker (τὸ ῥηθὲν διὰ Δανιὴλ τοῦ προφήτου). Matthew seems to clarify Mark here. But why does Mark not associate these matters with the OT prophecy as Matthew does? Is this a generalization by Mark, is it indeterminacy, or economy of style? In other words, is it deliberate and historical, or accidental and historical?[15] Did Jesus intend to be ambiguous to his disciples or does Mark economize, or does it become ambiguous through the passage of time? Chapter 5 will examine this further as a feature of the PD approach.

Deliberate Ambiguity. Caird makes an interesting comment about the cause of deliberate ambiguity: "Some deliberate uses of ambiguity must be called exploratory, because the speaker has not made up his mind between the two senses, but is discovering a new truth by investigating the

---

14. The category of giving the decreed end upon the desolations is not mentioned nor is "the one who destroys" or mention of wars being decreed and destruction (Dan 9:26). In the Septuagint, the object of the preposition ἐπί ("on," "against") is τὴν ἐρήμωσιν ("the desolations") which the end decree finally addresses.

15. The language of Daniel is flexible allowing multiple referents as the language is general. The NEB has the sense of the MT as "those abominations." In other translations the multiple referents and elasticity of the text in 27c is left unclear. The NIRV has the sense of "hated thing" *being set up*. The NIV has "an abomination." This is the referent (singular) that remains until the Lord brings the end he has ordered but the translation gives no sense of occurring desolations. The NET translates this as "abominations." Mark's allusion does not mention the temple directly whereas the translator of the Septuagint has made referential transfer to the temple (τὸ ἱερόν). Thus, it is unclear whether the predicted event in Mark Ὅταν δὲ ἴδητε ("but whenever you see") is related to an immediate event or if it is intended for some distant time.

interconnection between them."[16] If Mark writes first and is grappling with how the eschaton plays out, then this could account for why Matthew 24:3 uses the term and personal referent (σῆς παρουσίας καὶ συντελείας τοῦ αἰῶνος) and instead Mark refers to μέλλῃ ταῦτα συντελεῖσθαι πάντα (13:4). It is suggested that Mark may in some sense be doing "exploratory" thinking about the historical crisis and eschatological day. Or does Matthew draw out for his readers all implications in Mark's more ambiguous question in light of the passing of time since the writing of Mark's gospel.[17]

Grammatical Ambiguity. Caird has a detailed section on grammatical ambiguity especially involving genitive constructions, yet separates discussion about genitive constructions that have an important connection to eschatology from Hebrew idiom.[18] The fact that approximately 39 percent (12/31) of all genitive nouns and adjectives in Mark 13 are found in vv. 24 to 27 certainly adds to the level of ambiguity of the passage. Interpretation in this area requires a nuanced approach and examination of context. A few examples deserve mention here. In Mark 13:27, the preposition ἕως has as its object "extreme heaven" ἄκρου οὐρανοῦ. Is this to be read as the temporal conjunction "until" denoting the duration of time (contingency) with reference to the future gathering or as a spatial boundary "as far as" indicating the extent to which the future gathering will reach?[19] A spatial boundary (i.e., "from") is intended with the prior use of ἐκ and ἀπο.[20]

Mark 13:26 is another ambiguous passage where it is crucial to recognize its contribution to the conceptual thought of apocalyptic. The clause beginning with καὶ τότε ὄψονται, which has no additional subject noun is

16. Ibid., 105. See Wallace's discussion of the significance of genitives due to the wide variety of interpretations. See Wallace, *Greek Grammar*, 74–75.

17. Cf. Orchard and Riley, *Order of the Synoptics*, 82.

18. Caird, *Language*, 97–102.

19. BDAG, "ἕως," 423, lists five categories of usage for this preposition. §3a suggests ἕως denotes a limit reached *as far as* so a genitive of boundary in Mark 13:27. The first category which denotes "the end of a period of time" (§1bα.) lists where ἕως is used as a preposition with a genitive of time such as the kind of time envisaged in Matt 11:13; Mark 14:25 / Matt 26:29; Matt 1:17; Acts 1:22; Mark 13:19 / Matt 24:21 (ἀπ' ἀρχῆς κτίσεως ἣν ἔκτισεν ὁ θεὸς ἕως τοῦ νῦν καὶ οὐ μὴ γένηται). Under category §1aβ with the aorist subjunctive which indicates potential future action ἕως is used as a conjunction with a temporal nuance "until." Mark 12:36 / Matt 22:44 / Luke 20:43, LXX Ps 109:1; Mark 9:1; Mark 6:10 / Matt 10:23. Matt 2:13, 10:23, 22:44 are examples where the "commencement of an event is dependent on circumstances." Mark 13:27 does not involve a subjunctive aorist.

20. Wallace, *Exegetical Syntax*, 369, 371.

variously translated "men will see" (NIV), "they will see" (NJB) or "everyone will see" (NET). The subject is a clear contrast to the plural referent ὑμεῖς in v. 23 along with the second person plural imperative βλέπετε, and the pronoun ὑμῖν, modifying προείρηκα. In the original context, disciples of Jesus are the subject in both cases. The same group of "insiders" is in mind ἴδητε ("you see") in the opening section of v. 14 where a separate potential action is discussed and the section opens with a strong contrast δὲ ("but"). So it seems fair to translate ὄψονται generically as "people" or "everyone." Later it will be seen how second and third person plurals transfer well in translations and parallel passages when the future period in view is not limiting or bounded.

Finally, it is important to recognize that there is ambiguity in Mark 13:26 regarding the role of the Son of Man which suggests that there is more than one specific meaning in the text. Mark describes the commissioning of the angels with emphasis on the Son of Man's actions: καὶ τότε ἀποστελεῖ τοὺς ἀγγέλους καὶ ἐπισυνάξει τοὺς ἐκλεκτοὺς αὐτοῦ. Mark describes the action as ἐπισυνάξει. Matthew 24:31 changes the Greek text to ἐπισυνάξουσιν "they will gather" in order to clarify the sense (cf. "angels to gather" NJB). The question is, what associations are intended here by Mark? Does the Son of Man gather the elect through the agency of God's angels? This is significant because while Collins may be correct to say that the Son of Man was understood as an angel,[21] in the Christian Gospels the Son of Man is distinct. This clarifies its meaning vis-à-vis Judaism. The Son of Man sends God's angels. These are identified in some early MSS as "his" but confusion is seen when the task is to gather "his elect" τοὺς ἐκλεκτοὺς αὐτοῦ.

Vagueness. In order to understand the conceptual world of Mark 13 further, it is important to examine Caird's discussion on *vagueness* and *connotative* meaning as it relates to the Son of Man. Caird wishes to show the complexity of the various figures of speech and imagery that the biblical writers used. G. Vermes in his *Jesus the Jew* denies that the phrase *bar nasha* was in titular use in Jesus' day for Messiah and argues instead that

---

21. Also none of the Intertestamental texts give a complete picture of all Judaism's views about ὁ ἄγγελος; instead various associations and contextual meanings surface. For example, Tob 12:22 simply designates the reference as ἄγγελος θεοῦ. In Tob 5:4 the reader is told the angel is not immediately perceived as an "angel of God." In Sir 43:26 ὁ ἄγγελος carries the notion of the "messenger" and as a "guardian" in the Epistle of Jeremiah 1:6. Thus "angel" singularly does not equal "a heavenly being." These particular texts, however, illustrate that Israel's teaching accommodated a degree of ambiguity.

it was either a generic term for man or a circumlocutional self-reference.[22] Caird counters Vermes's understanding of Jesus' use of the Son of Man by two points. First, Vermes's argument does not consider why Jesus adopts this circumlocution or why Son of Man is Jesus' favorite self-designation.[23] Second, it is possible to convey a concept without its lexical term and that the phrase "Son of Man" can have "added connotative value."[24]

Periphrasis. Caird's discussion of periphrasis is helpful for part of Mark 13. Part 2 of *Language and Imagery* is devoted to Metaphor and Caird's concern is to show how direct or indirect the description of a particular referent can be by an author. The description of "the scepter" in Genesis 49:10 and the "key" in Isaiah 22:22 (cf. Rev 3:7) stand as a metonymy for authority calling a concept by the name of something familiar. Similarly in Colossians 1:16, θρόνοι ("thrones") which have their origin in the work of Christ, represent cosmic superpowers.[25] There are several important features of *periphrasis*, or circumlocution, as a figure of speech. Periphrasis can express more forcefully the persistence of a new state of things. It provides a means to express linear action in the future tense. Periphrasis also places emphasis on the duration of an action when used with the future tense.[26] In the case of first-century culture, Semitic idioms were recognized and translated into Greek. Their presence is an indication of the Semitic influence upon the Hellenistic language and wider corpus of Greek texts available during the first century.[27] Periphrasis does not necessarily connote a nonliteral status. Caird finds legitimate uses of periphrasis in non-apocalyptic passages. First Samuel 15:29 describes "the imminence of Israel" and Hebrews 1:4 refers to God as "the Majesty on high."

---

22. Vermes, *Jesus the Jew*, 188–91. See Vermes' preference to examine later literature first, e.g., 4 Ezra before 1 Enoch, and especially so if it relates to events pre-AD 70. Ibid., 172.

23. Caird, *Language*, 139.

24. For example, the Pauline and Lucan use of the term χάρις means the unmerited acts of God to sinners through Christ (Rom 1:5; 3:24; cf. Acts 15:11, 40; 16:2, 5). Once the Pauline sense of the word is understood the reader can examine the concept within a context. When one reads the book of Acts one recognizes all the saving acts of God as acts of grace, even when the word is not used in context.

25. Caird, *Language*, 136.

26. BDF, 3–4(§4); 179–180 (§352–53). See Matt 10:22.

27. BDF, 3–4(§4). Cf. Burkitt, "Mark 8.12 and ειν in Hellenistic Greek," 274–76. Moule, *Idiom Book*.

Eschatological Relationships and Jesus

In explaining the difference between sense and referent in figurative language, Caird lays out how language employing direct referents like "I" or "me" less direct terms and phrases that are more descriptive may be substituted. Each phrase is a substitute for a direct and literal reference; but it is better than an exact equivalent, since it has "connotative value."[28] For example, one can learn from 1 Samuel 25:24 the designation "your handmaid" spoken by Abigail to David is less direct than a simpler referent "I" but no less appropriate.[29] Second, the use of a periphrastic phrase establishes a relation as in the case when Abigail describes herself to David as "your handmaid" (1 Sam 25:24).

This point is important for explaining parallel uses of periphrasis which Caird does not discuss. In Psalms 69:34; 96:11 and 146:6, the phrase "all that is within them" denotes everything in the cosmos or that which fills "heaven and earth."[30] The ancient Near East was familiar with categorizing the cosmos in a twofold division. This twofold division of "earthly phenomena" (lightning, hail, snow, mist, wind, rain, etc.) and "heavenly phenomena" (sun, moon, stars, heavenly ocean) is striking in numerous texts (Ps 148; 104; Sir 43:1–33; Sg Three 29–68).[31]

For Caird, "Son of Man" in Daniel is a substitute for a direct referent and is therefore an important metaphor. Caird argues that it is not the Palestinian Aramaic of Jesus' day that is central to the meaning of the phrase, but the image from Daniel.[32] His argument that Daniel's Son of Man may have a messianic reading and that it is not ruled out by later Aramaic, is persuasive to many.[33] It is an illustration of synecdoche (use of general

---

28. Caird, *Language*, 138.

29. Ibid.

30. See Keel, *Symbolism of the Biblical World*, 56. See also Wright, *Early History of Heaven*, 118.

31. Keel, *Symbolism of the Biblical World*, 58. Cf. the concept of authority surrounding the "throne" which is associated with clouds in Sir 24:3-4. Wisdom says, "I came forth from the mouth of the Most High, and covered the earth like a mist. I dwelt in high places [in high heaven], and my throne was a pillar of cloud." Metzger, *Oxford Annotated Apocrypha*, 159. The second reference has nothing to do with earthly phenomenon of clouds and rain. It draws on the twofold division of Ps 148 and further develops the idea of clouds in cosmic heavenly sense, associated with the presence of the Most High and Heavenly host.

32. Caird, *Language*, 139.

33 Fitzmyer, review of *Aramaic Approach*, 417-28; Marshall, "Son of Man Debate," 348-49.

term for a particular one).³⁴ The direct referent is Israel which appears in Daniel 7:25 as "the holy ones of the Most High" who will "receive the kingdom" and in Daniel 7:27 as "the people of the holy ones of the Most High."

Caird suggests that Jesus deliberately exploited the ambiguity of the phrase Son of Man found in Daniel 7 and Psalm 8. Jesus ponders the destiny of man and Israel, "inviting his hearers to consider how his ministry was related to both these themes and what implications held for themselves."³⁵ On this point, PD insists that the Son of Man texts in apocalyptic passages find a direct prophetic fulfillment in Jesus.³⁶ Even though PD interprets that the figure of the Son of Man in Daniel as the eschatological judge, Caird's fundamental point about connotative value is important.³⁷ No matter what the kind or degree of reflection on the Son of Man saying in Daniel, the idea that this One could be the Messiah is not ruled out by Aramaic or by the context of Daniel 7.

Finally, Caird shows how the ambiguous quality of language may be unintended by a writer but may also be deliberate.³⁸ The cause of vagueness can be a particular style of speech for purpose of economy, and ambiguity can be used for "deliberate exploitation of multiple meaning."³⁹ Caird's discussion of linguistic awareness in chapter 11 is interesting for several reasons. First, he highlights the need to determine authorial intent especially when metaphorical or figurative language is used. This is a problem because even if one decides that a literal referent is not intended, one must still identify the figure of speech employed. Using the illustration in 1 Corinthians 2:6-8 of τῶν ἀρχόντων τοῦ αἰῶνος τούτου ("the rulers of this age") as waning in power, Caird discusses possible meanings. These could be (1) literal, as in Caiaphas and the Sanhedrin, Herod and Pilate; (2) same persons by synecdoche as typical representatives of the old order, or (3) τῶν ἀρχόντων as a metaphor of the "angelic principalities and

---

34. Cf. Barr's discussion that root meaning of a word is not necessarily an accurate guide to the meaning of a word in later literature. See Barr, *Semantics of Biblical Language*, 109.

35. Caird, *Language*, 139.

36. Bock, "Scripture Citing Scripture," 271.

37. See discussion below. Bock, *Blasphemy and Exaltation*, 201-3; Hengel, *Studies in Early Christology*, 185-283; Bock, "Scripture Citing Scripture," 271. Hengel is not a progressive dispensationalist.

38. Caird, *Language*, 91-94.

39. Ibid., 139.

powers" which "stand invisible behind the thrones of earthly princes."[40] He notes that in this passage the referent is the same regardless of figure of speech. Second, Caird sets out a "test" of intentionality.[41] Another text not discussed by Caird but relevant here is Mark 13:25. The term "powers" is ambiguous and could have the same function as in the Colossians passage αἱ δυνάμεις "powers" could be metonymy for the evil angels in the cosmos, or as in the above example, "powers" may by synecdoche indicate evil angels as typical representatives of the old order which Jesus will finally overthrow at his return.

Caird's position concerning the language associated with the Son of Man may require correction. Chapter 6 will explore how Mark's use of the periphrastic participle in 13:25 describes from an earthly perspective the stars falling from heaven and is compatible with traditional Jewish apocalyptic. Similarly, in Mark 13:26 there is a connotation from Daniel 7:13 that the Son of Man has authority and arrives with it.

Parataxis and Hebrew Idiom. It is important to relate Caird's thesis to his discussion on parataxis and Hebrew idiom. When the problem of identifying a referent to figurative language concerns texts of a cosmic and eschatological nature, Caird's discussion becomes increasingly complex. Caird's "rules" of intentionality are contentious. He discusses parataxis and prophetic hyperbole in chapter 5, "Hebrew Idiom and Hebrew Thought." His argument on the language of apocalyptic eschatology associates two factors: parataxis and his own category of "prophetic hyperbole." For Caird, this category includes all prophetic figurative speech employing overstatement which is characteristic of Hebrew prophets.

Two texts that are important here in his discussion as a whole, though not specifically linked in his discussion are Isaiah 13:9–11 and Mark 13. First, his category of "prophetic hyperbole" (nonliteral prophetic speech) is distinct from the general kind of hyperbole discussed in chapter 7.[42] Caird's understanding of prophetic hyperbole and parataxis is shaped by a number of considerations. Both reflect the Hebrew mindset of "absolutes." He states that "prophecy deals more often than not in absolutes" and so is not precise language.[43] Caird adduces, that Jeremiah 4:23–26, Isaiah 13:9:11; 34:1–3,

---

40. Ibid., 192.
41. Ibid., 191–93.
42. Ibid., 113.
43. Ibid., 112.

and 66:22-24 are not about the end of the world.[44] Isaiah uses symbols of world judgment to discuss the end of the Babylonian empire under the invading armies of Cyrus the Mede.[45] Caird does not explain how these passages evidence such a meaning or how applicable this is to other texts. A weakness in Caird's analysis of idioms occurs because he fails to note the parallel with Mark 13:24-27 and he does not mark out the similarities and differences in Christian literature.

Second, his section on parataxis seeks to explain how this feature of language relates to prophetic hyperbole. Caird argues that parataxis and prophetic hyperbole are the keys to understanding Mark 13. There are, however, several problems with Caird's claim which revolve around his unwillingness to distinguish between Jewish and Christian apocalyptic. He begins by defining this as "the placing of propositions or clauses one after another without indicating by connecting words the relation between them."[46] Next he identifies grammatical features of parataxis as a Hebrew idiom in general: (1) Parataxis is typical of Hebrew language in comparison to classical Greek and Latin which are heavily hypotactic languages, (2) Hebrew speakers were able to express logical connections, (3) Hebrew idiom "prefers the paratactical, [running] style,"[47] and (4) though a mark of colloquial speech, parataxis is not proof of naiveté or that "sustained argument is beyond the speaker."[48]

Caird argues that hyperbole and parataxis work together and hence he puts them together in one chapter. He further argues that the related functions of hyperbole and parataxis provide a "resolution" of the "inconsistencies of eschatology" in Mark 13:24-27 and beyond.[49] His argument about contradictory ideas in close proximity is used to explain how in Mark 13:24-27 the "premonitory sign" leads up to the day of the "Son of Man" but Mark 13:33 concludes with a warning suggesting imminence.[50] Paratactical thinking enables the ancient Hebrew to "set in close proximity

---

44. Ibid., 113-17.
45. Ibid., 114.
46. Ibid., 117.
47. Ibid., 118.
48. Ibid.
49. Ibid., 121.
50. Thus, in the instance of Mark 13, the principle phenomena observed relate to the tension of delay and imminence (Mark13:24-27 and 13:33).

Eschatological Relationships and Jesus

two different, even apparently contradictory, senses of a word."[51] What some source critics call a "composite origin and clumsy editing," Caird argues is natural.[52] The same tension holds true in 1 Thessalonians 1:10. Paul's injunction ἀναμένειν ("to wait for") at any moment in time, God's Son from heaven, is set against the seemingly contradictory statement in 2 Thessalonians 2:1–3. Here Paul affirms the readers are not to get excited because the Day of the Lord cannot happen until the man of lawlessness is revealed.[53] This contradiction is why the authenticity of 2 Thessalonians is doubted by some.[54]

There are two problems with Caird's argument in Mark 13. One is his general claim that "anyone who employs parataxis in expressions will think paratactically also."[55] He examines the discourse broadly in Mark 13:24–27. Yet there are several coordinate conjunctions linking clauses that signify Mark's capacity to see things separately.[56] This style is absent in the second section (Mark 13:32–37). Second these clauses have a sequence and have connecting words.[57] Thirdly, there is another phenomenon in Mark 13:24–27 which may be significant. This is the difference in antecedent circumstances. As Caird says, Mark is "not uneasy" about juxtaposing two seemingly contradictory statements. Caird's criteria can be used to evaluate Mark 13:24–27. It seems that paratactic and hyperbolic language in Mark function differently and not in complete agreement with OT idiom.[58] On the basis of Hebrew reading style, Caird implies that Mark 13 as a whole functions like Hebrew texts. This application of parataxis and prophetic hyperbole explains the juxtaposition and temporal tension in the text between vv. 24 and 33 but nothing else.[59]

Caird identifies a number of biblical metaphors that fit the view of their function as substitution or comparison.[60] He looks at only particular

---

51. Caird, *Language*, 119.
52. Ibid., 121.
53. Ibid. See below for discussion on the Son of Man.
54. See Perrin, *New Testament*; Ehrman, *New Testament*.
55. Caird, *Language*, 118.
56. There is one use of ἀλλά and seven uses of καί.
57. The subordinating clauses are introduced by the adverb τότε (13:26–27) indicating a temporal relation between them.
58. Caird, *Language*, 118.
59. Ibid.
60. Cf. Margolis, *Philosophy Looks at the Arts*, 551.

words and verbal expressions that occur in Mark 13. He assumes that a simple metaphorical statement is intended even though he uses the plural name "premonitory signs."[61] He also adduces that Mark's overall subject is not the time of the end so it is not true eschatology. The metaphorical meaning of the premonitory signs of the Coming of the Son of Man in their context is a major catastrophe which takes place in AD 70.

In sum, the problem when reading apocalyptic is in the holding together of many details and discerning the antecedents. There is a danger of a surface reading which glosses over the details. The problem restated, then, is (1) what is the best model[62] for understanding metaphor when the verbal framework is complex due to presence of multiple metaphors, and (2) how can one distinguish the antecedent circumstances and meaning of the figurative language in complex texts.

The other problem is his treatment of the subsidiary subjects in these sections and his idea that "connections between phrases are implicit and taken for granted."[63] True, there are no subordinating conjunctions in 24–27 and only eight coordinating conjunctions. Yet parataxis could be explored *within* the passage itself because the subjects of the clauses vary between clauses (vv. 24–27). For example, in v. 24, the sun is said to be darkened in the future and the moon will not give its light. In v. 25, the stars are said to fall from heaven, and the powers in the heavens to be shaken. In v. 26, "they" ("men" RSV; "people" NET) are said to see the Son of Man arriving in the clouds with great power and glory. Then, in v. 26, "He" (the Son of Man) is said to send out angels to gather his elect. Caird attempts to show that Hebraic style of "piling up of images" or the juxtaposition of images demonstrates nonliteral intention.[64] Caird seems so certain that the "speaker" in eschatology intends some "blurring of the edges between vehicle and tenor" in his use of metaphor that this becomes his third main proposition.[65] The problem with Caird's model is that it is too simplistic; it does not allow for the complexity of metaphorical statements incorporating several subjects which Mark uses.

In conclusion, from Caird's point of view, Mark's language about Jesus' apocalyptic teaching is set in the realm of the Hebrew thought and its

---

61. See the examples of Gen 49:10 and Isa 22:22 discussed on p. 106.
62. Is it substitution, comparison or interaction? See Margolis, *Philosophy*, 552.
63. Caird, *Language*, 118.
64. Ibid., 190.
65. Ibid., 256.

characteristics of periphrasis. Caird insists that there exists a close relation between the nature of Hebrew thought and the periphrastic style. Together these signal authorial intent that figurative language related to eschatology should not be taken as "literal." Consequently, Caird does not explore fine details. The content of the AE for Caird is summarized as follows: (1) Mark 13:2 concerns the "stones" and is hyperbole for massive destruction, (2) Mark 13:25 views cosmic "powers" as a metonymy for all evil angels in the cosmos, (3) The Son of Man in Mark 13:26 is a substitute for a direct referent in Daniel 7:25 and is therefore an important metaphor for Israel as the Holy ones of the Most High.

Evaluation

There are several benefits in Caird's approach to language. First, he recognizes temporal ambiguity and notices the temporal tension of apocalyptic in Jesus, Mark, and Paul. Second, he refutes the idea that there are multiple conflicting sources in the Jesus tradition behind Mark's text. There are some problems, however. First, Caird seems unaware that his approach to "testing" the author's intentions is not neutral.[66] For example, Caird's categories of "uses of language" in his chapter 1 set up a division between assumptions about authorial intent and the sense that words can or cannot have. On the one hand words that are informative or cognitive are classified as "referential." On the other hand, words that have a performative, expressive or cohesive use are classified as "commissive" (an act of commitment in actions, attitudes, and feelings).[67] Caird does not discuss the suitability of such fixed categories. Yet later he rejects the idea that metaphor is "optional embroidery" or that it can only be used (as some insist) in "emotive and evocative utterances which have no truth value."[68] This influences his interpretation of apocalyptic language. He writes: "Ordinary words may also be used without much regard to their connotation, but simply as identifying or mnemonic symbols."[69] Thus, writing about Ezra's vision that he "beheld, and lo! this Man flew with the clouds of heaven" (*4 Ezra* 13:3) he says that

---

66. See especially his conclusion to "linguistic awareness." Caird, *Language*, 186.

67. Caird, *Language*, 8. No discussion appears validating the grounds for such opposing assumptions about authorial intent.

68. Ibid., 132. For some proponents of the emotive theory of metaphor and its variations in Davidson and Beardsley, see Soskice, *Metaphor and Religious Language*, 26–44.

69. Caird, *Language*, 9.

the clouds have "no other function except to identify this figure with the similar visionary figure of Dan 7:13."[70] This does help us to read the imagery at a certain level. Caird, however, claims it is "over interpretation if we attempt to suck any further sense out of them." It is still unclear if he makes a hard distinction between the informative use of language on the one hand and their expressive use on the other. That would be a choice between the content of the figurative language and the referent of the figurative language. The table on his page eight seems to make that choice for the reader.[71]

Third, it is important to observe the distinctiveness of Mark's eschatology and its composite parts seen in the structure of Mark 13:24–27. When one considers Isaiah 13:10, for example, and the development of its themes in Mark's discussion, it is evident that Jesus is unique in his treatment of AE although from a traditional Jewish base. Moreover, it is hard to see how two figures of speech are so important that they control all the language of AE by stabilizing its meaning.[72]

Fourth, Caird seems overly selective in his examples; if they were broadened there might be an alternative conclusion that many categories of language apply to the eschatology of AE thus enriching the conceptual thought of the NT. Caird is surely wrong to argue that all apocalyptic imagery cannot affirm a variety of senses of meaning both informative and expressive. Caird commits the logical fallacy of the excluded middle. For example, the meaning of the clouds in Mark 13:26 is not necessarily exhausted by observing that it alludes to Daniel 7:13. Mark's perspective could be different from Daniel 7 while at the same time retaining the same connotations of authority and power in the Son of Man who is the eschatological judge.

However, Caird argues convincingly that the biblical writers were aware of the symbolic nature of the language they used. By highlighting questions on the function of language, Caird provides a valuable perspective on biblical criticism—but not in the area of AE. His insistence on the application of his categories suggests many ways to read the figurative language of the Gospels. The primary reasons for this outlook can be traced back to Caird's reaction to German scholarship. Schweitzer's theology of the end of the "literal" world is derived from a poor reading of the NT and an abuse of language. Collins correctly observes that as a

70. Ibid., 8.
71. Ibid.
72. See the discussion on p. 111.

result of his insistence on the symbolic character of the language (metaphor system), Caird is obliged to argue that it was not intended literally.[73] It is wrong to dismiss Caird's insights however. His discussion of language is helpful for Mark 13:24–27 and more generally the relationships of the parts of Mark's discourse.

Caird's Construct: The Framework and Handling of the Data

Mark 13:24–27 is clearly a problem passage for students of eschatological relationships. The goal of this section is to place the discussion of the previous section in the wider framework of Caird's construct. In part 3 of *Language and Imagery*, Caird correctly emphasizes the need to identify the referent where the language used is cosmic language associated with eschatology.[74] The discussion here focuses on three areas. First, it will be suggested that summaries of the main areas of Jesus' teaching are helpful. Caird draws on definitions and asks important questions about eschatological relationships in discussion of Judaism and Christianity and thus is a clear improvement on Meyer. The second goal is to examine the character of the "crisis" in Caird's construct and in particular his analysis of the relationship of Mark 13:2 to Mark 13:24–27. Here it will be suggested that the hermeneutical difficulty of understanding the relationship between Jesus' prediction of the historical crisis and that of the eschatological day in the Gospels is clearly demonstrated in certain Gospel passages. Caird, like Meyer, understands Jesus to be Israel's Messiah, yet as previously seen his hypotheses around language and eschatology are different from Meyer. Caird and Wright use Meyer's analysis of the historical crisis to make sense of John the Baptist and Jesus in the light of the restoration of Israel. In this, delay has a greater role, but the redemption of Israel's elect from suffering is not the basis of Jesus' teaching.

Caird's 1965 lecture reproduced in *Jesus and the Jewish Nation* outlines his theological construct from the Gospels.[75] His main hypothesis about eschatology and its key themes form the framework for his lectures. He argues first that Jesus presented his mission to Israel as a matter of urgency in light of a national crisis. His second is that Jesus' attitude and message

---

73. Collins, review of *Language*, 184.

74. Caird, *Language*, 56.

75. Caird, *Jesus and the Jewish Nation*, 3–22. A reprint of this section appears in Dunn and McKnight, *Historical Jesus in Recent Research*, 275–87.

does not exclude the Gentiles. His third theme is NT eschatology about the Day of the Son of Man. This latter theme is the primary focus of this study. Caird can be faulted on three grounds. One, the issue is that he is too dismissive of the judgment aspect of apocalyptic (e.g., Matt 3:7-10 / Luke 3:7-9). A second is his avoidance of transcendence and interpretation of symbolism as nonliteral, and the third, his lack of analysis of the synoptic parallels in the Olivet Discourse.

First, then, the framework Caird provides sets out his consideration of the data. One can take a thematic approach to Jesus' teaching, and link isolated texts in the Gospels. The variation of constructs shows that there is more than one way of doing this. The hermeneutical problem for each motif is that they select isolated texts, but they must interpret those texts within a coherent horizon. The main sets of texts that Caird lines up under each are listed below.

- Set 1: Jesus' ministry and urgent mission to the nation of Israel (Mark 1:2-11 and par.; Matt 10:5-6; Matt 10:23; Mark 11:15-19; 13:1-2; Luke 21:20-24)
- Set 2: Jesus' attitude and message involving Gentiles (Isa 2:2-3; 56:7; Mic 5:4; Dan 7:14; Zech 8:23; 9:9-10; Mark 9:1; 11:17; John 4:21-22; Acts 11:18; 3:19-21)
- Set 3: NT Eschatology about the Day of the Son of Man in Mark (Isa 11:1-9; Jer 4:23-25; Dan 4:17, 25, 32; 7:9-27; 12:7; Mark 13:24-27; Luke 17:31; 18:7-8)

The themes are fairly well documented with OT and NT texts. Set 1 focuses on the historical crisis going back to John the Baptist. The nation faces a "crisis." Set 2 texts focus on the acceptance of Gentiles to share in the gospel despite the reticence shown in the early church. Caird asks questions about the linkages between these sets. Linking set 2 with 1, he asks: "How does this comparatively optimistic picture of the bringing in of the Gentile nations fit with our earlier and more gloomy picture of the Jewish nation facing its last grim crisis?"[76] He also correlates passages in sets 2 and 3. It involves the correlation of a historical crisis and the eschatological day of the arrival of the Son of Man. The question asked is, "Was there a connexion between this eschatological crisis and the other national crisis

---

76. Caird, *Jesus and the Jewish Nation*, 13.

which . . . bulked so large in the teaching of Jesus?"[77] In his analysis of sets 1 and 3, Caird examines synoptic parallels (e.g., Mark 13:24–27 and Luke 17:31) but it is not his intention to consider the synoptic problem or relationships between these verses.[78]

Caird's framework and questions are important and not to be overlooked, but certain concerns remain. First, while asking helpful questions, Caird does not acknowledge the complexity of what he is attempting. Overall, the question is the need to explain how passages in set 1 as a whole link the historical crisis and the eschatological day mentioned in Mark 13:24–27. Yet it is necessary to explain why these passages discuss a historical event yet other passages go in a different direction? How does one explain that set 1 seems to exhibit a close relationship and what is exegetically defendable in Matthew and Paul (Mark 13:19 / Matt 24:21; 2 Thess 2:1–3) as explanations of delay. Such a task requires reflection as the reader can go one of two ways or take a "both and" approach. Is it accurate to say that the Gospels take one angle on historical events they portray? There is a fourth set of texts which Caird only alludes to in passing. In his *Victory of God*, Wright highlights this point and refers in a footnote to Caird's 1982 article. Wright argues that Caird makes "some analogies" toward Christology but in the end "lacks a full proposal."[79] In other words, if Caird had developed his proposal further this would represent a move from one of "representing Israel" to a "full blown Christology."[80] What he should have done is examine these set 4 texts and seek to correlate them into his construct. In contrast Wright, R. T. France, and PD do such an exercise. The second concern about Caird regards fulfillment. Caird's argument based on Luke 18:7–8 that rejection by national Israel means God will vindicate his elect "speedily" is questionable.[81] This does not mean that there is no divine judgment on Israel for its rejection of her Messiah. Caird's framework does

---

77. Ibid., 21.

78. Others take a different approach. Chapter 6 will examine David Wenham's thesis and argument of synoptic relationships particularly as it involves Mark 13:24–27. Wenham argues that finding the Markan priority hypothesis generally satisfactory, the synoptic relationships in key passages in the Olivet Discourse are not explained by borrowing, but to the fact that "Matthew and Luke have primitive non-Markan traditions in Markan sections." Wenham, *Rediscovery of Jesus' Eschatological Discourse*, 1, 6.

79. Wright, *Jesus and the Victory of God*, 615.

80. Ibid.

81. Caird, *Jesus and the Jewish Nation*, 21.

not allow for a final restoration of Israel. Some pertinent comments about the handling of the data in each theme are in order.

Jesus' Ministry and Urgent Mission to the Nation of Israel

The data on this first theme of Caird's include the above mentioned texts. Having identified the Gospel texts, Caird then correlates these passages together under the theme of an urgent national warning. In set 1 he recognizes "the consensus of all four Gospels" is that Jesus went to John to be baptized.[82] His argument that John's preaching about the object of "winnowing" not being about judgment but to "gather the wheat into the granary" (Matt 3:7–19 / Luke 3:7–9) is supported by Meyer. The bonfire is "purely incidental."[83] This is a call to identify true Israel. Yet to this arrival of the "the wrath to come" can hardly be viewed as a mere historical crisis as Caird suggests. Read this way, the crisis is historical, has its beginning with the message of John, and includes Jesus' temple denouncement (Mark 11:15–19). Matthew 10:23 is connected with the many sayings which predicted the fall of Jerusalem and the destruction of the temple.[84] Caird notes a common theme of urgency and asks why the haste? The reason for the assumed hurry is that the nation is at a "cross-roads."[85] Within this same set of texts lie the cleansing of the temple (Mark 11:15–19), the prediction about the temple stones (Mark 13:1–2), the picture of Jerusalem surrounded by armies (Luke 21:20–24), Jesus' lament over the city (Luke 13:34 / Matt 23:37), and the weeping women (Luke 23:27–31). He then makes this strong conclusion: "the haste of the mission" was directly connected with Jesus' many sayings in which he predicted the fall of Jerusalem by a foreign army and the destruction of the temple. "There can be no doubt that Jesus predicted the destruction of Jerusalem, and predicted it as the direct consequence of the rejection of his own preaching."[86]

---

82. Ibid., 6. See Matt 3:13–17 / Mark 1:9–11 / Luke 3:21–22 / John 1:29–34.
83. Ibid., 7.
84. Ibid., 8.
85. Ibid.
86. Ibid., 11.

Eschatological Relationships and Jesus

Jesus' Attitude and Message Involving the Gentiles

The second motif related to this construct is the message involving Gentiles. Meyer understood the "gathering" of the elect (Matt 13:24–30 and Mark 13:27) as a work in progress with its full accomplishment reserved until the completed reign of God.[87] Similarly, Caird argues that there is a disconnect between early church practice which was "devoid of all concern for the preaching of the gospel to the Gentiles" and Jesus' favorable teaching about Gentiles (Mark 11:17, cf. Isa 56:7; Zech 9:9–10). One cannot argue that it was a "universalism" which the church was slow to understand. Instead, it is found in eschatology where the Day of the Lord envisages the restoration of Israel and the inclusion of the nations in what signals "universal restoration" (Isa 2:2–3; Zech 8:23; Acts 3:19–21).[88] On the one hand, Caird understands that Jesus' mission was not a time "ripe for fulfillment" when God would "summon the nations from east and west" (Zech 8:21–23) because the immediate mission was to the "house of Israel" (Matt 10:5–6).[89] On the other hand, however, he sees the fulfillment of this promise in the *ecclesia*. PD differs from Caird here in seeing Acts 3:19–21's reference to the "restoration of all things" as meaning the future kingdom and restoration of Israel. Thus salvation history proceeds in two stages. His question above and observation of a delay in fulfillment in Jesus' teaching is well founded (Matt 10:5–6). His solution, however, to connect the Gentile blessing with the immediate crisis facing the nation of Israel seems to overlook a final restoration of all things which includes Israel in the future.

NT Eschatology and the Day of the Son of Man

The final motif analyzed is the eschatological Day described in Mark 13:24–27 or the coming of the Son of Man. Caird inquires about the relationship between Mark 13:1–2 in set 1 with Mark 13:24–26. He notes that it would greatly simplify the problem "if we could say that they were one and the same."[90]

There are two dimensions to Caird's view of this eschatological relationship. Both approaches involve his view of the function of language and

---

87. Meyer, *Aims of Jesus*, 214.
88. Caird, *Jesus and the Jewish Nation*, 15.
89. Ibid.
90. Ibid., 20.

his layered discussion of how it applies to this passage. One is a temporal question and raises the issue of what is valid: is a temporal tension intended in Mark 13:24–27? The other is historically and referentially related: Was the Day of the Son of Man to be an event in Israel's national history which fulfills prophecy? Caird asks and answers both questions in the affirmative because both are intrinsically related to the restoration of Israel.

First, when one reads Mark 13:24–25 and the subsequent passage of Mark 13:33 (Βλέπετε, ἀγρυπνεῖτε· οὐκ οἴδατε γὰρ πότε ὁ καιρός ἐστιν), one realizes that what is being highlighted is a temporal tension of the unknown time over the premonitory signs (vv. 24–25). Caird therefore rejects Dodd and Meyer's position on these two verses (a denial of authenticity) and argues the inclusion of the premonitory signs is intrinsically related to the restoration of Israel reflective of the temporal ambiguity.[91] Mark enumerates a "premonitory sign" that led up to the day of the "Son of Man" and then concludes with a warning in v. 33. Caird believes that the "resolution" of the nature of apocalyptic and the temporal tension within eschatology in Mark 13 is seen in parataxis. As mentioned, he argues that the resolution is merely that Mark is "not uneasy about this juxtaposition of incompatibles."[92] And so Mark leaves a juxtaposition of imminence and delay, something that Hebrew thought is happy to do.

One criticism is appropriate in response. This parataxis in the text only clarifies the temporal tension between vv. 24 and 33. The question becomes whether there are better explanations for the kind of ambiguity observed in the language of apocalyptic eschatology here. As noted above, parataxis could be explored further within vv. 24 to 27. The reason this exercise has not been undertaken is because of Caird's presuppositions about the functions of cosmic language. For Caird, Mark's account of Jesus' apocalyptic teaching is squarely in the realm of Hebrew thought and the characteristics of periphrasis he described. Caird is not interested in investigating the metaphorical transparency of apocalyptic language and insists that Mark would not wish the reader to explore connections or fine points of interest. In the context of the history of the discussion, this only means cosmic collapse. It represents a "hermeneutical blind spot" for Caird.

---

91. This is a rare situation for Meyer to see "secondary descriptions" in the tradition, but nevertheless it is a vital point of departure for Caird. For the details of where Meyer follows Manson, see Meyer, *Aims*, 209. Manson, *Teaching of Jesus*, 175–88. Here it is seen how Meyer's view on imminence and his less specific understanding of the son of man is maintained.

92. Caird, *Language*, 121.

Eschatological Relationships and Jesus

Second, Manson and Meyer's exclusion of the eschatological day from the premonitory signs is questioned by Caird because their view that the Son of Man is a pictorial symbol of the saints of the Most High, to stand for the manifestation of the kingdom of God on earth in a people wholly devoted to their heavenly king, ignores the possibility that the fall of Jerusalem is a fulfillment of prophecy (Dan 7:14).[93] In other words, the historical and referential question of whether the Day of the Son of Man is an event in Israel's national history is vital to Jesus.

Because Caird has redefined eschatology and argues there is no such thing as an *eschaton*, he is content to talk about national history as an event. Caird claims that since the nation has rejected God's Messenger and persecuted other Jews who responded, it is appropriate for God to give "an open demonstration that Jesus was right and the nation was wrong."[94] This analysis helps to explain why although Meyer avoids a closer study of Mark 13:24–27 and the coming of the Son of Man, Caird argues that the Day of the Son on Man is an event in Israel's national history. He, however, means within history and in reference to AD 70.[95]

Conclusion

In sum, Caird implies that Jesus' apocalyptic is stereotypically uniform and one dimensional, lacking in any development or clarification from Judaism. Caird acknowledges that Judaism held that one day the earth will end

---

93. See Manson, *Teaching of Jesus*, 277. Manson and Meyer's position is that the fall of Jerusalem is not a fulfillment of prophecy. Manson, *Teaching of Jesus*, 281. Meyer buys Manson's thesis in principle on Jesus and the remnant of Israel. Meyer, *Aims*, 211–12. Manson's view on the relation between Israel and judgment relies heavily on loyalty and obedience as the standard. See Manson, *Teaching of Jesus*, 175. This relation is unquestioned by Meyer. Meyer follows Manson's understanding of the Son of Man as pictorial symbol of the saints of the Most High which stands for the manifestation of the kingdom of God on earth among those devoted to their heavenly king. For the summary, see Manson, *Teaching of Jesus*, 180, 227. The horizon Manson follows is the interpretation of the Servant Songs Isaiah 40–55 as directed solely at Israel. On this basis Meyer declares the "epiphany of the Son of man comes unannounced like a sudden interruption (Matt 10:23; 24:27, 37; Luke 17:22–24, 26–30)" and that the day of the Son of Man is the counterpart after Caesarea Philippi to the reign of God in Jesus' public proclamation. Meyer, *Aims*, 209. This whole question of fulfillment of prophecy and its referents will be picked up in the PD discussion.

94. Caird, *Jesus and the Jewish Nation*, 20.

95. Ibid.

(Gen 8:22; Ps 72:7; Ps 102:25–26). However, in decrying the "intolerable deal of literalism in the interpretation of the imagery," he does ignore the issue of whether Jesus' apocalyptic language is direct or less direct in its referents in the same way that nonapocalyptic imagery can be understood when classified.[96] Finally, apocalyptic language is not allowed to become "transparent" because Caird does not allow for the discussion of simpler elements.[97] A key question is whether the meaning of the clouds and the Son of Man in Mark 13:26 (be it judgment, glory, rule, or authority) is exhausted by reference to AD 70.

Ben F. Meyer

Ben Meyer has been a large influence on Wright in two ways.[98] First, Wright endorses Meyer's structuring of his construct. Wright's outline in *Jesus and the Victory of God* in part 2, "Profile of a Prophet," and in part 3, "The Aims and Beliefs of Jesus," corresponds to Meyer's formula of describing Jesus' teaching in its two aspects of private teaching and public actions. This distinction is crucial for grasping Wright's understanding of Mark 13.[99] For Meyer the historical metanarrative pattern in the Gospel narratives is one of public pronouncement (often misunderstood but with an emphasis on God's immanence) followed by private explanation: "what Jesus says in public puzzles or startles his disciples, who question him in private on his meaning (Mark 4:10; 7:17; 10:23)."[100] Wright agrees that this applies to Jesus' teaching in Mark 13 and exemplifies his teaching about an imminent historical crisis. The word "metanarrative" is appropriate here. The constructs of Meyer, Caird and Wright identifies a narrative from Jesus' public ministry that overarches other narratives related to eschatology recorded in the Synoptic versions.[101]

---

96. Ibid., 17–18.

97. Compare what Caird says about the transparency of a language above. It is transparent "to the extent that the significance of its words may be deduced from a knowledge of their simpler elements." Caird, *Language*, 88.

98. The phrase "third quest" was invented by Wright and technically came into use during the early 1980s. However, Wright recognizes that Meyer's work in the later 1970s was significantly different from that of the New Quest. See Wright, *Challenge of Jesus*, 29.

99. Wright, *Victory of God*, 144. See also the discussion on the "guiding thread" for understanding Mark 13 in Wright, *Victory of God*, 512, 516.

100. Meyer, *Aims*, 141.

101. For discussion on the metanarrative controversy, see Breisach, *On the Future*

Second, Wright outlines five questions that are researched in the third quest period. These are: (1) How does Jesus fit into Judaism of his day? (2) What are his aims? (3) Why did he die? (4) How did the early church come into being, and why did it take shape? And (5) Why are the Gospels what they are?[102] Meyer's extensive work in questions two and three has convinced Wright.[103] Meyer's influence in the third quest is also evident in his emphasis on the theme of restoration and the detailed question of whether Jesus intended to found a church.[104] Wright says, "The peculiar idea of Jesus 'founding' a community designed to outlast his death gives way to a more nuanced, and perfectly credible, first-century Jewish one."[105] Finally, Wright also largely accepts Meyer's concept and use of "imminence."[106]

Apocalyptic Eschatology in Wright's Theological Construct

Placing Wright in the Third Quest: A Summary

A general question to consider before investigating Wright is how he differs from other students of Caird's such as Marcus Borg. Of particular interest here is the terminology used in the third quest.

There is basic confusion over terminology and categories of describing eschatology and apocalyptic because many writers assume a simple division. Wright and Borg both follow Caird in understanding the cataclysmic end of the world as nonliteral and metaphorical language. They differ, however, over the apocalyptic teaching of Jesus. When Borg in 1986 declared "a non-eschatological Jesus," he was not denying that Jesus believed in eschatology of future judgment or hope of the resurrection.[107] Rather he departed from his mentor by denying the authenticity of the apocalyptic Son of

---

of History, 122. Metanarrative by definition indicates a "narrative that overarched other narratives." The literary analysis Wright uses is a modified version of A. J. Griemas' narrative analysis, to show a typical story comprises three movements. Wright, *People of God*, 71.

102. Wright, *Victory of God*, 89–116.

103. Meyer is mentioned along with nineteen other Third Quest writers who are considered important. Ibid., 84.

104. Ibid., 103.

105. Ibid., 104.

106. Ibid., 208.

107. Borg, "Orthodoxy Reconsidered," 207–17; Borg, "Temperate Case for a Non-Eschatological Jesus," 81–102; Borg and Wright, *Meaning of Jesus*.

Man sayings. Jesus did not use the language of AE.[108] Wright follows Caird (although not uncritically) and applies metaphorical language to Jesus in Mark 13:24–27, and then relates it to AD 70, but Borg sees it as secondary.[109] Wright does not see himself as reinterpreting apocalyptic, whereas Borg does.[110] One reason is because Wright embraces "imminence."

Thus, there is still confusion over terminology in the third quest. One key question is whether the subject is eschatology in general or AE in particular.[111] For Caird however, the question is not a matter of paradigms or the avoidance of AE, but the issue of how to interpret language and metaphor. Wright follows Caird in this respect.

Description of Wright's Theological Construct and Themes

This section seeks to describe features of Wright's interpretive model and then asks about his objectives. The goal is to show that Wright borrows from Caird in his understanding of the historical crisis. Wright in essence uses Caird's definition of eschatology and his conceptual categories. After the literary aspects, Wright recognizes three other hermeneutical contexts to understanding apocalyptic: the personal, the social, and historical. By drawing on Meyer's and Sanders' work on Jesus' temple actions (Mark 11:15–17 / Matt 21:12–13 / Luke 19:45–46 / John 2:13–17), Wright's construct gains in detail, but questions remain as to the validity of his claims about the nature of the historical crisis.[112] Wright collates teaching from

---

108. For examples, see Miller, *Apocalyptic Jesus*, 42, 43 51. This point is clear here. Both Borg and Crossan affirm that Jesus was eschatological but they deny Jesus spoke the language of AE. Often times the issue is about paradigm titles so that "Jesus is not an apocalyptic prophet." Borg's doctoral dissertation, *Conflict, Holiness, and Politics in the Teaching of Jesus*, completed in 1972 under Caird, challenged what Borg calls the "apocalyptic paradigm" for understanding the historical Jesus. See Miller, *Debate*, 32. See also Borg, *Conflict, Holiness and Politics*.

109. See Miller, *Debate*, 42.

110. Wright, *Victory of God*, 95.

111. Others to use eschatology and AE interchangeably include Eddy, "Jesus as Diogenes?," 449–69.

112. Both Meyers and Sanders view Jesus' temple actions in line with the theme of restoration. Meyer sees Jesus' actions as a "cleansing" and argues for a new messianic community while Sanders argues for the temple's eschatological restoration and Jesus' temple actions as "an acted parable." See Sanders, *Jesus and Judaism*, 363–69; Meyer, "Expiation Motif in the Eucharistic Words"; Meyer, "Appointed Deed, Appointed Doer," 157, 164; Meyer, *Aims*, 198–202. On the other hand Borg and Wright strongly argue the case

Eschatological Relationships and Jesus

Jesus' public ministry in a way that clarifies Jesus' immediate theme of judgment on the temple but does not clarify long-term restoration. Wright's understanding of the historical accounts in Josephus (especially *Ant.* 12.322; *War* 6:312–15) is also important in light of the character of negative apocalyptic. This section examines the relationship of suffering and the construct of the exile. Wright's thesis of the continuing exile, while recognizing a negative aspect of apocalyptic, is nonetheless too broad for understanding Jewish apocalyptic. In terms of the framework, Wright's concept of the restoration of Israel from the exile is his driving motif, and his understanding of Jesus' teaching revolves around this. It involves four areas: (1) the future hope of the end of the exile, (2) the central theme of judgment on Jerusalem, (3) the coming of the "Son of Man" and (4) the delay of the Parousia.

Two books by Wright, *New Testament and the People of God* and *Jesus and the Victory of God*, extend his argument beyond Caird's construct. These discuss Wright's hypothesis on the global scope of the kingdom. The former book traces the OT and intertestamental literature, and the meaning of apocalyptic. It brings analysis from literal, personal, social, and historical contexts to his definition of apocalyptic. The discussion can be limited to five main subjects. First is the notion of the ongoing exile. Second, Wright's agreement with Caird's argument that AD 70 spells judgment on the nation because of the rejection of her Messiah and vindication of the true Israel. In this, he sees a relationship between the national crisis and Mark 13 but denies any literal aspect to Mark's focus that is also transcendent. Third, where Caird understands the language categories of prophetic hyperbole and parataxis to point to a metaphorical "end," Wright continues this thought in his discussion of language about AD 70. Wright takes two chapters to argue that this language of prophecy corresponds to an actual referent to the destruction of the temple in AD 70. Fourth, understood correctly in his Jewish context (and bearing in mind the motif of restoration), Jesus is Israel's savior. Fifth, Wright states that Mark 13 has been misunderstood to teach the second coming of Jesus. Both pietism's view that Jesus predicted his return at the end of time and Weiss's view of the prediction of the end of the world are incorrect.[113] He recoils from the import of the theological language of the "second coming" as a concept in the Gospels.

---

for Jesus' temple actions as an acted parable of judgment and Wright affirms a messianic community replaces the temple. See Wright, *Challenge of Jesus*, 65. Borg, *Conflict*, xvi.

113. Wright, *Victory of God*, 341.

Antecedents and Apocalyptic Literature

Wright understands apocalyptic lexically to mean the "unveiling" of things otherwise kept secret.[114] Wright's understanding of the themes in apocalyptic is best understood by exploring his distinction between negative aspects and positive hope of Second Temple Judaism.[115] For Wright, the negative aspect of "apocalyptic" in Jesus' day was that many, if not most, Jews regarded the exile as "still continuing."[116] His argument is that the exile is the ultimate backdrop to the narrative of Jesus' teaching. It is the "central drama" that Israel believed herself to be acting out.[117] The people had returned in a geographical sense, but "the great prophecies of restoration" had not yet come true.[118] Positively, many if not most Second Temple Jews hoped for the new exodus seen as "the final return from exile."[119] The question which chapter 6 will examine is, whether this is the best construct for conceiving of the ambiguity of apocalyptic which is what some call "positive and negative apocalyptic" in historical setting?[120] The unveiling of reality for people in the intertestamental period from the perspective of Jewish writers aware of the events they recorded in the apocalypses does not correlate directly with the theme of continuing exile. Thus, apocalyptic reflects a context of social deprivation.[121]

First, Wright's thesis on the exile needs to be discussed. Wright argues that to speak of the Temple or Land is to evoke the image of the exile and restoration.[122] His argument is that most Jews in Jesus' day regarded the exile as central drama which Israel believed herself to be "living out." It is not made in a vacuum but builds off (1) signs, and (2) the temple.[123] Though the Jews had physically returned to the land, the great prophecies of restoration had not yet been fulfilled. The Jewish hope of "the kingdom of God" was a

---

114. Wright, *New Testament and the People of God*, 252–56, 288.
115. Wright, *Victory of God*, 36.
116. Ibid., 126.
117. Ibid., 127.
118. Ibid., 126.
119. Ibid., 209.
120. For these terms, see Körtner, *End of the World*, 195. Part of Körtner's definition of "positive apocalyptic" and anxiety applies to Second Temple writings which explore the meaning of specific historical events (167 BC) while holding to covenant nomism and deliverance.
121. Wright, *People of God*, 287.
122. See chap. 10, "Hope of Israel," in *People of God*, 280–338.
123. Wright, *Victory of God*, 126–27.

periphrastic phrase for talking about "Israel's god becoming king."[124] Jesus understood his own career as that of a prophet announcing that the god of Israel was "at last becoming king." Wright goes on to argue that Jewish hope therefore has as its two focal points the return of Israel from exile and the return of Yahweh to Zion (chap. 13 and 14).[125] Thus for Jesus' Jewish contemporaries, both these themes relate "closely and obviously to the temple."[126]

The problem is that Wright distinguishes mystical speculation and political subversion from his discussion of the key issues of Temple, Land, and Torah.[127] He acknowledges that apocalyptic flourished in Hasmonean and Roman periods, but does not quote directly from them in his works. This is a prelude to his discussion on "representation" which has prominence over the category of historical context and which would have benefited from further investigation. He distinguishes symbolic representation (the sea = evil or chaos) sociological representation, where a person or group is deemed to represent or stand in for another individual or group, and metaphorical representation.[128]

Second, Jesus created controversy over the law. Wright recognizes controversy between Jesus and Israel took shape over many "symbols" such as the Sabbath, food, nation, family, and temple.[129] Wright essentially agrees with Sanders that the controversy of Jesus' message regarding law and the kingdom of God was a significant first step in the conflict which led to his death. Though Jesus did not speak against the law (Matt 5:17), he challenged the adequacy of the "Mosaic dispensation at various points."[130] When one reads Matthew's list of antitheses (Matt 5:21–47) and other related sayings

---

124. Ibid., 203. The spelling of "god" when referring to YHWH varies for Wright and needs to be seen in the context of Jewish monotheism and pagan religions. Wright frequently refers to YHWH as the "covenant god," "kingdom of this god," and the "creator god" while affirming the polemical statement explicit in Ps 96:5 that "the gods of the people are idols: YHWH [i.e., Israel's God] made the heavens." See Wright, *Who Was Jesus?*, 49.

125. There are several precise symbols of this return (1) this means a return to restored land and restored people (Isa 35:1–2, 5–6, 10; Matt 11:4–6 / Luke 7:22–3), (2) redefined family (Mark 3:31–5), (3) redefined Torah, and (4) rebuilt temple. See *Victory of God*, 428–32.

126. Wright, *Victory of God*, 415.

127. Wright, *People of God*, 289; cf. 285.

128. See n103.

129. Wright, *Victory of God*, 385–405.

130. See Sanders, *Jesus and Judaism*, 255–64. Wright, *Victory of God*, 377.

Antecedents and Apocalyptic Literature

(Matt 19:3–9) on divorce and Sabbath hand washing (Matt 15:1–20 / Mark 7:1–28) there is evidence that Jesus called for a total response of faith and an insistence on divine righteousness. He radicalized the law rather than abrogated it. Thus, Jesus' pronouncement on the law, his announcement of the kingdom and the fact that he personally spoke for Israel's God and disrupted the temple combined to set about his death.[131]

Similarly, Jesus' temple actions affirmed him as the Messiah. Here, Wright stands firmly with other third quest scholars who place the temple as the "central agenda to understanding Jesus."[132] If Wright's definition of eschatology and the meaning he gives to apocalyptic are the primary grounds for his differences with Meyer, then a secondary agent is his treatment of Jesus' temple activity, his riddles, and prophecy. Wright interacts with Sanders and lays out an inexplicable link between Jesus' messianic aims and the claims to his message and actions regarding the temple. The key historical questions are, what precisely did Jesus do in the temple, why did he do it, and what did he intend to accomplish and symbolize by it?[133]

In chapter 11, "The Meaning of Messiah," Wright draws together three stories of temple actions around the themes of symbolism and controversy. The key to understanding Wright's construct is his understanding of Jesus' symbolic link between (1) the temple "cleansing" and (2) temple riddle saying, and (3) temple prophecy, which he relates to his threefold message and aim of Jesus' threefold prophetic announcement: (1) the return from exile, (2) the defeat of evil, and (3) the return of Yahweh to Zion. In chapter 9, "Symbol and Controversy," Wright summarizes Chilton and Evans's view on the temple action as a "cleansing" and Sanders's view as "an acted parable" and then follows Sanders.[134] He says:

> Jesus intended to symbolize the imminent destruction of the temple. He believed that Israel's god was in the process of judging and redeeming his people, not just as one such incident among many but as the climax of Israel's whole history. The judgment on the temple would take the form of destruction by Rome, which (like Babylon, according to Jeremiah) *would be the agent of the wrath of YHWH.* The specific reasons for this judgment were, broadly, Israel's failure to obey YHWH's call to be his people (chapters 7,

---

131. Wright, *Victory of God*, 377.
132. Ibid., 405.
133. Ibid.
134. Ibid., 413–17. See also, Chilton and Evans, *Jesus in Context*.

8 above); and more narrowly, Israel's large-scale commitment to national rebellion, coupled with her failure to enact justice within her own society, not least within the temple-system itself. I thus agree with Sanders that Jesus symbolized the destruction of the temple; but I agree also with Sanders's critics (e.g., Bauckham, Evans) that this was more than a mere intention to replace the present Temple with a new one. It included a critique of the present Temple. This critique, though, was itself part of Jesus' eschatological programme. That is, after all, what we might expect from a prophet.[135]

Thus, on the cryptic riddle, Wright follows the metanarrative of Meyer and others that Jesus called for the destruction of the literal temple.[136]

Third, Wright traces the theme of the return of the king. The term "coming" or "arrival" in Mark 13 for the disciples and first-century Judaism meant Jesus' arrival in his enthronement as king.[137] When the disciples were questioning Jesus (Matt 24:3 / Mark 13:3–4) they were "pressing Jesus to give them details of his plan for becoming king, as David had become king in the city."[138] In other words, the disciples were longing for the "end of Israel's period of mourning and exile" and the beginning of a new age as the climax of Israel's history.[139] Jesus' prediction encompasses both Mark 13:2 and Mark 13:24–27. The "end" is Jerusalem's destruction and ruin. Wright quotes Caird's definition of eschatology that it "involves events for which end-of-the-world language is the only set of metaphors adequate to express the significance of what will happen, but resulting in a new and quite different phase within space-time history."[140] In support of this view of vindication, Wright provides a full section on the subject of the "start of woes" (Mark 13:5–13) and the "signs of emergency" (13:14–23). He examines the prediction of the destruction of the temple and the motif of YHWH's victory over Jerusalem as the "final acting out" of the predictions made against Babylon and calls Jerusalem the "great pagan city."[141] Finally, he points out

---

135. Wright, *Victory of God*, 417–18.
136. Meyer, *Aims*, 205–209.
137. Wright, *Victory of God*, 346.
138. Ibid.
139. Ibid.
140. Ibid., 208.
141. Ibid., 346–60.

Antecedents and Apocalyptic Literature

that Luke's reading of Mark is "quite clear"[142] concluding with the concept of the "vindication of the Son of Man."[143]

Wright's Use of Daniel and Background Themes

Two remaining themes are investigated here. One is Wright's interpretation of Daniel. The other is his analysis of Josephus. In both areas Wright follows Caird. His analysis of Mark's language is questionable.

First, Wright argues the Son of Man imagery in Daniel was seen as messianic in the first century. In Daniel's story the "son of man" as a human figure is surrounded by beasts and functions as a "symbol for Israel."[144] He holds that Genesis 2 is the basis for the idea that the people of God are "the true humanity" and the pagan nations are beasts and Israel will be vindicated over them. 4 Ezra 11–12 makes reference to the collective symbol of "the Lion of Judah" triumphing over the "Eagle of Rome"[145] and 2 Baruch 35–40 validates this claim.[146] Furthermore, Wright is adamant that the "son of Man" from Daniel 2, 7, and 9 does not have a literal referent but is a composite "messianic picture."[147] He argues that to read the text to mean that Son of Man is intended to be a historical individual who represented Israel as a nation (in the sense of sociological representation) misinterprets Israel's worldview and also confuses categories. He provides a complex discussion on the first-century Jewish worldview and explores how many concepts and ideas the ancient reader would understand.[148] He sees the meaning of messiahship as a symbolic picture of Yahweh's judgment and vindication which Jesus' ministry affirms and the events of AD 70 validate. Wright follows Caird in understanding the "son of Man" as a

---

142. Ibid., 359.

143. Ibid., 360.

144. Wright, *People of God*, 292.

145. Wright, *Victory of God*, 514.

146. For his understanding of first-century political patrons in describing the gospel and its claims, see Wright, *What Saint Paul Really Said*, 151–54.

147. Wright, *Victory of God*, 514.

148. A later question is how the NT handles the moves. The OT remains the foundational history for the early church and the Gospel writers. The answer PD gives is that the NT Gospels take different angles on historical events which the OT portrays prophetically. This is part of the discontinuity between Christianity and Judaism. Matthew also has parallels which draw out the implications in Mark's discourse.

collective symbol for Israel and that this is an important starting point for reading Jesus' apocalyptic discourse.[149]

Second, Wright develops this notion by arguing that the first-century view of the Messiah is derived from a reading of the book of Daniel as a whole. He argues that Josephus' cryptic mention of an "ambiguous oracle" refers to a widely believed messianic oracle.[150] Taken together, Daniel 2, 7, and 9 provide a messianic prophecy that became the impetus for Jewish revolt. Wright holds that Josephus alludes to this in his comment of an "ambiguous oracle... found in their sacred writing" (Jos. *War* 6:312–15).[151]

Several criticisms may be made. First, in arguing this interpretation of Daniel, Wright accepts the Jews incited war and political revolt but rejects the presence of a more specific pattern that is characteristic of apocalyptic. Second, Wright's analysis fails to observe that Josephus's use of Daniel's prophecy refers to both of these "destructions" and that although they occur under different circumstances Josephus alludes to fundamental similarities in them both.[152] Wright's use of Daniel sidesteps the possibility that Josephus sees a common pattern in two historical periods. In other words, he does not set the text in one milieu; meaning is not temporal. Josephus makes reference to the temple desecration in 167 BC in the Seleucid era with the comment that this was predicted by Daniel (*Ant.* 12.322).[153] Josephus emphasizes at least two themes to the first-century mindset according to Josephus: the susceptibility for desolation (*War* 6:296) and the divine preservation of the Jews (*War* 6:310). If Josephus sees a "pattern" that he believed to be operative in two time frames then it is the tension between ἀνοίας καὶ κακῶν ("folly and evil") and divine salvation.[154] Josephus posits that ἐννοῶν ("thoughtful reflection") enables one to recognize God's sovereignty and concern to preserve his people thus removing their fears and the reality of the effect of evil as a result of a sequence of actions based on human ignorance (*War* 6:310). Josephus quite clearly believes the Jewish revolt was fueled by Jewish interpretation of the oracle of Daniel. However, such confidence in the desired outcome, under the circumstances, was

---

149. Wright, *Victory of God*, 513.
150. Wright, *People of God*, 314.
151. Wright, *Victory of God*, 514; Wright, *People of God*, 312–14.
152. Wright, *People of God*, 314.
153. Other passages present a survey from the exile. See *Ant.* 11.1–2.
154. For Josephus, only the destruction and suffering in AD 70 is of the Jew's own accord.

clearly unjustified (*Ant.* 6:315). Thus Josephus correctly critiques a behavior that reacts to a Jewish apocalyptic scenario, seemingly as foolishness.[155]

Wright focuses on Josephus's comments in *War* 6:312–15, relating to AD 70. His failure to mention 167 BC is questionable given his main thesis about the exile. It implies that a non-specific historical era explains his themes focused on "restoration" and he relates selected passages to the kingdom in general to support his notion (*T. Mos.* 10:1–10; *Wis* 3:7). It is essential to address Josephus's comments on the "ambiguous oracle" that incited the Jews to war to AD 70. First, he mentions a ruler and this is interpreted by Josephus to mean the Emperor Vespasian.[156] Second, Josephus's perspective comes after two periods of intense persecution for the Jews. While Josephus relates Daniel to both 167 BC and AD 70, this does not prove that most Jews recognized fulfillment of the prophecy in the events in 167 BC as Wright suggests, or that they would agree with his view of the Son of Man. It also demonstrates that this text can relate well to two periods.

Assessment

Three criticisms are pertinent here. First, Wright does not ask if Mark 13:24–27 refers to different events from the one predicated in Mark 13:2, and 4. Instead he holds that Jesus teaches what any Jewish prophet after Daniel would see as Yahweh's vindication. He sees this as "earth-shattering" language which does not describe either the end of the space-time universe or a transcendent figure who is "about to come floating, cloudborne, towards earth."[157] Second, Wright does not ask, what is the relation between Jesus' temple action, his riddle, and his prophecy of the destruction of the temple. Instead, along with R. Bauckham, he views the Second Temple expectation of the temple's "demolition as divine judgment" (Mic 3:12; Jer 7:26; *Sib. Or.* 3:265–81; 4:115–18; *Apoc. Abr.* 27; *2 Bar* 1–8; *4 Bar* 1–4).[158] The third problem is his view of exile. It is contrary to the traditional Jewish

---

155. See *War* 6:290–295. These incidents and their interpretation by the common people, which Josephus refutes, are expressed in mythological language. Similarly, the idea that the Jews had the freedom to choose prosperity and win it by revolt against Rome was misguided (*War* 6:310).

156. Wright, *People of God*, 304.

157. Wright, *People of God*, 285; *Victory of God*, 515. Wright's first point is correct: the language does not signify the end of the space-time universe i.e., not a total cosmic collapse.

158. Ibid., 415. See Bauckham, *Jewish World around the New Testament*, 186.

Eschatological Relationships and Jesus

apocalyptic which anticipates the direct intervention by God against Gentile oppression in a day of crisis. These three problems cannot be separated.

Wright argues that the Daniel text carried a clear messianic significance for Israel. In his interpretation of Mark 13 he poses the question, what happens when one integrates the picture of Jesus' messianic claims with Jesus prophetic warnings?[159] Wright refers particularly to Daniel. First, Daniel 9:26, 11:30–32 and 12:11 deal with the destruction and desolation of the sanctuary at the hands of the Gentiles. Each passage predicts the cessation of regular sacrifices and the setting up of the abomination and "is linked to the activity of the anointed one."[160] In Daniel 7:13–14 the four "beasts" represent Gentile empires.[161]

The Gentiles feature prominently in Wright's construct. His interpretation is not overly complicated since apocalyptic is traditionally conceived to consist of negative and positive apocalyptic.[162] It is likely that he is correct to say that the book of Daniel was read centrally as a "revolutionary" kingdom of God text in which Israel's true representatives would be vindicated after their trial and suffering at the hands of pagans.[163] But other factors exist. First, for Wright to expect a first-century reader to make both sociological and literary moves is demanding.[164] If a passage like Daniel 9:24–27 has in mind the complete picture of Messiah presented in the whole book and if it is a "very sharp" picture as Wright suggests, then why is there confusion in Second Temple Judaism over the Son of Man? Furthermore, if the key to interpreting Daniel is not the original meaning, nor the precise meaning of Aramaic phrases in the second century BC or the first century AD, but the narrative sequence of Daniel and the ways in which that nar-

---

159. Wright, *Victory of God*, 510.

160. Ibid., 512.

161. Wright, *People of God*, 291. For the view that holds the four beast-empires are interpreted as Babylon, Persia, Greece and Rome, see also France, *Jesus and the Old Testament*, 185.

162. Körtner, *End of the World*, 195.

163. Wright, *Victory of God*, 517.

164. Wright, *People of God*, 283–92. The moves are: (1) that Judaism had a firm grasp of the return from exile and creation motifs; (2) that sociologically these notions equate completely to the apocalyptic mindset itself, which though admittedly is broadly distributed, requires no further attention to antecedents; that these motifs found in apocalyptic are the only plausible alternative to the notion that Second Temple century Judaism expected a literal end of the world and a divine Messiah figure from heaven; (3) that certain descriptions of heavenly figures bear no obvious link to transcendent realities; and (4) that Israel held that the Son of Man stood for herself.

rative sequence was invoked, then why does Jesus not evoke this image of exile with his contemporaries?[165] On the contrary, Mark seems to be giving a redaction about the exile motif, not Jesus.[166] Furthermore, toward the end of his analysis Wright notes *1 Enoch* 37–71 has a different messianic development of Daniel but does not mention that *1 Enoch* portrays an individual person. Turning to the signs in Mark 13:24–27, he argues the exile theme fits apocalyptic language in general and that it is characteristic to use cosmic otherworldly language to cloak worldly realities with theological and spiritual significance.[167] Jesus explains in the private discourse of Mark 13 what has been said and done cryptically in public through "grand scale works."[168] Isaiah 13:10 and 34:4, both quoted in Mark 13:24–27, speak of the sun being darkened, and stars falling from the heaven. Each in their own contexts refers to "startling and cosmically significant events such as the fall of great empires, within the space time world." But why is it anachronistic to maintain a heaven-earth distinction? Dualism is older than the first century. Like Caird, Wright does not indicate how apocalyptic language is the appropriate vehicle for the devastating message Jesus had come to announce.[169]

Furthermore, it is crucial to recognize that Mark's order of events is different from what Wright suggests. Wright reverses the order of events listed in the scenario. Wright begins with the great tribulation, then the false messiahs arising, and then mentions the disciples hauled before magistrates.[170] It is important to realize that the ambiguity of language concerning Daniel's "one like a Son of Man" does divide Israel.[171] 1 Enoch clarifies the figure of the Son of Man as a human figure. The text is by its very nature vague and so it invited speculation by Second Temple Judaism. Appeals to worldview do not alleviate the problem of the nature of revelation or the response to it. The ambiguity of language and the quest for understanding drive these moves in the text. Furthermore, it is important to examine Jubilees for antecedent ideas about negative and positive apocalyptic in post 167 BC

---

165. Wright, *Victory of God*, 512.

166. See Mark 1:1–2. Watts, "Consolation or Confrontation"; Watts, *Isaiah's New Exodus*.

167. Wright, *Victory of God*, 515.

168. Ibid., 512.

169. Ibid., 513.

170. Ibid., 349.

171. See n19.

Judaism, rather than apply a broad "exile" motif.[172] Following Caird, Wright has a good grasp of literary form and linguistic aspects of apocalyptic, and his discussion on metaphor is helpful.[173] But he works with late apocalyptic examples (*2 Baruch* and *4 Ezra*) when discussing particular historical and social settings.[174] Wright is correct to say that apocalyptic language employs complex and highly colored metaphors in order to describe events in alternative terms. This involves layers of meaning and special metaphors from the exodus which would come readily to mind.[175] Like Caird, Wright recognizes that all apocalyptic writing does not necessarily have the same or even parallel kinds or layers of meaning, and that the exact meaning of figurative language is sometimes hard to determine.[176] Sometimes language as *Apoc. Abr.* 19, 20 is a straightforward description of a heavenly reality.[177] It is clear then that the issue of referential meaning remains open.

Wright's Development and Differences with Meyer's Construct

Meyer and Wright share similar presuppositions about the historical Jesus; he was a prophet who saw himself as Israel's promised Messiah; his teaching included apocalyptic discourses. However, Wright's content and direction about the theme of Israel's restoration differs from that of Meyer in several ways. First, extended metaphor of the exile is essential to Wright's paradigm as the historical exile-restoration theme is to the apocalyptic mindset. Wright begins with Jesus' parable of the Prodigal Son in Luke

---

172. For example, see the climax of evil and the final assault of Gentile nations (*Jub* 23:22–25). The type of antecedent used in the Jubilees narrative relating to the "Gentiles" is one that is not expressed in the text. However, a punishment by a "sword" (v. 23) that is to be administered by the Gentiles (v. 23) refers to a retribution on ungodly people. The language is in harmony with chaotic social times present in the Maccabean uprising. See Lietaert Peerbolte, *Antecedents of Antichrist*, 242. See 1 Macc 2 on profaning of the temple and 1 Macc 3:52 on destroying the Jews. The interpretation of Dan 7:21 reveal how sensitive to the time of the end the Jews were in reading the OT. Compare also the rise of eschatology in the fifth century and interpretation of Revelation after the fall of Rome.

173. Wright, *People of God*, 286–86.

174. Ibid., 282, 288. The book of Jubilees does a similar thing with a negative and positive apocalyptic message. Where is the comment on its antecedents in Wright?

175. Ibid., 282–83.

176. Ibid., 283.

177. Ibid., 284.

15:11–32 because "this is the story of exile and restoration"[178] and because the "metaphors for the exodus" would easily come to his readers' minds.[179] As Israel goes off into Gentile country, becomes a slave, and then is brought back to her own land, so will the true Israel. As Babylon took the people of Israel into captivity and then fell and the people returned, so too will God's people experience salvation.

Wright presents a fairly detailed discussion of worldviews and mindsets in first-century thinking, whereas Meyer does not. Worldviews are lenses through which society views the world, and as such they represent a set of basic beliefs and aims of individuals and groups.[180] Wright argues that Jesus introduced a paradigm shift when he challenged the worldview of his contemporaries with poignant symbols.[181] Meyer in *Probleme einer präzedenzlosen geschichtlichen Situation* presented apocalyptic literature in relation to the crisis of Jesus' passion. The resurrection and Parousia are not distinguished. Meyer's hermeneutic emphasizes Jesus' temple cleansing and statement "destroy this temple" (John 2:19) as both event and acted statement. This text governs much of Meyer's thinking. Wright sees it more broadly because of his insistence on a theological-historical interpretation of the ongoing crisis of the exile in the land of Israel. AE is applied to the imminent restoration of Israel and salvation in Jesus which focuses on the future unfolding in AD 70. Wright sees prophecy in Jesus' teaching and distinguishes between Jesus' rejection, death, and resurrection and the events of AD 70. Furthermore, AD 70 is the climactic judgment on Israel in their homeland because of their rejection of the Messiah.

A further criticism of Wright's interpretation is appropriate. Given his opening analysis of the exile and the Seleucid era, he simplifies the unprecedented historical situation to a broad theological-historical theme rather than an acute problem in Israel's history. The extended period of "negative apocalyptic" scenarios in Second Temple Judaism, however, known as *das zeitalter der Angst* in Jewish apocalyptic relates to a more specific crisis than that which Wright summarizes. The mindset of *apokalyptische Angst* evidenced in literature around 167 BC is surely rooted in the temple desecration, not exile with its religious disappointment and hope. Wright has played down traditional apocalyptic teaching.

178. Wright, *Victory of God*, 126.
179. Wright, *People of God*, 283.
180. Wright, *Victory of God*, 138.
181. Ibid., 141–42.

Conclusion

Wright asks, did Jesus use apocalyptic imagery in his preaching, and if so, how? He affirms that Jesus did. Wright does not view his construct as a radical reinterpretation of apocalyptic literature in the way Borg does.[182] Nevertheless it is clear that Wright follows Caird in redefining eschatology and overlooks the historical problems of positive and negative apocalyptic. Wright views the eschatological horizon of Mark 13:24–27 on the same historical plane as Mark 11 and Mark 13:2. Caird and Wright recognize a temporal tension in Mark 13 which Meyer ignores. Meyer reinterprets the "end" in order to avoid a temporal tension of the signs that would otherwise lead up to an instant cataclysmic end. Caird and Wright live with the ambiguity of apocalyptic language and a temporal tension, but explain AE as nonliteral or they reinterpret final judgment in relative terms but through political entities associated with the language of myth which would be better placed under Pauline categories. Wright also refers to Meyer's emphasis of imminence across Jesus' teaching in general, and points to the hope for restoration while recognizing the prediction of separate events in resurrection and AD 70.

Wright also recognizes a fourth set of texts which Caird does not interact with in significant ways in his construct. In the next chapter, it will be seen that like R. T. France, Wright and PD have attempted to change the debate in order to deal with the text in its literary setting. There is not the space to examine these texts exegetically. However, they must be correlated into a coherent construct. If the relationship between history and Mark's transcendent concerns is puzzling enough, then there is a further text in this fourth set, Mark 14:62, which complicates and enriches the topic and requires further decisions. Did Mark mean an arrival of the Son of Man to God as hope of vindication or did he envisage the Son of Man arriving again from heaven to earth?[183]

---

182. Ibid., 95.
183. See also Dunn, "He Will Come Again," 42–56.

5

The Approach of Progressive Dispensationalism to Eschatological Relationships

Introduction

IN THIS CHAPTER, a final theological construct is examined. The purpose is not to construct a full description of PD.[1] Instead the initial goal is to describe PD and the role of typology in eschatology. Then it will examine the key points of PD regarding the scope and interpretation of the Olivet Discourse and the figurative language of Mark 13:24–27 in particular. I will propose that there are two important points to understanding the eschatological relationships in the Gospels. The first is that the Synoptic Gospels present different angles or perspectives concerning Jesus' prophetic teaching. The second is that the distinctive hermeneutical feature of the PD approach to understanding the use of the Old Testament in the New is the

---

1. For a description of the history of the movement of dispensationalism, review of in-house revisions, and distinctives of PD regarding salvation history in contrast to non-dispensational systems, see Blaising and Bock, *Dispensationalism, Israel and the Church*, 13–34; Blaising and Bock, *Progressive Dispensationalism*, 46–51; Saucy, *Case for Progressive Dispensationalism*, 13–35. For discussion of hermeneutical differences in method with other forms of dispensationalism, see Bateman, *Three Central Issues*, 85–118. For a response to the various categories in PD and the complementary relationships proposed for the kingdom, see Ryrie, *Dispensationalism*, rev. ed., 189–212.

concept of "pattern and prophecy." The nature of these relationships, which impact the time of fulfillment and consummation, cannot be overlooked by readers if an understanding of Mark's discourse is to be grasped. The chapter will conclude by assessing the validity of pattern typology and by exploring some of the key issues in restoration eschatology such as the consistency and nature of apocalyptic. This will be important for chapter 6 which returns to the question of the nature of figurative language in Mark 13:24–27.[2]

A Progressive Dispensational Construct

Description, Definitions, and Issues of PD

Robert L. Saucy writes, "Anyone who asserts not only the restoration of Israel as a national entity but also a future role for that nation in God's kingdom program has been generally identified as dispensationalist."[3] For the purposes of this study this feature of eschatology is what distinguishes PD from Meyer's and Wright's constructs. The addition of "progressive" to the title serves to link the movement to the lineage of dispensational theology and to highlight differences between it and other versions of dispensationalism which are variously called "classic" and "revised."[4] The

---

2. This discussion is in a separate chapter in order to simplify the study. In review, the last chapter showed the following. First, that Caird has three sets of texts in which to examine eschatological relationships and history. Wright sees an additional fourth set. Caird and Wright agree that some language intends a straightforward description of a heavenly reality. Here, it is seen that Wright applies this to understanding Mark 14:62. The text relies on spatial dualism and the referent is debated. The background not covered in detail is that Jesus speculates about his exaltation at his trial. Importantly though Mark presents Christology from a history to heaven perspective. So the issue of referential meaning does remain open and to be determined with the apocalyptic language of Mark 13:24–27.

3. Saucy, *Case*, 9.

4. The term "dispensation" refers to different arrangements by which God regulates the way people relate to him. Blaising and Bock, *Progressive Dispensationalism*, 14, 48. Charles Ryrie says the essence of dispensationalism is "the distinction between Israel and the church." Ryrie, *Dispensationalism Today*, 47. How this relationship is described by dispensationalists in biblical theology is debated. Traditional dispensationalism advocates "stable meaning" and a hard distinction between Israel and the Church. PD sees a more "complementary relationship" between the present and future dispensations. For understanding of "single meaning" and "restricted meaning" which led to the major premise that the author has a stable meaning, see Johnson, *Expository Hermeneutics*, 34–35, 50.

The Approach of Progressive Dispensationalism

name "progressive dispensationalism" derives from the understanding of dispensations as not "simply *different* arrangements between God and humankind, but as *successive* arrangement in *progressive* revelation and the accomplishment of redemption."[5]

Early writings of the movement include the 1992 co-editing by Blaising and Bock of their *Dispensationalism, Israel and the Church* which set out the main issues of discussion. This was followed in 1993 by *Progressive Dispensationalism* by the same authors. The more systematic theological version by Saucy *The Case For Progressive Dispensationalism* appeared the same year. In a 1983 paper, *The Time of the Fulfillment of the Messianic Prophecies*, Saucy has asserted the future restoration of Israel and treated the messianic prophecies as fulfilled during the present church age and future age according "to [the] natural interpretation of all prophecies."[6] Darrell Bock's commentaries on *Luke* in 1994 and *Mark* in 2005 discuss structural and exegetical issues concerning the Olivet Discourse. In the former, Bock summarizes the PD position on prophecy and in the later he expresses his most recent thoughts on Mark's discourse.[7]

A key question is the definition of the church. PD views the church not as an anthropological category in the same class as terms like "Israel" and "Gentiles" or "Gentile people." In this sense the church is not another "people-group." Rather the church represents redeemed humanity on the earth (both Jew and Gentile) in the present age, as opposed to national Israel and the unsaved Gentiles (Eph 2:15).[8] Like all dispensationalists, PD believes God is working in the church today and in a future dispensation he will have a role for national Israel again.

The PD approach to Scripture is also important for understanding eschatology. Progressive dispensationalists write extensively on methods of interpreting Scripture. Their understanding of biblical and theological interpretation has several features. First, Craig Blaising argues that PD is not an abandonment of "literal" interpretation for "spiritual" interpretation.

---

5. Blaising and Bock, *Progressive Dispensationalism*, 48, italics theirs. See also Thomas, "Hermeneutics of Progressive Dispensationalism," 79–95.

6. Saucy, "Time of the Fulfillment," 11.

7. Bock, *Luke: 9:51—24:53*, 1656–57; Turner and Bock, *Gospel of Matthew, Gospel of Mark*, 515–24.

8. Blaising and Bock, *Progressive Dispensationalism*, 49–50. See also Blaising and Bock, *Israel and the Church*, 392. In denying there are separate programs for the church and Israel PD understands God's salvation plan will be fulfilled for both in history in respective roles according to the distinctions revealed in Scripture. Saucy, *Case*, 28.

Instead, "progressive dispensationalism is a development of 'literal' interpretation into a more consistent historical-literary interpretation" which allows for a complementary hermeneutic of interpretation.[9] Second, PD recognizes the importance of intertextual features such as typology along with historical and literary hermeneutics (grammar, lexicography, structural and compositional discussion, and genre) in the interpretation of the NT.[10] Third, it recognizes the important role of biblical theology which is "manifested in the progress of revelation as it impacts the interpretation of any individual passage."[11] This thematic approach in PD includes the study of related concepts, not just "individual terms."[12] For example, the thematic approach which PD adopts on the "Day of the Lord" incorporates many related concepts and terms. A key emphasis of PD is that the early church places a high focus on eschatological hope.[13] Commenting on the Day of the Lord, Blaising and Bock write: "what the church expects to happen at the coming of Jesus correlates generally with the Old Testament predictions regarding the coming of the kingdom (1 Thess 1:10; Tit 2:13; Phil 3:20; 1 Pet 1:13; Rev 1:7; 22:12, 20; 1 Cor 16:22).[14] It will be a day of the Lord, a time of wrath and judgment against sin and evil (1 Thess 5:1-9; 2 Pet 2:9; 3:7-12; Rev 6:17; 16:14) and is equated to "the Day of our Lord Jesus Christ (1 Cor 1:8)."[15] This applies particularly to the debate of Mark's restoration eschatology where Wright denies that there is any future for Israel. How PD treats the Synoptic Gospels in relation to the wider subject of the church's eschatological hope will be examined. On the basis of this general portrait of PD, the source-critical issues of Mark 13 are now examined.

---

9. Blaising and Bock, *Progressive Dispensationalism*, 52.

10. Blaising and Bock, *Israel and the Church*, 380.

11. Ibid.

12. Ibid. For the theme of Israel's national and political promises traced through Lukan theology and Luke's anticipated future dispensation, see Bock, "Reign of the Lord Christ," 37-67.

13. On the centrality of Christ's return in the earliest Christian documents (e.g., 1 Cor 16:22) see Dunn, "He Will Come Again," 42. Dunn is not a dispensationalist.

14. Blaising and Bock, *Progressive Dispensationalism*, 262.

15. Ibid.

The Approach of Progressive Dispensationalism

Eschatological Relationships and Source Criticism Debate

One vital element of the discussion regarding the subject of the Fall of Jerusalem and the return of the Son of Man is their literary nature as described in the Synoptic discourses. A broad summary of the eschatological relationships and the source question is required because the debate turns on how Mark's ambiguity or potential ambiguity should be understood. The goal is to gain a broad understanding of the issues by attempting to place PD in relationship to the critical debate over the sources. Much that has been written on the issue of sources will not be covered here.[16]

Views on Eschatological Relationships

One view tends to dismiss the ambiguities in the passage. The basis for this interpretation can be twofold: (1) either the assumption is made that complex historical and literary referents are implausible,[17] or (2) the interpreter assumes the hermeneutical maxim: "one meaning many applications."[18] This leads to a choice being made in favor either of AD 70 or the final Day of the Lord as the intended focus of prophecy.[19] The majority of critical scholars hold to the first position while traditional dispensationalism takes the

---

16. For a discussion on source issues, literary questions, and structure of the Olivet Discourse, see Carson, "Matthew," 488–95. For a short but helpful review of past source-critical and tradition-critical approaches by redaction critics, see Wenham, *Rediscovery of Jesus' Eschatological Discourse*, 2–5.

17. R. C. Sproul contends that Mark portrays Jesus as speaking true prophecy. Mark's record of prophecy, however, differs markedly from ancient prophecies like those of the Oracles of Delphi which are "exercises in the art of studied ambiguity." See Sproul, *Last Days according to Jesus*, 13. Intended ambiguity, he claims, is merely akin to predictions found in modern daily horoscopes which are sufficiently broad or ambiguous to allow for random fulfillments. Chapter 4 of this study also noted that critical historical grammatical methodology has the assumption that a text is fixed in a single historical mileau.

For a detailed description of the features and function of Greek oracles, see Aune, *Prophecy in Early Christianity*, 51. Aune notes that the ambiguity in such oracles contributed to the widespread belief that an oracle would be fulfilled, even if in a "totally unexpected manner" and that the obscurity of these oracles meant that any particular interpretation was held with "some skepticism until the fulfillment was obvious." Noteworthy too is the recognition of conditional oracles which are introduced by the particles "if" and "when," and the fact that most oracles were given in response to specific questions posed by enquirers, Aune, *Prophecy*, 60–66.

18. See Ramm, *Protestant Biblical Interpretation*, 113.

19. See Carson's article for laying out both sides. Carson, "Matthew," 488–95.

second position. It is fair to say that too often traditional dispensationalists have argued the Olivet Discourse (OD) is only about the Second Advent. A second approach recognizes the inherent ambiguity and complexity in Mark's structure of the passage and moves forward to interpret his intended meaning while maintaining the temporal tension.

In his commentary on *Matthew*, Carson makes several helpful points in arguing against critics who too quickly focus on the disparate material and assume the presence of a number of separate sources that have not been well integrated by the evangelist-redactor.[20] First, too many details in these various theories "seem unconvincing and fail to deal adequately with how each synoptist thought of the material he was editing."[21] Second, an *a priori* case for the apparent textual differences can be based, not on the synoptist's "failure to integrate separate sources," but on its condensed and selected reporting of a "much longer unified discourse delivered by Jesus."[22] Add to this the current scholarly emphasis that inconsistencies found in Jewish apocalyptic are not irreconcilable abnormalities (as some former scholars thought) and so Mark is consistent with Jewish apocalyptic literature in his style.[23]

Adopting the second approach, D. A. Carson (not a dispensationalist) recognizes intended ambiguity when he describes the "tightly intertwined" subjects inherent in the discourse.[24] Similarly, Darrell Bock notes that Jesus "wove" two subjects "together here because their nature will be similar."[25] In this way PD emphasizes the theological cohesion in the Olivet

---

20. Ibid., 491. Carson labels this the "unifying method" solution.

21. Ibid.

22. Ibid.

23. E.g., R. H. Charles. T. W. Manson wrote that "there was a sense in which the language of Apocalyptic remained a foreign language to him." F. C. Burkitt, in commenting on Charles's lack of commitment to the Jewish author, says, "He was unwilling to believe that such a person could have entertained conceptions which to Charles's trained and logical western mind were 'mutually exclusive.' His favourite explanation was to postulate interpolations and a multiplicity of sources, each of which may be supposed to have been written from a single and consistent point of view." See Burkitt, "Robert Henry Charles," 443. Cited also by Barr, "Jewish Apocalyptic in Recent Scholarly Study," 32. For a critique on Charles's theory on literary structure, see Burkitt, *Jewish and Christian Apocalypses*, 44–50. For further details and Collin's critique on Charles's "presupposed doctrinal consistency," see Collins, *Apocalyptic Imagination*, 14–15.

24. Carson, "Matthew," 491.

25. Turner and Bock, *Gospel of Matthew, Gospel of Mark*, 524. Others see two events "linked conceptually." See Garrett, "Type, Typology," 786.

The Approach of Progressive Dispensationalism

Discourse, while as mediating theologians, they recognized that aspects of the traditional position needed modifying. For example, in "The Trial and Death of Jesus in N. T. Wright's Jesus and the Victory of God," Darrell Bock argues that "too little importance" is traditionally given to the significance of the fall in AD 70.[26] PD recognizes that there are eschatological relationships between history and apocalyptic to explore in the text which go beyond the source criticism debates and which do not equate the content of Jesus' prediction with current events.[27]

Summary

Carson's comment on skeptical critical scholarship's "unifying method" to this solution of the source problem is important. As the primary criticism under which everything else is subsumed, the AD 70 interpretation influences all ideas on redactional change. The "little apocalypse"[28] theory advanced by T. Colani, and modified since by scholars, fails to see any cohesion or coherence in Mark. This leads to the notion of ad hoc redactional changes in various traditions (e.g., as seen in Käsemann's construct in Matthew's gospel[29]). Carson rightly explores an alternative perspective. However, Carson too quickly dismisses the dispensational view of the OD when he criticizes it as "historically implausible" that Jesus would predict judgment and couch his message in terms of dealing with Jerusalem's temple crisis a second time.[30] PD shares with other interpreters understanding about the theological cohesion of the OD at the source level. Once this basic framing for viewing the discourse is established, the second most important element PD draws attention to is the use of the OT in the NT. The concept of pattern prophecy in particular answers Carson's concerns about history in Mark.

---

26. Bock, "Trial and Death of Jesus," 120.

27. For some tight disagreement on matters of fulfillment between "historicist" premillennial and "futurist" premillennial, see Blaising and Bock, *Progressive Dispensationalism*, 19.

28. Colani, *Jésus Christ*; Geddert, "Apocalyptic Teaching," 20–27.

29. Käsemann, "On the Subject of Primitive Christian Apocalyptic."

30. See Carson, "Matthew," 495.

The Role of Typology

The biblical meaning and use of typology is an important issue for PD as it is for all scholars concerned about understanding the relationship between the OT and the NT. The subject has seen much debate.[31] The initial goal here is to survey the non-dispensational position on typology then to describe the terms used by PD which add to the debate by advancing the discussion from the PD perspective. Saucy's introductory remarks on the biblical meaning and use of typology are helpful. This is followed by Bock's understanding of "typological-prophetic" interpretation.

Typology in the Wider Context of Biblical Studies

Foulkes and Daniélou: "Foreshadowing"

Among commentators a wide range of approaches to biblical typology exists. For some like Francis Foulkes, "type exists" because meaning extrinsic to the text is read into it.[32] From this skeptical perspective, typological hermeneutics is seen as a necessary method to unite the Testaments.[33] Foulkes understands typology as a "foreshadowing" with a backwards glance reading of Scripture. Perceived this way, typology is a "reading into Scripture." Typology finds meaning that is not there "in that it reads in the light of the fulfillment of the history." In this way he says the reader "recognizes the incompleteness" of the OT.[34] In his *The New Testament and the Theology of History* Jean Daniélou also adopts a model of typology as one of "foreshadowing." He writes: "The basis of typological interpretation of history is the notion that events and institutions of one age 'foreshadow' those of a following age."[35] From

---

31. See Feinberg, "Hermeneutics of Discontinuity," 120n39 and n40. For the misunderstanding of the "complementary hermeneutic" of PD as *sensus plenior* (i.e., "fuller meaning"), see Thomas, "Hermeneutics of Progressive Dispensationalism," 91–92. Thomas argues that the hermeneutics of PD represents a "significant discontinuity" to dispensationalism and that attempts to include traditional pre-understandings, and the interpreter's historical context and reasoning make the PD approach "more provisional in its conclusions." Thomas, "Hermeneutics," 82–83.

32. Foulkes, *Acts of God*, 38–39.

33. Feinberg, *Continuity and Discontinuity*, 120–21.

34. Foulkes, *Acts of God*, 38–39. On author's intended meaning, cf. France, *Jesus and the Old Testament*, 41.

35. Daniélou, "New Testament and the Theology of History," 28. Cf. Daniélou, *From Shadows to Reality*.

The Approach of Progressive Dispensationalism

this model of type to antitype fulfillment Daniélou defends a Christological and eschatological reading. For example, Christian hope is secured because of the Christ event (Rom 6:10; 8:16–17; Heb 9:12; Luke 23:43; John 3:18; 1 Cor 15:45).[36] However, there seems little evidence that "foreshadowing" is the appropriate model under all circumstances.

Whitman: "Allegory"

Others, such as J. Whitman, dismiss the concept of typology and prefer the vocabulary of "allegory" and "symbol."[37] Whitman argues that the meaning of words and shifts in interpretation are themselves historical events which require assessment. Whitman singles out the concepts of "allegory" and "symbol" as adequate to "imply changing views about the relation between text and time." He goes on to rule out typology as prophetic when he says, "Prefiguration is now often called *typology*," but the term in early Christianity most "frequently associated with this alignment of events is *allegory*."[38] Importantly for this discussion, Whitman views typology through a Pauline lens that interprets "Paul's broad chronological orientation" of successive historical periods as the only framework necessary to understanding typology. In other words, these large periods of history are the norm in comparing the Old Covenant to the New Covenant.[39] Whitman incorrectly dismisses the concept of pattern/typology, however, though he inadvertently raises the issue of whether typology should be treated monolithically.

France: "Correspondence"

R. T. France on the other hand describes typology as a discipline distinct from "allegory." For France, typology is "essentially the recognition of a correspondence between New and Old Testament events, based on a conviction of the unchanging character of the principles of God's working."[40] Moreover, it represents a subsequent understanding and description of the

---

36. Daniélou, "Theology of History," 28.
37. Whitman, "From the Textual to the Temporal," 161.
38. Ibid., 164. See also Lubac, "'Typologie' et 'allégorisme,'" 187.
39. Whitman, "Textual to Temporal," 165–64.
40. France, *Jesus and the Old Testament*, 40.

NT event in terms of the old model.[41] France's definition is that typology is "theological reflection in light of later events" and he sees OT events and people as "apt parallel[s] to those of Jesus" and his time rather than a method of exegesis.[42] Bock affirms this vocabulary of "correspondence" and relates it to the shared presupposition Judaism has with Christianity for discerning "pattern in history."[43] This is also important for understanding the history-kerygma discussion and needs to be developed.

Goppelt: "Theological Correction"

Finally, L. Goppelt in discussing the use of the OT in the New introduces a new vocabulary. For example, Goppelt refers to the relationship between Christ and Adam (Rom 5:14) and the inauguration of a new creation, as "typological correction."[44] For Bock, this biblical illustration reflects belief in "the one in the many" in which a "single member of a community can represent the whole."[45] He adds: "Adam is used by Paul as a representative of all humanity, just as Christ represents redeemed humanity (Rom 5:12–21; 1 Cor 15:20–23, 45–49).[46]

Summary

These then are some of the ways biblical typology is viewed and the elements and issues involved. The pattern of the ancient mythical worldview with its emphasis on the cosmic battle between the Creator and forces of chaos re-emerges in Second Temple Judaism in modified form and is behind apocalyptic.[47] When this pattern is factored in, a variety of options for interpreting typology become evident.[48] The question remains, how does this relate to Mark's narrative? The PD approach to typology is now considered.

41. Ibid.
42. Ibid., 42.
43. Bock, "Scripture Citing Scripture," 262. The first shared theological presupposition is the Bible is God's word. Bock, *Scripture Citing Scripture*, 261.
44. Goppelt, *Typos*, 130.
45. Bock, "Scripture Citing Scripture," 261.
46. Ibid.
47. For a description of how redemption is viewed in cosmic terms under a renewed mythical pattern in Second Judaism, see Stone, "Three Transformations in Judaism," 466.
48. Everything is classifiable into one of two categories: order and chaos. Further,

The Approach of Progressive Dispensationalism

Robert L. Saucy

In *The Case for Progressive Dispensationalism*, Saucy draws from David Baker's description of a type as "a biblical event, person or institution which serves as an example or pattern for other events, persons or institution."[49] He goes on to define typology as the study of the "general historical and theological correspondence" between types as a key relationship taught in Scripture.[50] Although not interacting with Wright directly, Saucy articulates the PD position in opposition to the replacement view of Meyer, Caird, Wright, and Reformed and Roman Catholic theology in general. Describing this view, Saucy defines a type as a "shadow pointing forward to the reality of an antitype."[51] Understood as such, it would mean, that the coming of the reality of Christ brings the "existence of the type to an end."[52] This reflects the reformed view that "the shadow was absorbed into the reality [namely, Christ]."[53] In contrast, PD concludes that the relationship and analogies between Israel and the church understand Israel as a type of the church. However the correspondence with God's actions among OT Israel does not deny a continuing role for that nation in the future.

Darrell L. Bock

In a 1987 update of his PhD thesis, "Proclamation from Prophecy and Pattern," Darrell L. Bock describes the debate on Luke's use of the Old Testament in recent study and presents his view of how Luke uses the OT.[54] The goal of the work is to examine key passages in which Luke uses the OT (to

---

myth sees this ensuing struggle occurs according to a predestined pattern in the world since creation. There is one pattern: Chaos is doomed.

49. Baker, "Typology and the Christian Use of the Old Testament," 153.
50. Saucy, *Case*, 32.
51. Ibid.
52. Ibid.
53. Ibid. Cf. also Goppelt, *Typos*, 107–11. From the Synoptic Gospels Goppelt argues that the church is related to Israel in redemptive history and in a typological way but also in replacement of Israel. He does not explain however why the move from the Old Covenant and the inauguration of the New through Christ's death necessitates the end of a future role for Israel. Here too belongs France's conclusion on the survey of types. He claims in general that the "disasters of Israel are foreshadowings of the imminent punishment of those who reject him" (Mark 13:14; Matt 23:38; Luke 21:24; 23:30). France, *Jesus and the Old Testament*, 75.
54. Bock, *Proclamation from Prophecy and Pattern*.

connect the OT passage to the Jesus event) in order to understand Luke's Christology.⁵⁵ Relevant for this discussion is the section on three guiding questions. These are: (1) the "manner" in which the OT passage is used, (2) "motivations or theological presuppositions" and (3) "theological assertions" made by the use of the OT. These areas of study are pertinent to understanding Luke's typological presentations and Christology. Bock maintains that there are a variety of different usages of typology and so it is a mistake to take typology just one way.⁵⁶ In *Proclamation from Prophecy and Pattern*, Bock distinguishes six other uses or classifications of OT use over against prophetic-pattern, which is why the typological link, when anticipated, must be identified.⁵⁷

In his summary essay in *Three Views of the Millennium*, Bock rejects the function of typology as "shadow" which Foulkes and others hold.⁵⁸ Instead, he articulates his support for the messianic hope and promise typology perspective of Goppelt's *Typos: The Interpretation of the Old Testament in the New*, and Davidson's *Typology in Scripture: A Study of Hermeneutical τύπος Structures*.⁵⁹ Acknowledging these works and others, Bock lays out four further points of clarification about typology.

Prophecy

First, drawing from Daniélou's work, Bock argues for "typology as prophecy." In *Prophecy and Pattern*, Bock shows that while typology is often retrospective (and the pattern can not be recognized until it is repeated) it is still prophetic "because at its foundation is the idea that God works in certain patterns in working out his salvation."⁶⁰ Bock defines pattern and prophecy as: "God's pattern of salvation . . . reactivated in a present fulfillment." This

---

55. Ibid., 47.

56. Ibid., 49, 51. Here the focus is on considering an author's use of typology and not limiting interpretation to "only one class." See also "Types of Usage" in Bock, "Scripture Citing Scripture," 271.

57. Ibid., 49. These are: (1) analogy, (2) illustration, (3) legal proof, (4) a proof passage, (5) explanatory or hermeneutical use, and (6) prophetic or direct prophetic.

58. Bock, "Summary Essay," 282.

59. Davidson, *Typology in Scripture*; Goppelt, *Typos*.

60. Bock, *Prophecy and Pattern*, 291n24. Cf. Whitman, "Textual to Temporal," 161.

The Approach of Progressive Dispensationalism

fulfillment happens in accordance with "messianic hope and promise" and according to the pattern of God's activity in salvation history.[61]

Escalation

Second, typology is not analogy. This is one of the most pertinent distinctions Bock makes. For example, Bock treats typology in Luke 1–24, Acts 2–5 and 7–13 as separate from "analogy" in that the latter expresses a "more general" parallel than typology, because the patterns are less marked and the movement from "lesser to greater event is absent."[62] Bock makes three important statements about this distinction. First, analogy "compares" but typology "escalates." Second, analogy is frequently "not sufficiently distinguished" from the classification of typology. Third, it is misleading to call both types of texts typological, and the two kinds should be distinguished since typology is prophetic while analogy is not.[63] This aspect of typology is a crucial hermeneutical key for interpreting passages like Isaiah 7 in the NT.

Salvation History

Third, Bock argues it is accurate to say typology "is a way of thinking" about God's outworking plan through history as it "moves to consummation."[64] Texts that reflect this pattern can be called "typological-prophetic" as they present the "realization of a pattern" which is a crucial issue for interpretation.[65] This typology is not a form of spiritual interpretation but that which refers to "patterns of resemblance between persons and events in earlier history to persons and events in later history. Bock affirms that the tension is no different than that of other themes in biblical theology. For example the Day of the Lord judgment revealed by the OT prophets is a type of a future, eschatological Day of the Lord.[66] Similarly, the "throne of David" looks one day to a period of Jesus' reign on the earth as Son of David (Acts

---

61. Bock, *Prophecy and Pattern*, 49.
62. Ibid., 50.
63. Ibid.
64. Ibid., 292.
65. Blaising and Bock, *Progressive Dispensationalism*, 102.
66. Ibid., 53.

3:19–22).⁶⁷ The added dimension of apocalyptic with its emphasis on intervention from "above" in the context of conflict and its temporal tension presents a problem for typology.

Multiple Referents

Bock is clear that different subjects can relate to "pattern" with multiple referents. In a footnote in *Prophecy from Pattern*, he says, "Many of the initial OT texts found in typological category are texts of promise tied to ideas of deliverance, kingship, or other key concepts that have eschatological overtones and suggest patterns of salvation in themselves."⁶⁸ In "Scripture Citing Scripture" he says: "Types in the sense we are using it refers to events or the function of an office. The OT tends to apply this imagery to the concept of creation and re-creation or to the theme of Exodus and new Exodus. So when Isaiah spoke of a new Exodus in Isaiah 40, he referred to the redemption of the nation out of exile, and yet his language also applies to what ultimate redemption would look like."⁶⁹ He goes on to say that the idea of "multiple referents" being ultimately fulfilled in a unique way is a key to understanding the NT use of the OT. For example, the NT extends "Creation and Exodus imagery" to other categories, "such as promises made to righteous sufferers, or promises made to the king, so that when these promises are realized in Jesus, they are realized in him uniquely."⁷⁰ This is where the church and Judaism "parted company" because what Judaism thought was unrealized, the church saw "fulfilled in Christ."⁷¹ As Bock notes the issue is that typology is not always retrospective.

Many have established the presence of typology in history. Bock articulates the importance of three issues that affect pattern. These are dual authorship and language referent and progressive revelation. Bock argues that given the flexibility of language the use of generic terminology makes it possible for a writer "to address two or more events in the same utterance."⁷² For example, the language-referent situation in Isaiah 7:14

---

67. Bock, "Hermeneutics of Progressive Dispensationalism," 88.
68. Bock, *Prophecy and Pattern*, 291n124.
69. Bock, "Scripture Citing Scripture," 262.
70. Ibid.
71. Ibid.
72. Ibid., 265.

The Approach of Progressive Dispensationalism

read typologically reveals how a "multiple-context situation would work."[73] Bock writes: "in the short term, the referent must be one that Ahaz could experience about a sign child. Isa 7:15–17 appears to give timing for the original promise that ties it to the defeat and judgment of Ahaz, although assuring that the Davidic house will still be preserved, keeping an element of futurity to the promise. So Isaiah points to a woman who is currently a virgin (referent: some unidentified woman in the court) who will give birth to a child. That child's arrival is the sign, represents 'God with us,' and starts the clock ticking on Ahaz's judgment. The child contextually would probably be Maher-Shalal-Hash-Baz (Isa 8:1–4)."[74] Bock continues, "the text as a potential pattern text points to a 'type' of sign child that has a second, escalated realization in Jesus."[75] Bock adds that the language of the text has not changed in Matthew's account but the referents and their "force" have "shifted slightly" to reveal the escalation (Matthew's account of a virgin birth). Bock concludes: "This kind of interaction is how language-referent and multiple settings can combine to allow God to develop the force of a text in the process of revelation through a pattern fulfillment. In doing so, God's design within history is heightened even more than in direct prediction, for now his hand is present in at least two settings, showing his sovereignty over history at a variety of points."[76]

In sum, Bock describes "typological-prophetic" usage as that which expresses a peculiar pattern or link with a movement from the "lesser OT person or event to the greater NT person or event."[77] He holds that Judaism and Christianity recognize pattern in history and that there are a variety of classifications for understanding the function of typology in the Old and New Testaments. From this, one can deduce that Isaiah is a potential hermeneutical key for understanding Mark 13. In a more recent work on dispensational hermeneutics, *Interpreting the New Testament Text: Introduction to the Art and Science of Exegesis*, Bock addresses the issues of whether typology is always retrospective and argues that it is not.[78] God has still designed the correspondence even though the pattern is not

---

73. Ibid., 266.
74. Ibid.
75. Ibid.
76. Ibid.
77. Ibid.
78. Bock, "Scripture Citing Scripture," 272.

anticipated or looked for humanly speaking until the fulfillment makes the working out of the pattern apparent.

Summary of Mark 13 and Apocalyptic Relationships

In Bock's commentary on *Mark* he gives an up to date interpretation and reflection on the OD since he wrote his commentary on *Luke*.[79] This section presents a summary of the major exegetical points Bock presents in *Mark*. Four motifs or themes are selected above others: (1) Temple destruction, (2) Abomination of desolation, (3) Tribulation, and (4) Transcendent events (the Premonitory Signs, Arrival of the Son of Man, and the Gathering of the Elect). While these themes belong together at the literary level based on common context, certain differences are noted. In contrast to Meyer and Wright, Bock isolates these themes in the context of Mark because they represent different aspects of prophetic fulfillment in history. Furthermore, PD advocates a distinct mutualism or dependence in theory and practice between events two and three and sees them as a distinctive eschatological relationship.

Jesus' Prediction of the Temple's Destruction (vv. 1–7)

Jesus' prediction of the temple's destruction derives from the disciples' question (v. 1) and leads to his Olivet speech. Bock identifies vv. 1–7 as an important group for several reasons. First, the utterance in v. 2 that "not one stone will be left on top of another" speaks of these local "buildings being completely demolished."[80] The figurative language here does not speak of an absolute or cataclysmic end of the world or even of literal destruction of every stone, but rather Mark's language intends to convey a complete collapse, ending the function of the temple.[81] Second, the disciples' question twice centered on the plural ταῦτα ("these things") indicates that Jesus' remarks deal with "more than the temple."[82] Third, the mention of the prediction of wars, and rumors of wars, means the "temple will be destroyed

---

79. Bock, *Luke: 9:51—24:53*; Turner and Bock, *Gospel of Matthew, Gospel of Mark*.
80. Turner and Bock, *Gospel of Matthew, Gospel of Mark*, 515.
81. Though see Zech 14:21 for final end-time restoration envisaged with the temple.
82. Turner and Bock, *Gospel of Matthew, Gospel of Mark*, 517.

in a period of chaos."[83] Fourth, Bock's understanding of the discourse to v. 7 shows there is a temporal tension to explore. On Mark's statement ἀλλ' οὔπω τὸ τέλος ("but the end will not follow immediately)" Bock writes: "Jesus said that such chaos would still not indicate the end. This is Mark's first direct mention of the end."[84] Bock therefore adduces that the temple's destruction was related to the end time. This means that Mark is grappling with the problem of how the prediction of the temple's destruction is related to the end. Bock's statement about the relationship between the temple and the end emphasizes the inherent relational ambiguity, yet at the same time expresses certainty that the two events are not identical: "How that relationship was to work was not yet detailed, except that the events that pointed to the Temple's destruction would not indicate the end. This remark made it clear that there were many events to come before the return of the Son of Man, which was Jesus' indirect way to refer to himself."[85]

The Abomination of Desolation (v. 14)

The first distinctive theme that can be isolated is the future abomination of desolation. It is also related to history in Mark's thinking because this is the initial fulfillment of Daniel's prophecy in the era of the Maccabeans. Bock's discussion on the abomination of desolation in Mark 13:14 follows his historical study on Second Temple Judaism.[86] Bock's explanatory rendering of the Greek on "the sacrilegious object that causes desolation standing where he should not be" is drawn from Daniel 12:11. Bock's commentary repeats the position articulated in *Luke* about the reference in the prophecy of Daniel to the "desecration of the Holy of Holies." He writes: "The historical example at the root of the image is Daniel's prophetic prediction of Antiochus Epiphanes and his desecration of the Temple in 167 BC (see

---

83. Ibid.

84. Ibid.

85. Ibid. Cf. comments on Mark 13:13. The "end" here refers to the end of "an individual's journey" not to "the final point on the eschatological calendar." Bock, *Gospel of Mark*, 517.

86. Bock, *Studying the Historical Jesus*, 85–90. Bock's argument in this book is clear, though a survey, as it traces the national situation when Israel is "caught politically between Egypt and Syria" and the "arrival of Hellenism" and its challenge to the Jewish Faith.

Macc 1:54; 2 Macc 6:2; other passages in Daniel note the theme; Dan 8:13; 9:27; 11:31)."[87]

Three points can be observed here from Bock's interpretation. First, the referents in the PD view differ from Meyer's and Wright's constructs. Second, the temporal antecedent to Jesus' teaching on Daniel predates the first century, and is significant for understanding the pattern inherent in Mark's discourse.[88] Third, it is reasonable to identify the hermeneutical key of pattern-escalation discernable in the NT intertextuality with Isaiah as applicable. Furthermore, Whitman's theory of typology errs in that it overlooks an existing historical pattern to which Mark's context alludes.

Tribulation, θλῖψις (v. 19)

On Mark 13:19 Bock has a sizable note and subsequent commentary.[89] Bock makes three points with his emphasis falling on a future period of suffering. First, the tribulation of those days will be "unprecedented." At such a time it will be necessary "to flee" but Jesus predicts this may be "difficult."[90] Second, the term, which also appears in Revelation 1:9 and 7:14, refers to a "time of disturbance." Third, the decisive time to which the description points in Mark is the "world rebellion described in Daniel 12:1" which as an "event" mentioned in the discourse "appears . . . at the very end of the speech's timeframe.[91] Bock is able to maintain this reading of Daniel's seventieth week without equating the exile/suffering to "the extension of the seventy years of Babylonian exile to the seventy weeks of years of exile included . . . of time when Jews were back in the land worshipping in the rebuilt temple."[92] This is significantly different from Wright.

---

87. Turner and Bock, *Gospel of Matthew, Gospel of Mark*, 517; cf. 521.
88. Cf. Whitman, "Textual to Temporal," 161–76.
89. Turner and Bock, *Gospel of Matthew, Gospel of Mark*, 521–22.
90. Ibid., 518.
91. Ibid.
92. Newman, *Jesus and the Restoration of Israel*, 260.

The Approach of Progressive Dispensationalism

Transcendent Events (The Premonitory Signs, Arrival of the Son of Man, and Gathering vv. 24-27)

Bock's focus begins with the cosmic significance of Mark's words that "the sun will be darkened, the moon will give no light." The "stars" will fall from the sky. "Starts falling" is not taken literally as this would threaten life itself on earth. Instead, these are astronomical signs and events that precede the arrival of the Son of Man.[93] Along with Lane, he highlights the OT source of themes of cosmic change and judgment. First, as Isaiah 13:10; Ezekiel 32:7; Joel 2:10, 2:31, 3:15, and Amos 8:9 show, connected to the cosmic imagery in Mark 13:24 is the picture of "creation in alternation."[94] The key point is plain: "One reason why no one will need to look for the return of the Son of Man and the vindication he brings is that there will be cosmic signs to signal his arrival"[95] (cf. Luke 17:24). Second, in Mark 13:25, the emphasis is on judgment theology from the OT. Bock highlights that Isaiah 34:4 is cited by Mark when he says, "The stars will fall from the sky and the bodies in the heavens will be shaken," and notes, "This OT theme carried over into Judaism (Judg 5:5; Ps 18:7, 114:7; Amos 9:5; Mic 1:4; Nah 1:5; Hab 3:6; *Testament of Moses* 10:1-5; *1 Enoch* 57:2)."[96] The tenor of Bock's statements follows Evans when he says, "As with the entire speech, these themes were common in texts about the coming judgment."[97]

Connected to the arrival of the Son of Man is the commissioning of the angels (13:27). Bock explains that "he will send out his angels to gather his chosen ones from all over the world" affirms that the "major point" of the arrival of the Son of Man according to Mark is to "vindicate the elect."[98] Furthermore, Bock draws on Second Temple literature to argue that this Marcan theme of gathering from "all corners of the earth" is intrinsically related to the OT message and to the conceptual thought of Judaism. He cites twelve texts in support of this notion: Deut 30:3-4; Ps 50:3-5; Isa 43:6, 66:8; Jer 32:37; Zech 2:6, 10; Tob 14:10; *1 En* 62:13-14; *Pss. of Sol.* 8:28, 11:1-4,

---

93. Bock notes that Josephus records that when the temple burned, a bright star resembling a sword stood over the city and that comets were visible for a year (*Jewish War* 6.5.1-3). Bock, *Luke*, 1667.

94. Turner and Bock, *Gospel of Matthew, Gospel of Mark*, 518; Lane, *Gospel according to Mark*, 475.

95. Turner and Bock, *Gospel of Matthew, Gospel of Mark*, 518.

96. Ibid.

97. Ibid. See Evans, *Mark 8:27—16:20*, 328.

98. Turner and Bock, *Gospel of Matthew, Gospel of Mark*, 518.

17:28.⁹⁹ Bock concludes that with this gathering of the ἐκλεκτός ("elect") who are present at the time of the Son of Man's return, God's people are vindicated. In conclusion, he notes that Jesus ends the discussion of the signs at v. 28 and begins to "summarize" (13:28–36).¹⁰⁰

Pattern in Mark

The final goal is to assess how Bock interprets "pattern" in Mark's Olivet Discourse. What is its basis? If typology is not "foreshadowing" and involves "correspondence" then what does that look like in Mark? In order to understand the PD view of relationships one must trace discussions on persecution. Bock presents evidence that the theme of persecution is a pattern in Mark. First, Bock separates discussion on persecution with certain signs to mark the "onset of the end times" (13:7–8) from the tribulation (13:19).¹⁰¹ The character of this former time and the provisions for this time are spelled out by Jesus. The onset of the end times is marked by persecution at the hands of governors and kings because disciples are followers of Christ (13:9). A reader of Mark will need to discern what Jesus' words mean historically when he or she uses terms like literal and figurative. This persecution will lead to "witness" and widespread travel of the gospel "into the world" (Acts; Rom 1:5, 8; 10:18; 15:18–24; Col 1:5–6, 23). The spiritual enablement for this witness in the face of persecution is because the Holy Spirit is "poured out" (Isa 11:1–2; Joel 2:28–29). Disciples need not fear because God is with them by the Spirit, and there is an indicator that the "messianic age" is realized.¹⁰² Thus, with such divine power and responsibility to deliver the gospel, Jesus ends the first part of his speech with a "call to persevere" (13:13). Bock compares this "exhortation" with Revelation's statement of the "one who overcomes" (Rev 2:7, 11, 17, 26; 3:5, 12, 21; 21:7).¹⁰³

On the other hand, the events described in 13:14 onwards are distinctive of a future period of time. The division occurs at v. 14 because the desecration described in the following verses is not fulfilled in the first century but awaits a future period. Thus Bock treats the remainder of the speech as

99. Ibid.
100. Ibid., 519.
101. Ibid., 520.
102. Ibid.
103. Ibid.

The Approach of Progressive Dispensationalism

yet to be realized and gives three reasons for this. First, the speech refers to a specific event that will "trigger" the end time. Second, the term "abomination" which relates to an event that the text predicts, refers to "shameful acts associated with a place of sacrifice or idolatry (Deut 7:25–26; 1 Kgs 14:24; 2 Kgs 23:13; 2 Chr 15:8; Jer 16:18; Ezek 5:11; *TDNT* 1:598–600)."[104] Bock goes on to explain Mark's reference to desolation in Mark 13 in terms of the famous historical account which Antiochus Epiphanes performed in 167 BC when he erected an altar in the temple and subsequently sacrificed a pig to Zeus.[105] This act "became a model" for the later abomination of desecration mentioned in the Gospel (Matt 24:15), and is distinct from "the destruction of the temple" in terms which Daniel 11:31 predicts.[106] Third, Jesus indicated that when the temple is invaded and a Gentile stands in the Holy Place "the prediction about the Temple was about to occur." Furthermore, in opposition to Lane's suggestion that a future reference is excluded because there are four first-century contenders, Bock notes with Evans that these referents are disqualified. He writes: "Pilate and Caligula never carried out their plan and the Zealots do not fit the description. Titus visited the temple *after* it was destroyed, so there was *no altar to desecrate*."[107] Fourth, the abomination that causes desolation will lead to great tribulation (v. 19). The content of this section of the speech in relation to the Son of Man's return means that "this time is decisively tied to the vindication of the saints."[108] Fifth, the remark concerning the tribulation's uniqueness compared to any period that "precedes or succeeds it" implies that this event will not occur near to the end of history, but to "something before then."[109] This last point rules out Weiss's understanding of an "absolute" end (cosmic collapse) as Mark's framework continues history beyond the crisis.

---

104. Ibid., 521.

105. Bock, *Studying the Historical Jesus*, 85; Turner and Bock, *Gospel of Matthew, Gospel of Mark*, 522.

106. Bock, *Studying the Historical Jesus*, 85.

107. Turner and Bock, *Gospel of Matthew, Gospel of Mark*, 521, italics mine. Cf. Lane who lists a high priest "Phanni" as a probable first century referent. Lane, *Gospel according to Mark*, 467–69. Cf. also David Turner's comments on the parallel in Matthew, Turner and Bock, *Gospel of Matthew, Gospel of Mark*, 313–15.

108. Turner and Bock, *Gospel of Matthew, Gospel of Mark*, 521.

109. Ibid.

The Significance of Figurative Language

Bock's understanding of the passage also rests on the interpretation of the figurative language. In his commentary on Mark, Bock's defense of the physical return of Christ is controlled by several factors. First, he warns against reducing the "image" in v. 24 about the "stars will fall from the sky, and the powers in the heaven will be shaken" to "metaphor."[110] This lesson is learned from Caird's mistake. The reason is because "the return of the Son of Man will bring about a change in the world order even at its most basic physical level."[111] In his Luke commentary, Bock draws on the OT allusion to Daniel when he says Luke "includes the allusion to the clouds because it is the key image of authority (note also clouds in Acts 1:9)."[112] His commentary refers to Driver on the subject of the figure in Daniel who comes "with the clouds of heaven" as one of "superhuman majesty and state."[113] Bock adds, "The association of a figure 'riding on the clouds' or with clouds is normally tied to the authority of God or the gods in the OT (Exod 14:20; 34:5; Num 10:34; Ps 104:3; Isa 19:1)."[114] Jesus' mention of the Son of Man is a reference to this "regal individual." Here is a figure related to the consummation arriving "with great authority like a deity."[115]

Bock also interacts with R. T. France and Wright in the debate over referents and meaning of symbolic language. France argues the language of Daniel and Mark is not about a "visible descent" or return of the Son of Man, but describes Jesus and the church as being given "transcendent power" and authority when the "temple is destroyed."[116] Like Wright, France has a complex argument and involves exegesis in its literary setting and the correlation of texts around the themes of exaltation, authority and

---

110. Ibid., 522.

111. Ibid.

112. Bock, *Luke: 9:51—24:53*, 1686.

113. Driver, *Book of Daniel*, 88.

114. Bock, *Luke: 9:51—24:53*, 1685. Bock identifies the Jewish "Son of Man" imagery (Dan 7:13) and the fact that it is used to describe his "universal worship in the kingdom" as "corporate individual interplay" which focuses on the "king who heads the community." Thus a reference to Israel exclusively is unlikely. Compare also the phrase "representative head" used for the Son of man.

115. Ibid., 1686.

116. On Mark 13:26, see Turner and Bock, *Gospel of Matthew, Gospel of Mark*, 522; France, *Gospel of Mark*, 535. See also "Sharing the Throne of God," in Wright, *Victory of God*, 615, 624–29, esp. 643–44.

The Approach of Progressive Dispensationalism

the arrival.[117] He also holds Mark 14:62 refers entirely to Jesus' vindication. France sets his proposal around the language of "power" in "Mark 9:1, ἐν δυνάμει; Mark 13:26, μετὰ δυνάμεως πολλῆς καὶ δόξης; and Mark 14:62, ἐκ δεξιῶν καθήμενον τῆς δυνάμεως. He also noted the theme of glory in Mark 8:38.[118] Bock makes three points in reply. First, France's interpretation does not clearly explain "how the gathering at the Son of Man's coming constitutes the kind of vindication anticipated in the OT."[119] Second, like Evans, Bock argues that France's interpretation is "undercut" by the idea that this event follows a time of "unprecedented tribulation."[120] Furthermore, Bock's reply to Wright in *The Trial and Death of Jesus* elaborates further on similar themes that France raises and which Bock comments on more briefly in his Mark commentary. The idea that these texts speak exclusively about the perceptions of transcendent power is doubtful for three reasons. First, it removes the source for the church's later eschatological hope (Acts 1:1–9; 3:19–22; Acts 10:42; 17:31; 1 Cor 15:20–28; Rev 19–22).[121] Second, some things Jesus claimed go beyond the exile imagery or "alter it" so that "other imagery might be a better summary description" of what Mark claims.[122] This comment is certainly valid since Wright declares that it is a "serious misjudging" of its first-century meaning to see Mark 14:62 as "a reference to Jesus flying down towards the earth" just as it would it be "a crass literalism" to expect a "physical seeing by Caiaphas" of "Jesus physically sitting on a throne."[123] Third, it overlooks a normal Jewish way of reading history and pattern which Christianity uses (Ps 110:1).[124] However, as it will be seen, there is some agreement between Bock and Wright on the themes of the return of Yahweh to Zion and the defeat of evil.

---

117. This is the fourth set of data which Wright, France and PD acknowledge. Mark 14:62 is a pivotal text and both Wright and France accept a gloss of two-into-one. However distinctions need to be made between "exaltation" and "arrival." Mark connects these two ideas with καί ("and"), so consequently they should not be bundled together. These two are different in kind. These two events are mutually dependent in terms of authority not in terms of imminence. Christologically, one confirms the other but they are not one event mutually dependent.

118. France, *Gospel of Mark*, 535.

119. Turner and Bock, *Gospel of Matthew, Gospel of Mark*, 522.

120. Ibid. See Evans, *Mark 8:27—16:20*, 328–29.

121. Bock, "Trial and Death of Jesus," 121.

122. Ibid., 117.

123. Wright, *Jesus and the Victory of God*, 643.

124. Bock, "Trial and Death of Jesus," 124.

Assessment

Restoration Eschatology: The Wider Context of Understanding Eschatological Relationships

The previous chapters highlighted how Meyer and Wright approach the relationship between history and Mark's transcendent concerns in their interpretation of Jesus' prophecies about the temple. Now the PD perspective and that of Bock in particular has been summarized. This section looks at four points under the theme of restoration eschatology by Wright on the one hand and Bock on the other. A comparison of their wider understanding of restoration eschatology and on their reading of apocalyptic is helpful. The four issues are: (1) apocalyptic structure, (2) narrative history (exile), (3) chronological sequence in the book of Daniel, and (4) referents and historical fulfillment in key texts with ER.

Apocalyptic Structure and Sequence

PD does not differ fundamentally from the basic apocalyptic structure of suffering and vindication that Wright presents.[125] For example, Bock does not argue that Wright's proposal is a "denial of eschatology and apocalyptic"[126] or that it is "escapist" in the sense that God is not acting "in history through Jesus."[127] Furthermore, Wright like PD speaks of apocalyptic as looking for ultimate vindication. He recognizes that "Israel's oppression" at the hands of Gentile foreigners is central to understanding apocalyptic.[128] This is the concept of positive and negative apocalyptic.

Two motifs placed into this framework by Wright are also accepted by PD. Bock also affirms the temple "shows a recalcitrant and corrupt present system, ripe for judgment" and that Jesus declares that it will "pass away" for a time, not permanently as Wright argues.[129] Second, concerning Jesus' last week of ministry, PD affirms that Jesus did foresee both the defeat of

---

125. It has been stressed by Travis that "at the heart of apocalyptic faith is its "movement towards the future." See Travis, "Value of Apocalyptic," 76.

126. Newman, *Jesus and the Restoration*, 119.

127. Ibid., 111.

128. Ibid., 257.

129. Ibid., 114.

The Approach of Progressive Dispensationalism

evil and the return of Yahweh. The solution Jesus presented to the Jewish establishment is that "salvation comes through Jesus the Messiah."[130]

Historical Narrative (Exile)

It is important to realize that PD is not opposed to Wright's theme of restoration and motifs of "new exodus."[131] Therefore there is no need to argue that most Jews did not think the "exile" was still continuing in Jesus' time. Rather the question of reading apocalyptic turns on hermeneutics and exegesis of specific texts. Wright's response to critical assessment of his view on the "new exodus" motif symbolically lived out in Second Temple history reveals the influence of E. P. Sanders: "restoration eschatology . . . is an appropriately loose term to denote various movements that could locate their different agendas within the broad hope that Israel's god would act decisively to restore the people's fortunes and to reestablish them as in the days of old."[132] Wright goes on to argue that the "larger narrative history" which Jews lived under in Second Temple Judaism and in time of Jesus included an unbroken hope for deliverance from Gentile oppression. This much is true, but it needs to be explained in light of the character of OT apocalyptic and its conceptual framework.

Chronological Sequence

There are clear points at which Wright and PD disagree. One issue raised in the last chapter is the claim by Wright that apocalyptic is linked to a broad period of history. Wright's perspective here is taken directly from the condensed schema in Daniel 9:24–27. He says: "Daniel 9 declares that the period of exile has continued long after the Babylonian exile and that it will be brought to its climax in the strange events which concern the abomination of desolation and the cessation of sacrifice, and, yet more strangely, 'an anointed one' who 'shall be cut off and shall have nothing' (Dan 9:26); and, not strangely at all, the time when the 'troops of the prince who is

---

130. Ibid.

131. For support of various studies that explore methods and themes with the OT in the NT, see e.g., "New Exodus," in Bock, "Scripture Citing Scripture," 264. For others who use the "exile" motif as a paradigm of the eschaton about the nature of Christian hope, see Dunn, "He Will Come Again," 43.

132. Newman, *Jesus and the Restoration*, 254.

to come shall destroy the city and the sanctuary' (Dan 9:26)."[133] Wright also believes that this interpretation of the scheme of Daniel 9:24–27 offers a "specific chronological sequence" that is coherent enough to sustain this narrative world.[134] He thus equates the "prolongation of the period of exile" (the theory that Jeremiah's prophecy is reinterpreted or reapplied) as representing the "70 years of Daniel."[135] Thus, Wright's concept of "exile" as a possible historical phenomenon is based on interpretation of apocalyptic from the OT and Judaism suggesting an extended "period of history" of national suffering looking for a "climax."[136] In contrast, PD places an emphasis on apocalyptic tribulation as a special period in the future. The basis of this interpretation is the character of Daniel's and Jesus' teachings of unprecedented turmoil and their use of pattern escalation hermeneutics. PD shows a difference lies in understanding the meaning and referents of Daniel's seventieth week, the Day of the Lord, the final consummation of restoration of Israel/elect, the end of transgression, end to sin and the atonement of iniquity of Israel, all of which Daniel affirms (Dan 9:24). The key distinction to note here is that PD holds the NT can do more with the Old through progressive revelation, and never less.

Referents and Historical Fulfillment

PD understands that a difference exists between short-term persecution and predicted distant suffering which relates to Israel in the "Great Tribulation." This will be so severe in the tribulation that God will shorten the time (Mark 13:20). PD affirms that specific requirements are revealed in Mark 13:14 for the desolation described in Daniel. Other suggested referents of the desecration (e.g., by Lane[137]) lie outside the apocalyptic pattern of crisis followed by restoration which Bock calls the "final decisive resolution."[138]

133. Ibid., 259.
134. Ibid., 257–58.
135. Ibid., 259.
136. Ibid.

137. See Lane, *Gospel according to Mark*, 276. Josephus contemplated fulfilment in Gaius Caligula's attempt to erect a statue of himself in Jerusalem's temple in AD 40 (*Ant* 18.257–60, 261–88) and then in the destruction of the temple in AD 66–70 (*Ant*. 10.276). Restoration is a less prominent theme in Josephus. Nevertheless, it is noteworthy that Josephus recognized the subsequent restoration of the sacrificial system by Judas Maccabeus after the desecration by Antiochus Epiphanies (*Ant*. 12.321–24).

138. Bock, "Trial and Death of Jesus," 120.

The Approach of Progressive Dispensationalism

Thus, with respect to prophetic and apocalyptic hope and its various motifs, PD differs fundamentally on historical *fulfillment* because it identifies different *referents*. This impacts not only how the OT promises relate to Jesus' teaching about the "elect" but on how one reads the NT realistically in terms of traits inherent in the present age.[139]

Furthermore, according to the Synoptic Gospels historical fulfillment is also linked to the Day of the Lord. This key eschatological theme is emphasized in the OD as Jesus' "coming in judgment" at the end of the age.[140] It is important to understand the kind of time envisaged in the coming in judgment. The time of Jesus' coming will feature "trouble and distress, of great evil and persecution."[141] Matthew 24:15 (Mark 13:14; cf. Luke 21:20) highlights many "themes, features and literary citations" from OT prophecies concerning the coming Day of the Lord and makes "explicit reference" to Daniel's vision of a coming time of great suffering marked by the activity of one "perpetrating an abomination of desolation."[142] Blaising and Bock therefore adduce that Jesus integrated "the prophets' notion of a coming Day of the Lord with Daniel's vision of a coming time of trouble."[143] This results in a "synthetic prediction of evil and judgment" which represents the historical context of the Christ's coming.[144]

The Validity of Typological-Prophetic Interpretation

The final question is whether there is reasonable evidence in support of the PD position that pattern-prophecy is indeed what Mark is presenting. There is evidence that the "certain signs" which will mark the "onset of the end time" (13:7–8) are distinct from Mark's later transcendent concerns (13:24–27). There is enough ambiguity here to suggest that this theme fits with a pattern-prophecy hermeneutic. First, Jesus' image of ἀρχὴ ὠδίνων ταῦτα ("beginning of birth pangs"; cf. Mark 1:1) carries this notion of the

---

139. Cf. Ladd, "Why Not Prophetic-Apocalyptic," 192–200. Ladd (Historic Premillennialism) holds the trait of "pessimism" was one of the basic differences between prophecy and apocalyptic. For support of "pessimism toward the present age" as the dominant trait of apocalyptic, see Osborne, *Hermeneutical Spiral*, 226.

140. Blaising and Bock, *Progressive Dispensationalism*, 238.

141. Ibid., 239.

142. Ibid.

143. Ibid.

144. Ibid.

onset of a distinct phase of salvation history. It is commonly agreed that these general persecutions are not extraordinary. Second, understanding the "tribulation period" as specific and "open" and not linked to the crisis of AD 70 is reasonable. Further, the reference to an antecedent in an abomination which was extraordinary in Second Temple history is sound exegetically and shows the pattern is not simply one of "type to antitype" or of "shadow to reality" (cf. 1 John 2:18; 2 John 1:7). Third, Jesus' statement that this θλῖψις ("tribulation") will be unique οὐ γέγονεν ἀπ' ἀρχῆς κόσμου ἕως τοῦ νῦν οὐδ' οὐ μὴ γένηται ("unlike any period that precedes from the beginning of creation that God created until now") fits this pattern interpretation and means that it is distinct from "general persecution" occurring in every generation. Furthermore, if the abomination is the trigger to further eschatological events, then suffering at this magnitude does not fit today's circumstances. Finally, Bock's observation of a "repetitive pattern" in the second mention of false prophecy in Mark 13:21–23 and Matthew 24:23–28 which further emphasizes the warning in Mark 13:5–6 and Matthew 24:4–5, is convincing.[145]

Conclusion

This chapter sought to show how interpretation of themes in the OD is linked to one's position on the relationship between history and Mark's transcendent interests which includes the arrival of the Son of Man. If the view is taken that there is no ambiguity in Mark's account then a choice is required to settle the eschatological problem. Fulfillment of the prophecy must be located either to AD 70 or the Parousia. However, if one recognizes Marcan ambiguity as intended by the author, then the hermeneutical issues are significantly different. The relationships become discernable not by deciding demarcations *a priori* in the text between AD 70 and the Parousia but by exploring the patterns in OT prophecy. The PD approach uses this line of reasoning. The goal of the next chapter is to explore Mark's figurative language in the context of Second Temple Judaism in order to ascertain its character and conceptual framework. When apocalyptic language is no longer assumed *a priori* to be "figurative" then the content of the sermon may be seen as emphasizing the continuity and discontinuity between Judaism and Mark's version of Christian teaching.

---

145. Bock, *Luke*, 1683.

6

Hermeneutics and Exegesis of Mark 13:1–2 and 13:24–27

Introduction

CHAPTER 4 ARGUED THAT there is a pattern relationship between the predicted events of AD 70 (Mark 13:1–2) and end-time events described in Mark 13:24–27 which look beyond AD 70. It is the opposite of Caird's position, which associates a pattern with the language but rejects any relative comparison which is not merely figurative or loosely connected to political themes in the final fulfillment. This chapter explores the hermeneutical and exegetical issues underlying this thesis in order to understand who Jesus is, and his view of the future. It is necessary to examine five areas in the key passages: (1) questions about form and tradition, (2) the structure and imagery of Mark 13:1–2 and 13:24–27, (3) the eschatological relationships in these passages, and (4) their interpretation. Then, (5) the pattern in Jesus' teaching is identified and four themes in the discourse are traced. By tracing the development of these themes (suffering, salvation, and signs) from Jesus' discourse in the parallel accounts the different temporal perspectives are highlighted. This is followed by exploring the mission in Matthew 10:23.

All three Synoptic Gospels recognize the pattern. It will be seen that Luke focuses on AD 70 while Matthew focuses on Jesus' Parousia. The synoptic parallels are possible because the structure of the tradition includes unrestricted forms (notably the "look-you" second person plural imperatives) and restricted third person singular and plural forms that signal one-off events. This structure allows the tradition to be transferred to another *Sitz im Leben* and thus it allows the theological implications of Jesus' sermon to be highlighted. The resulting elasticity of the Discourse may be tested on the level of meaning of the shared referents and the textual world of AE within Judaism and the Jesus tradition. By observing specific similarities and differences across the synoptic parallels it is possible to assess these shared meanings for their theological, cultural implications.[1] This section will conclude briefly by analyzing points where Mark's text correlates with other NT passages.

The future teaching of Jesus and specifically his role as the eschatological Son of Man is essential to consider. As teacher and prophet Jesus highlights the typological-prophetic pattern (the category followed) that links the historical crisis to the Day of the Son of Man. Apocalyptic reveals what is otherwise a secret. Cosmic topics are adduced and issues are present in Mark's discourse as he moves to describe the descent of the Son of Man "from above" to bring final restoration to the righteous. The cosmic imagery, which is often described as myth relates to a historical base. This does not mean that Mark's discourse is made up. This kind of language and its function is important because it relates to what is otherwise a secret: the *universal in-breaking* of God's kingdom revealing Jesus' power and authority.

The Prediction of the Destruction of the Temple
(Matt 24:1-2 / Mark 13:1-2 / Luke 21:5-6)

Form and Tradition

Mark 13 opens with a conversation between Jesus and some of his disciples over the destruction of the Jerusalem temple. Matthew and Luke describe the saying about the temple's destruction with slightly different emphases than Mark. The main verbal agreements of the opening section are τοῦ

---

1. The work on cultural differences is stimulated by the work of Pym, *Translation and Text Transfer*. It will be shown that the conceptual framework of apocalyptic transfers to all traditions. This is the forward moving characteristic of apocalyptic, or a forward sequence of events, in which suffering is followed by final vindication. Second, that variations exist on themes in the OD because they are localized. For example, Mark has less material on the judgment of Israel's enemies and a simpler focus on restoration.

Hermeneutics and Exegesis

ἱεροῦ ("the temple"), and the third-person singular speaker (εἶπεν) as Jesus. Mark's Greek is simple. This opening section has a vocative of address ("teacher") yet lacks complex subjects and titles in comparison to Mark 1:1 and Revelation 1:1.[2] The subject of the temple saying is λίθος ("stones") and οἰκοδομάς, ("buildings"). The disciples ask a direct question to Jesus (αὐτῷ) and Jesus answers with a prediction. Details on who asks the questions vary. Luke's version records "some spoke" while Matthew and Mark's versions point to the disciples' enquiry. As the subject matter and literary framework of this section of the narrative is the same in three versions, there is no doubt that Jesus' sayings are the source.

Structure and Imagery

The structure and imagery highlights a use of dramatic figurative language in a historical setting. The metaphorical statement in question is οὐ μὴ ἀφεθῇ ὧδε λίθος ἐπὶ λίθον ὃς οὐ μὴ καταλυθῇ: "Not one stone will be left on another; all will be thrown down." The referencing to the λίθοι in the figurative language is direct.[3] Matthew's version is explicit when he adds τὰς οἰκοδομὰς τοῦ ἱεροῦ (Matt 24:1). Luke and Matthew (Luke 21:5 / Matt 24:3) agree the resulting destruction will be distinctive (καταλυθήσεται, literally "it will be torn down").[4]

The imagery in the opening scene only hints that apocalyptic may be introduced later in the discourse. There are several factors supporting this view. History related to the temple is clearly included in apocalyptic literature. Judaism expected that the nation would face catastrophe and that the temple would be damaged (Dan 9:17, 20–27).[5] Furthermore, this figurative

---

2. There are no first person subjects ("I-here-now") in Mark 13 that commonly portray a note of finality attached to judgment in the JAT. The sixteen imperatives spread throughout the discourse begin in v. 3 (e.g., βλέπετε). They point to the literary integrity of the discourse, signal participation of disciples, and indicate that the tradition circulated orally as a unit before it was written. These second person imperatives also allow Mark's discourse to be transferred into other cultural contexts (e.g., Matthean community) and developed according to the Jesus tradition and certain apocalyptic themes. On the significance of sixteen imperatives and other differences with the JAT, see Cranfield, *Gospel according to Saint Mark*, 388. Beasley-Murray, "Rise and Fall of the Little Apocalypse Theory," 348. Morris, *Apocalyptic*, 88. On the lack of strong eschatological motifs in aphoristic sayings, see Piper, *Wisdom in the Q-Tradition*, 9.

3. See also *Pss. Sol.* 2:1.

4. BDAG, 521 (s.v. καταλύω "a demolition process").

5. The writer of Daniel looks back on the events of 586 BC yet he expects that

language is itself coded. This is suggested grammatically in the lack of instrumental datives explaining how the destruction occurs. Moreover, tales of war typically used hyperbolic language to support the imagery of destruction.[6]

Eschatological Relationships

A wider framework of eschatology is not evident here. The principle subject of the Discourse is the destruction of the temple but this is not exclusive. A complex metaphor constructed from a historical base would require a change in the main subject. It is plausible that Mark exploits the figurative language associated with war to introduce a complex metaphor that will include apocalyptic predictions that appear in non-parallel events. An eschatological framework, in which a future tribulation and signs need to be experienced prior to the final restoration, is therefore a possibility. Furthermore, the possibility of temple destruction implies a possible cyclic scenario as history attests.

Interpretation

The language about the destruction of the temple cannot be assumed to be "literal" or "absolute." Jesus teaches about God's plan. So when Jesus asserts in hyperbole that "no stone will be left upon another," it is intended as a judgment statement. The disciples are privy to the saying but it is directed at the religious establishment. The reference to destruction is specific. The resulting meaning of the metaphor is that Mark means nothing less than a catastrophic destruction of the Jerusalem temple (Mark 14:58, 15:29).[7] Jesus, no doubt,

---

Judaism will triumph. This concept is the crucial other half of the story of the Day of the Lord (Isa 27:1, 12; Zech 12–14). The messianic woes must be endured before deliverance (Isa 13:6–10; 26:17; 34:4; Dan 7; 9:20–27; 12:1–4). The writer of *1 Enoch* shows great awareness of suffering associated with the Gentiles. In *1 En* 103:1–2, 14–15, "the sinners" are Gentiles who bring terrible suffering to the "righteous." *1 En* 96:1–3 associates the day of the Lord ("those days") with the condemnation ("woe") of the wicked and hope for the righteous. The wicked are apostate Israel. *1 En* 1:1–2 gives a blessing for the elect who have endured "suffering" and witness the removal of the ungodly ones. In *1 En* 5:7–8 the elect triumph over the wicked. In *1 En* 91:6 oppression and injustice are followed by divine judgment. The scheme of suffering followed by deliverance, and the destinies of both groups are established by divine decree.

6. BDAG, 156. See Reader and Chvala-Smith, *Severed Hand and the Upright Corpse*, 197–99. Heater, "Destruction Genre in the Prophets."

7. See also Acts 6:14. Jesus' temple actions are also telling, Mark 11:15–19; 12:9.

had in mind a major disruption not a permanent end for the temple.⁸ The implication of Jesus' prediction is that the Jewish religious system, for now, is coming to an end, resulting in social upheaval for Judaism at large.

The Coming of the Son of Man
(Matt 24:29–31 / Mark 13:24–27 / Luke 21:25–28)

Form and Tradition

The saying on the premonitory signs and the coming of the Son of Man are preserved in Matthew and Luke in similar but also distinct versions. The form of the Marcan version including its three scenes has been retained entirely by Matthew and two scenes are retained by Luke. The order of the premonitory signs is the same in all three Gospels. The paratactic links of the different signs with καὶ from the source text are preserved in scene one. Similarly, scene two introduced by καὶ τότε ὄψονται is retained in all three gospels, and Matthew follows Mark with καὶ τότε ἀποστελεῖ in scene three. The eschatological association concerning the gathering of the elect is of less importance and significance to Luke. The shaking of "powers" in the heavens is the climactic "sign" in all three versions. Similarly, the climax in all three narratives is the coming of the Son of Man. This indicates the unit is not handed down as an independent logion. Slight rewording and expansion in the versions, however, have taken place.⁹

The similarities in basic form and Semitisms show the tradition is old. Moreover, the logical breaks indicated by καί are part of paratactic structure that lays events side by side in typical Jewish fashion. This is evidence of Jewish origin. The sayings contrast "power" in the manner of Judaism's tradition, yet the differences in the gospel tradition point to the sayings unit being unique to Jesus. There is no reason to suppose that the differences of Mark's approach to those in JAT writings are secondary.¹⁰

8. Zech 14.

9. Matthew's version follows Mark for the most part but Luke's account is shorter. After v. 29 in Matthew's account a further description of the sign of the Son of Man is added with καί: "then will appear the sign of the Son of Man in heaven . . . all the tribes of the earth will mourn." Luke's version has a shorter description of signs and omits any mention of gathering the elect. After v. 25 in the Lukan account a further prediction and explanation of suffering on earth is attached with καί: "and upon the earth distress of nations in perplexity at the roaring of the sea and the waves, then men fainting with fear and from the expectation of what is coming on the world."

10. Isa 13:9–11; 14; 34:1–3; 66:22–24; Jer 4:23–26. Note the climatic word on Babylon.

Structure, OT Allusions, and Imagery

The saying in Mark 13:24-27 is subdivided into three scenes not found as a unit in the JAT. The premonitory signs are followed by witness to the coming of the Son of Man, and then the sending of the angels to gather the elect. In v. 24, the first scene uses a contrast (ἀλλά) to introduce the signs. The remaining two scenes are each introduced by the coordinating conjunction καὶ τότε and the adverb τότε (vv. 26 and 27) which maintain the logical and temporal links to the events that follow.[11] Thus, the apocalyptic signs are signs of the "coming of the Son of Man" and signal a tight calendar of events. The first καὶ τότε in v. 26 links the Son of Man section temporally to the preceding signs. The second καὶ τότε introducing v. 27 links the activity of the Son of Man to the subsequent commissioning of the angels to gather the elect. The first three subjects in vv. 24-25a of Mark's construct ("sun," "moon," and "stars") reflect the Semitic style of the LXX. The paratactic structure using καί found in the prophets (e.g., LXX Isa 13:10; cf. Isa 24:4) is rearranged so that the unified saying from Isaiah 13:10 remains but the subjects are changed with stars mentioned last and with the sun and moon first. A parallel is also evident with Joel 2:10 which mentions the sun, moon, and stars. In Joel, the scene is one of "darkness"; the stars fail to shine but in Mark they are "falling." Mark does not mention ἡ ἡμέρα τοῦ κυρίου (Joel 2:11; LXX) but the allusions to eschatology in his account are clear.

Table 3. Use of Isaiah in Mark 13

LXX Isaiah 13:10, 13:13 and Isaiah 34:4 MT	Mark 13:24-25a and 25b
οἱ γὰρ ἀστέρες τοῦ οὐρανοῦ καὶ ὁ Ὠρίων καὶ πᾶς ὁ κόσμος τοῦ οὐρανοῦ τὸ φῶς οὐ δώσουσιν καὶ σκοτισθήσεται τοῦ ἡλίου ἀνατέλλοντος καὶ ἡ σελήνη οὐ δώσει τὸ φῶς αὐτῆς ὁ γὰρ οὐρανὸς θυμωθήσεται καὶ ἡ γῆ σεισθήσεται וְנָמַק כָּל־צְבָא	Ἀλλὰ ἐν ἐκείναις ταῖς ἡμέραις μετὰ τὴν θλῖψιν ἐκείνην ὁ ἥλιος σκοτισθήσεται, καὶ ἡ σελήνη οὐ δώσει τὸ φέγγος αὐτῆς καὶ οἱ ἀστέρες ἔσονται ἐκ τοῦ οὐρανοῦ πίπτοντες, καὶ αἱ δυνάμεις αἱ ἐν τοῖς οὐρανοῖς σαλευθήσονται.

---

11. BDAG, 1012 (s.v. τότε, §2).

Isaiah 13 is a key background text to Mark 13:24–25a. Twice we see an exchange of verbs with Isaiah 13:10 LXX (σκοτισθήσεται / οὐ δώσει) and exchange in antecedent (αὐτῆς) and in coordinating conjunction (καί). The first καί links the first two subjects, the sun and moon. The second καί in v. 25 describes the third subject in this cosmic scene as "stars of the sky." The allusion to stars "falling" is closer to early apocalyptic texts (Isa 34:4 LXX; πίπτει). This passage predicts that the stars of heaven will wither ὡς ("like") leaves that wither and fall from a tree. The image of the heavens "trembling" in Isaiah is like that found in various psalms. Elsewhere in Judaism it is found in wisdom literature written prior to the Maccabean revolt in 185 BC.[12] The third καί introduces a fourth subject αἱ δυνάμεις ("powers") and functions as a climax to the signs and has no direct allusion in the LXX.[13] In spite of the rearrangement within the OT saying and the inclusion of the saying on the powers being shaken (Isa 34:4 MT / Mark 13:25b), the basic OT meaning is the same. However, Mark adduces both cosmic and spiritual realms in the signs logion of Jesus that he formulates.

The context of Isaiah 13 is an oracle concerning Babylon which is further identified with "sinners" (13:10). Babylon is rich because she has "silver" and "gold" and she is the powerful "jewel of the kingdoms." The passage describes a time of terror and wrath because evil will no longer go unpunished in the Day of the Lord. God will bring disaster against Babylon and she will lose her power and glory on that Day (13:19–20). That day will also reveal cosmic upheaval involving the sun, moon, and stars (13:10). Such descriptions of cosmic upheaval are followed consistently in the JAT.[14] Natural phenomena are not overlooked, however, in the ancient Near East. Clay Assyrian tablets record a significant cosmic event—a total solar eclipse over Nineveh, June 15, 763 BC.[15]

---

12. Ps 17:8; 81:5. Sir 16:18 ἰδοὺ ὁ οὐρανὸς καὶ ὁ οὐρανὸς τοῦ οὐρανοῦ ἄβυσσος καὶ γῆ ἐν τῇ ἐπισκοπῇ αὐτοῦ σαλευθήσονται. See BDAG, 911 (s.v. σαλεύω, 1 "cause to move to and fro"). Cf. also Sir 48:19; Rev 6:13.

13. In the LXX Ps 102:21 αἱ δυνάμεις refers to "armies" (NJB) "warriors" (NET), "hosts" (RSV). See also 2 Chron 26:11; 1 En 4:10; 1 Macc 7:2; 3:42. Cf. LXX Ps 148:2 "heavenly hosts" (RSV), "heavenly assembly" (NJB).

14. Sometimes nature is viewed as perfect in contrast to sinners in pre-Maccabean times before Hellenism intensified: "Everything functions in the way God has ordered" (1 En 5:2–3). Elsewhere nature is changed: "in those days... luminaries shall faint and tremble" (1 En 102:1–3). Some wisdom literature (Sir 16:18) predicts the sky and heavens shake when God comes to "punish sinners." In all cases a contrast between the wicked and righteous and between cosmic powers and the environment is envisaged.

15. Bury et al., Cambridge Ancient History, 149.

ESCHATOLOGICAL RELATIONSHIPS AND JESUS

Figurative Language

Three metaphorical expressions involving seven subjects in the discourse deserve examination to support the interpretation of an interactive metaphor. Mark's use of the OT in fresh circumstances invites their assessment. The first metaphorical expression is found in reference to the premonitory signs involving the first three subjects (vv. 24–25). The reference to the series is a direct one, referring to the "sun," "moon," and "stars." The periphrastic participle in 13:25 describes the stars falling from heaven from an earthly perspective. This meaning contrasts to the vision of the "stars" in 1 *Enoch* 86–87 in which fallen angels are described allegorically as stars. In contrast, to the first three signs, the fourth sign of the future shaking of "the powers in the heavens" is less direct. The heavens were viewed as spiritual forces (*1 En* 40:9; 65:6; 82:7–8; 91:16; 92:19; *Jub* 1:29; 49:2; *Mart. Ascen. Isa* 2:2) and so the shaking of the "heavenly bodies" (NIV) indicates a rattling of power in the spiritual realm. This apocalyptic climax of the cosmic signs signals a further shift in power in the wider environment.

The second metaphorical expression involves the fifth group of subjects as future participants (v. 26). The saying is formulated so that the subject is not explicitly named. The third person plural is neutral not allegorical (ὄψονται; literally, "they will see").[16] The referencing is direct and refers to "all people" who witness the coming of the Son of Man. This moves the discourse to a universal level in contrast to the earlier discourse which indicated the disciples' participation in the events. For example, v. 5 (βλέπετε μή τις ὑμᾶς πλανήσῃ).[17] The object of the verb is τὸν υἱὸν τοῦ ἀνθρώπου. The background imagery is the heavenly realm from Daniel 7:13–14. The theme of "riding on clouds" is an issue for Wright and is a key Jewish theme that impacts Mark 13:26.[18] The point of the figure "riding on clouds" is not primarily heavenly cloud travel. Rather, it represents the authority and access of a unique individual before the throne in the heavenly court.[19] The outworking of this presentation from Daniel 7:13–14

---

16. Cf. *1 En* 89:20, the rescue of the sheep (Israel) by the Lord.

17. We notes there is an indicative boundary signaling a change in recipients from shared to indefinite transfer where the subject becomes so general it almost always does not include the disciples.

18. See Bock, *Blasphemy and Exaltation*, 201.

19. Cf. Acts 1:6–11 and 1 Thess 4:14 as examples of progressive revelation on this issue of ascending and descending in clouds. Acts:1:6 says Jesus will return the same way he ascended.

is assumed in the saying. In Mark, the introduction of a subsidiary subject of "all people" who see the Son of Man in a definitive fashion, points to an eschatological framework.

The final metaphorical expression is the gathering of the elect by angels (v. 27).[20] The gathering of the elect or righteous is an OT theme (Deut 30:4; Isa 11:11, 16; 27:12; Ezek 39:27).[21] But certain features can be understood as highly figurative and indirect: the Son of Man sends his angels ἐκ τῶν τεσσάρων ἀνέμων ἀπ' ἄκρου γῆς ἕως ἄκρου οὐρανοῦ. The saying οἱ τέσσαρες ἄνεμοι ("four winds") is common in Judaism and can mean "the four directions or cardinal points" and typically appears in the LXX and Josephus to describe cosmic and earthly boundaries (Ezek 37:9; Dan 7:2; Zech 2:10; 1 Ch 9:24; Jos *Ant.* 8.80; cf. Job 28:25; 1 Enoch 18:2-3; cf.76:1-12).[22] Three spatial relationships are figuratively envisaged: (1) ἐκ ("from") the four winds, (2) ἀπό ("from") the boundary of the earth, and (3) ἕως ("until") the boundary of the sky. The spatial characteristic of this gathering is an activity that moves from one end of the earth to the other.

The gathering of the τοὺς ἐκλεκτοὺς ("elect") is presumably a referent focused on this group in contrast with the sinners (cf. Mark 13:20, 22; *1 En* 1:1).[23] Mark does not elaborate. The saying, however, sets up a contrast between those who are righteous and the pitiful circumstances following the temple desecration and human plunder (Mark 13:14-18).[24] The vindication of the righteous is therefore presented as a central theme of the return of the Son of Man and a goal of kingdom consummation.

---

20. The concept of the future vindication of the elect or chosen people was present in the first century (*T. Mos.* 4:2; 12:12-13).

21. See also, Meyer, "Many (= All) Are Called"; Meyer, *Christus Faber*, 90.

22. See BDAG, 77 (ἄνεμος §2) for the figurative sense. Cf. §1, wind as a blowing atmospheric phenomenon (Matt 14:24; Mark 6:48; Matt 14:30; Mark 4:39, etc.). The Book of Watchers begins with Enoch's ascent to heaven (14:8-16:3) and then return to earth at the start of chapter 17-19 for his first earthly journey. In 18:1-2 he arrives at the ends of the earth where he saw the "treasuries" or storehouse of all the winds and the foundations of the earth. Enoch learns the function of the four winds is to support the foundation of the earth, and the firmament of heaven, and heaven itself (*1 En* 18:1-5). See Bautch, *Study of the Geography*, 100.

23. Bauckham notes the "elect" and "sinners" accompanying the admonitions and woes in *1 Enoch* is a "contrast between the ways of life of two categories of people" (1:1 others). Bauckham, "Apocalypses," 146. Written prior to the Maccabean revolt the sinners in the *Epistle of Enoch* are probably not Gentiles but Jewish apostates.

24. Note in v. 18 the genitive of time: ceimw/noj ("during winter").

Eschatological Relationships

Four crucial statements of the discourse from Jesus' teaching can be highlighted in connection with the three-part scene/framework as the consisted basis of the synoptic texts. Each scene has a connection to an eschatological "location" of power in the cosmos or on earth. Within the logion there are three "location" sayings and one saying of "accompanying power." The deployment of traditional Jewish location markers in the text is another reason for assessing them.

Scene 1. The "time" saying, viewed as relatively remote, begins with: Ἀλλ' ἐν ἐκείναις ταῖς ἡμέραις.[25] Mark's Greek in v. 24 places the emphasis on specific circumstances that form a sharp contrast to the suffering mentioned in v. 19. In this saying Jesus identifies a different period from that of the temple's desecration as a period of cosmic activity. This remoteness is reinforced by reference to the same "suffering" from v. 19. Somehow the cosmic activity that unfolds is μετά ("after") suffering and something that precludes a parallel event to Mark 13:1–2. Instead this is part of the prelude to restoration; something that is expressed by the eschatologically distant object, τὴν θλῖψιν ἐκείνην (cf. v.19). This presupposes that Jesus knew about the OT "messianic woes" (Isa 13).

The double saying of the "sky" and "heavens" forms the second eschatological "location" and functions with a third, in v. 26. It is focused on "seeing." The saying presumes an eschatological process where events are visible. This is made clear in v. 26 where the human participation is made explicit. At the same time at which the sun and moon cease to shine (v. 24) two other cosmic events occur. First is a saying about the third subject with the metaphorical expression "the stars will be falling from the sky." This is an image of cosmic alteration not total collapse. Jesus alludes to Isaiah, and uses this metaphor directly to describe the natural place where one sees stars fall: ἐκ ("from") the sky. Second, is a saying about how the powers will be shaken in the heavens. This saying unfolds the place where the fading cosmic powers will be shaken and represents the fourth subject in the unit. The eschatological collapse occurs ἐν ("in") the heavens. What, then, is the relationship between location and the contrast of AE? Going into the imagery of scene one (cosmic signs) is a Gentile rule which emerged from the temple desecration, unprecedented suffering. The signs of scene one therefore signal the approach of a change in power.

---

25. BDAG, 302 (s.v. ἐκείναις).

Hermeneutics and Exegesis

Scene 2. The "seeing" saying represents the third eschatological location leading out of the cosmic activity. The fifth subject (ὄψονται = all people) is definitively identified as a group of participants. Jesus asserts, using the figurative language from the prophet Daniel of the heavenly scene and authority to act as a prelude to restoration. "Riding on clouds" is separate to "coming in clouds." Daniel's image is changed. In Mark's account many people on earth will see the coming of the Son of Man "in clouds." In general, a restoration is envisaged. A fuller grasp of the function presupposes an understanding of the Son of Man in the prophet Daniel. Mark does not formulate this primarily in terms of specific advantages or disadvantages for recipients but with regard to the Son of Man's universal coming.[26]

The "accompanying power" saying requires examination for its eschatological relation to the coming of the Son of Man. Jesus asserts, in the language of Daniel 7:13, that he is the eschatological judge. This claim, and the challenging contrast between Gentile rule and his own rule, on behalf of his elect is now made clear. This saying of the Son of Man's visible coming with a change of power is evident from the use of the prepositional phrase: μετὰ δυνάμεως πολλῆς καὶ δόξης. Determining the meaning of this phrase depends on a solution to the following problems. First, what is the nature of the phrase?[27] The genitive is personal, indicating a personal coming accompanied with great power and great glory.[28] It is clear that divine authority accompanies the Son of Man from the object of the preposition: μετά ("with") great power and glory. Second, the temporal terms μετὰ τὴν θλῖψιν ἐκείνην (v. 24) and καὶ τότε (v. 26) indicate the coming as somehow related to the restoration of those who have experienced suffering. Third, v. 26 is not an early church allegory for receiving power. That view flattens a true apocalyptic contrast. Rather, Jesus asserts the contrast between all power, whether in the cosmic or spiritual realms, and the authority and power of the Son of Man to bring restoration and judgment. The contrast is not between church and Israel but the apocalyptic contrast between old and new environments and old and new orders and powers. Mark 13:2 and 13:24, each introduced by kai, need not be taken as parallel, because the contrast in 13:24 is not between the power of Judaism and that power transferred to disciples. Such a reading is contrary to Mark's gospel (Mark

---

26. Compare n9.
27. BDAG, 637 (s.v. μετά, §A3b).
28. See Mounce, *Basics of Biblical Greek Grammar*, 61n16. Mounce notes the object with the genitive is usually a "person or a personal concept."

8:31). Furthermore, since those who "see" are distinct from disciples (Mark 13:3; Βλέπετε) the phrase μετὰ δυνάμεως πολλῆς καὶ δόξης cannot mean that Christians have power and glory as France argues.

Scene 3. The third scene (v. 27) presents two corresponding eschatological actions that follow in time. Mark's style is typically minimalistic. Both sayings are formulated so that the subject is not explicitly named for the verbs ἀποστελεῖ τοὺς ἀγγέλους, "he will send angels," nor the next clause (which is linked by καί) ἐπισυνάξει τοὺς ἐκλεκτοὺς αὐτου, "he will gather his elect." The antecedent of the subject in the verbal ending is the "Son of Man" (v. 26). The activity described here, while still abstract, echoes the promises made in Daniel 9:26–27 (LXX) concerning the completion or end to the troubles which the elect experience, and which the end-time decree addresses. Responsibility designated to the Son of Man is operative here through this public display of gathering the elect.[29] Mark 13:14 has not specifically mentioned any decreed end to desolations. However, this is the second instance where Mark envisages a universal event connected with restoration and judgment. The gathering is cosmic in its scope and determinative because it is authorized by the Son of Man. The saying is given an equivalent expression and expansion in Matthew's version where the gathering occurs with "a loud trumpet call." Matthew has understood the saying as another eschatological sign (cf. Isa 27:12–13; Zech 9:14). It is very Jewish (*Pss. Sol* 8:1; 1 Macc 4:13) and taken together suggests that his tradition has implicit knowledge residing in his community about these events. Luke omits this saying and instead offers a description of redemption. Thus the Synoptic Gospels reflect a culture of belonging in which eschatological relationships are developed appropriately to levels of each community's understanding. ER are expanded thematically in Matthew and explained with a descriptive gloss in Luke.[30]

As the conclusion of the cosmic signs, the events of the coming and gathering are dramatic. The apocalyptic prediction presupposes a local proximity and visual activity which (1) relies upon a spatial dualism, (2) has an eschatological connection supported by Jewish background, (3) requires a thematic movement from negative apocalyptic to positive apocalyptic, (4)

---

29. BDAG, 974 (s.v. συντέλεια) and BDAG, 242–43 (s. v. δίδωμι, §13, 7) "to grant by formal action" and "appoint to special responsibility." Cf. Luke 21:24 for a more concrete image of the troubles. In the Septuagint, the object of the preposition ἐπὶ ("on," "against") is τὴν ἐρήμωσιν ("the desolations") which the end decree finally addresses. Mark 13:14 does not specifically mention a decree to end desolations.

30. Aland, §292. Note the switch to the second person plural personal pronouns.

Hermeneutics and Exegesis

allows for equivalent expression and expansion in other versions, and (5) leads to a change of environment and power as part of end-time restoration.

Interpretation

Apocalyptic reveals what is otherwise a secret. The resultant meaning in Mark 13:24–27 is the visible descent of the Son of Man. The contrast is not between "suffering" and "the reception of power" for the disciples or for Jesus. The implications of Jesus' words are encouraging. The contrast revealed is an apocalyptic theme; the change between old and new environments, and old and new orders and powers that lead to the restoration of Israel. Jesus presents himself at the center of God's redemption plan for Israel. The "Son of Man" is Jesus' favorite title for himself. Jesus exercises his authority to commission his angels to gather the elect, thus implying a time when Israel again has a central role in God's plan. Somehow he will bring about their vindication against Gentile powers when he comes visibly with divine power and glory.

Identifying a Pattern in Jesus' Teaching

Before the thesis that AD 70 is like the end can be validated as short-term and long-term points of fulfillment, it is first necessary to identify a pattern in Jesus' future teaching. Has an initial period of the messianic woes predicted in Daniel 9 already been fulfilled? What will the end-time tribulation look like? The purpose here is not to examine the pericope in detail but merely to identify the pattern in Jesus' teaching to affirm this is Jesus' view of the future. It is recognized in three ways. The passages are assessed in the reverse order in which they appear in the OD.

The Desolating Sacrilege (v. 14)

In v. 14, Mark says, "But when you see the desolating sacrilege set up where it ought not to be (let the reader understand), then let those who are in Judea flee to the mountains." This imagery is related to what occurred in 167 BC when the temple was desecrated and shows continuity with the OT prediction of Daniel 9:2 concerning the ἐρημώσεως Ιερουσαλημ ("desolation of Jerusalem" resulting in the exile) and τῶν ἐρημώσεων ("those abominations")

Daniel 9:27. While some thought the Daniel passage was fulfilled, Jesus teaches, from his perspective, that there will be another desecration.[31] In other words, Jesus has a complementary perspective that views the text of Daniel 9 from the stand point of later events (connected with the text's origin) and, short-term events not connected to the text originally. So is Jesus solely dependent upon a Jewish apocalyptic standpoint to view Daniel 9 in light of AD 70? No. His role as teacher and as Messiah is the basis for indicating that AD 70 is like the end. Jesus simply recognizes the pattern for the end in what Jewish groups in the Maccabean wars assumed was the final event. Mark recognizes this pattern and uses a strong contrast (δέ) to introduce an event that is portrayed as less certain for the disciples.

There is good reason to hold that a typological historical pattern is in view from apocalyptic Daniel 9, and therefore that the prediction in Mark 13:2 is relative not absolute. First, the language in Daniel 9 is flexible allowing multiple referents as the language is general.[32] Second, the use of Daniel in Mark 13 is difficult and appears arbitrary. The text of Mark 13:14 does not preserve generally the categories defined by Daniel 9:27. This is not considered an explicit citation of Daniel 9:27 in the Greek Jewish Scriptures (OG) and so an historical pattern may apply. Third, Mark does not have "I–here–now language" typical of Jewish apocalypses, which give the impression the imminent climax of history has been revealed. Mark's allusion does not mention the temple directly whereas the translator of the Septuagint has made a referential transfer to the temple (τὸ ἱερὸν). Thus, it is unclear whether the predicted event is related Ὅταν δὲ ἴδητε (Mar 13:14, "but whenever you see") to an immediate absolute event or whether it is relative and intended for some distant time. Given this ambiguity it is best to see two periods of time are delineated: the time from the temple destruction leading to general persecution and the time after the act of desecration. Mark's parenthetical comment, ("let the reader understand") must be adduced as pivotal to the literary start of eschatological distant events; it requires discernment to identify the sequence of catastrophic events that follow. Here is where the synoptic writers go in different directions.

---

31. 1 Thess shows Paul was aware of this theme of desecration, and he expands it.

32. The NEB has the sense of the MT as "those abominations." In other translations the multiple referents and elasticity of the text in 27c is left unclear. The NIRV has sense of "hated thing" *being set up*. The NIV has "an abomination." This is the referent (singular) that remains until the Lord brings the end he has ordered. There is no sense of occurring desolations. The MT could be translated "those abominations." The NET translates this as "abominations."

The End Is Not Yet (v. 7)

A second point states that the eschatological day is not the same as the historical crisis because certain signs point to times of wars, and rumors of wars, and persecutions, yet "the end is not yet" (Mark 13:7). Mark has already described AD 70 in vv. 1–2 but proceeds to mention for the first time in v. 7 that these things are "not the end." So Jesus clearly anticipated a future period which is called τὸ τέλος. The important point is that Jesus' teaching has two periods in mind. With these two periods the similarities help define the pattern of events between the initial and final fulfillment.

The Disciples' Questions to Jesus (v. 4)

The evangelists have phrased the disciples' questions differently to suit the expansion in the discourse associated with the pattern that Jesus gave, as short-term prophecy, and as a final fulfillment that awaits.

In vv. 3–8 Mark describes the disciples' question to Jesus. Mark reads: πότε ταῦτα ἔσται καὶ τί τὸ σημεῖον ὅταν μέλλῃ ταῦτα συντελεῖσθαι πάντα ("when will these things happen? And what will be the sign that *all these things* are about to take place?"). Here a difference is noted with Luke. The short-term fulfillment is stated more explicitly with Luke: πότε οὖν ταῦτα ἔσται καὶ τί τὸ σημεῖον ὅταν μέλλῃ ταῦτα γίνεσθαι "When will this be, and what will be the sign when these things (tau/ta) are about to take place" (Luke 21:7).

Matthew's version says, "What will be the sign of your coming and the end of the age" (Matt 24:3). Matthew highlights that what was originally promised in Daniel (the time of the end) is not excluded. But this is a separate issue that needs validating if the discussion is to be advanced. The issue is that Matt 10, associated with the eschatological day in Matt 24, has a parallel in Luke (Matt 10:17 / Luke 21:12), and Luke tends to emphasize AD 70. Nevertheless, the typological prophetic pattern of Jesus is expressed differently in the synoptic accounts, but together the evangelists' perspectives show that God's program is continuing.

The Development of Themes from Jesus' Discourse

The tracing of these themes highlights the theological, literary and temporal differences in the Synoptic Gospels. Appendix 1 sets out to sketch a synoptic framework within which verbal actions may be used in interpreting the patterns in eschatology.

1. Delay

The idea of suffering/judgment is developed by Luke in 21:20 to highlight that the events predicted about temple desecration relate to Israel's historical crisis (Mark 13:1–2). The next major move in Mark's sequence is the desolating sacrilege (§290). Some say that Mark and Matthew (Mark 13:14 / Matt 24:15) take their referent from Luke 21:20 on the city surrounded. But there is no justification for overlooking the allusion to Daniel and the introductory apocalyptic setting which is part of biblical typology. What would Mark's readers make of such an interpretation without Luke giving them the referent. Luke has changed the referent to Jerusalem and warns about fleeing the city before the day of vengeance.[33] The time of fulfillment is uncertain to Jesus.[34] Initial fulfillment occurred in AD 70: "but when you see Jerusalem surrounded by armies, then know that its desolation has come near." This verse shows an expansion of the messianic woes theme. Understanding Jesus' perspective of a pattern in OT prophecy, which adds a short-term fulfillment, makes this possible. Luke therefore focuses on the short-term crisis for Israel even though its activities are patterned around the future time of "unequalled distress" or tribulation recorded in Mark (§290; Mark 13:14–20; Matthew 24:15–22; Luke 21:20–24). God sent his Messiah but the people rejected him.[35] Later when the end-time tribulation comes before the Son of Man is revealed, there will be greater suffering as Mark and Matthew attest (Mark 13:19 / Matt 24:21; cf. Dan 12:1).

2. Imminence

Luke 21:20 also functions literarily in the first section of Luke's gospel which describes Jesus' journey to Jerusalem (Luke 1–19). How did Luke handle the theme of imminence here? Did Luke see delay as well? Chapter 17 responds to this question and reveals Luke's literary and Christological

---

33. "God will punish Jerusalem" (NIRV).

34. Note Luke follows Mark's indefiniteness: "but whenever you see . . ." (21:20). A study of Mark's use of characterization and mood in the story reveals the verbal action described is not a shared transfer situation. See appendix 2.

35. Luke 13:33–35; John 1:11.

insights about the role of the Son of Man. This passage reiterates, at some length, the signs sayings prior to the day when the Son of Man is revealed, with accounts that parallel Matthew in their scope (Luke 17:24 = Matt 24:27; Luke 17:26–30 = Matt 24:37–39). Even though Luke writes from within a largely short-term perspective, it can be adduced that final fulfillment is present also with the end-time descent of the Son of Man, not AD 70. This is clear for several reasons. First, Luke's use of parataxis (καὶ τότε ὄψονται: Mark 13:26 = Matt 24:30 = Luke 21:27) at the same place in his version, is consistent with the Jesus tradition and functions to signal a parallel event to the other evangelists. Second, the language of "lifting heads" to see redemption is literal for seeing the descent not metaphorical for understanding an enthronement or transfer of power to the disciples. Luke presents Jesus' enthronement as an unobserved fact not an observable event revealed for people to see (Luke 22:54–71 / Mark 14:53–67).

A further confirmation of the pattern and Luke's commitment to final fulfillment is adduced from the saying denying the arrival of the Son of Man in short-term events that were realized in AD 70; the issue is one of imminence. The context in Luke is one where the reader might expect to see such deliverance: "the days are coming when you will desire to see one of the days of the Son of Man, and you will not see it" (Luke 17:22). This reading of delay and imminence is consistent with the pattern in Jesus' teaching. Luke simply presents it differently from his literary perspective.

Another way Luke 21:20 functions literarily in the gospel is through Luke's highlight on Jerusalem as the place of short-term judgment: "when you see Jerusalem surrounded by armies . . . its destruction (ἐρήμωσις) has arrived." First, the order of the temptation accounts varies and closes with Jesus' temptation on the pinnacle of the temple (Luke 4:9–13). Second, Luke places an emphasis on Jesus' sorrow over Jerusalem's approaching desolation at the hand of her enemies (Matt 23:37–39 / Luke 13:34–35; and Luke 19:41–44). In other words, Jesus knows Israel will be judged for her rejection of the Messiah. So, Luke balances his short-term focus on the signs which in the context of his version of the OD relate to the temple's destruction realized in AD 70 with a long-term perspective. In short, Luke 17 and 21 shows that Luke's long-term perspective passages are complementary to his short-term perspective passages.

3. Signs

Treatment of this third theme helps highlight the hermeneutics of short-term fulfillment coming out of Jesus' discourse. Luke emphasizes the short-term aspects of the pattern in Jesus' discourse. This becomes clear in Luke 21:25–28. Jesus taught that AD 70 is like the end. Knowing Jesus' ministry at the outset, Luke in contrast to Mark and Matthew, associates the end-time signs with the future events of AD 70 (note v. 25: Καὶ ἔσται σημεῖα). Historically, Josephus recounts that when the Jerusalem temple burned, a bright star like a sword stood over the city and that comets were visible for a year (Jos. *War* 6.5.1–3). The future fulfillment of such a sign is in keeping with such cosmic changes on display in the first century; where it differs will be in its intensity. When people see the signs they will be able to recognize the pattern. In this way, Jesus' typological interpretation of Daniel's prophecy is not retrospective. The signs are also not to be taken literally. And so one would not expect literal stars (other suns) to fall to the earth as this event would have detrimental consequences for life on earth. Jesus is not predicting the literal end-of-the-world at this point in time.

How are these differences expressed in their details of the pattern in Jesus' teaching? Luke developed the idea of short-term aspects of the pattern more intentionally than Mark and more explicitly than Jesus. Jesus' teaching is in line with Daniel's prophecy predicting the great end-time suffering. But by having Mark's perspective, his own tradition material, and the hindsight of viewing Jesus' ministry as a whole, Luke developed Jesus' prophecy toward its short-term meaning involving the scenario of AD 70 while retaining the original meaning of Daniel 9 that points to the end-time. In short, chapter 17 of Luke shows that the original intent of Daniel's prophecy is not lost.

In sum, Meyer's and Wright's observations of the short-term line of Jesus' prophecy are valid because it is correct to highlight short-term referents from Jesus' sermon found in Luke and certain passages in Matthew. However, the construct fails to grasp the problem and presence of an indeterminate pattern in Jewish prophecy and Jesus' teaching which shows continuity and discontinuity with Israel. The recognition of a final fulfillment within Jesus' teaching is essential to placing the OD and parallel passages in the framework that Jesus indicated.

Hermeneutics and Exegesis

1. The Development of the Theme of the Vindication of the Righteous in Matthew 10:23 and Jesus' Pattern-Typological Teaching

The question that remains: if the "coming" described in Matthew 10:23 is fulfilled in AD 70?

Having established Luke takes a predominantly short-term view of Jesus' teaching in the use of Jesus' pattern the remaining question is what does Matthew do? Specifically how does Matthew develop the theme of the salvation of the righteous remnant in Matthew 10:23? This section makes some observations related to the topic, then it examines how Matthew develops the theme concerning the disciples' mission, and finally it explores the differences in Matthew as another example of Jesus' teaching of two ages by exploring another theme in Luke (God's visitation) which also highlights differences between Christianity and Judaism. It is important to show that the nature of the pattern can encompass events in AD 70 and the end-time. Are the themes necessarily highlighted in both the short and long-term fulfillment? No. It will be shown that the pattern in Jesus' teaching is not always retrospective in all the themes with a prophetic-typological interpretation. In other words, the various events related to the historical crisis and the coming of the Son of Man are distinguished in the pattern of fulfillment in Matthew 10. So the themes of suffering and the proclamation of the message of salvation are fundamental to the pattern not the return of the Son of Man which stands as a unique event in the future.

Peculiar Issues Concerning the Pattern in Matthew

The issue of explaining how Jesus' pattern operates in Matthew is vital to the topic of eschatological relationships and Jesus. It is observed that Matthew is more explicit than Mark concerning the use of such terms as Parousia, end of the age and how the righteous will be reached. Related to these observations is the issue of entry into the future kingdom. Earlier discussion noted that Mark does not mention how the righteous will be reached in his treatment of the restoration of Israel; only the result. Even here the gathering is in "code" form and involves ministering angels. This is clear because both sayings are formulated so that the subject is not explicitly named for the verbs Καὶ τότε ἀποστελεῖ τοὺς ἀγγέλους αὐτοῦ, "he will send angels," nor the next clause (which is linked by καί) ἐπισυνάξει τοὺς ἐκλεκτοὺς αὐτοῦ, "he will gather his elect" (Mark 13:27). Nevertheless, Mark clearly identifies τοὺς ἐκλεκτοὺς ("the elect") in his text as the well known recipients of God's salvation in the Day of the Lord.[36] However faith through grace is always a prerequisite of entry into the kingdom in Jesus' teaching as the constructs have noted. It will be no different in the consummation of the kingdom of God. PD holds that the gospel goes to all because Jesus is Lord of all. Entry, however, into the kingdom and the realization of God's rule is not operative without faith and this is significant for the future judgment also (Matt 13:24–30).

The Development of the Theme of the Righteous in Matthew 10

The idea of the vindication of the righteous is developed in Matthew 10:23 according to Matthew's understanding of Jesus' pattern and by an emphasis on Jesus' mission given to the twelve disciples. Understanding Matthew's development of this theme in relation to Luke's and in light of the pattern revealed in Mark is important to understanding how the pattern is developed differently. The acceptable part of a compromise on the question of AD 70 and the future end-time crisis is therefore based not on a general pattern per se but the specific development of the pattern according to each theme. Discrimination between themes helps identify the nature of the pattern in Jesus' teaching. The synoptic framework in appendix 1 seeks to outline the key themes and their relationships in the Synoptic Gospels. Differentiation in the treatment of themes is therefore essential to advancing the discussion on the pattern in Jesus' future teaching in several ways.

First, Donald Carson and PD both agree where the differences are with regard to AD 70 and the Parousia according to Luke and Matthew. The problem occurs when one works with Matthew singularly. Specifically, is Matthew's "coming" in 10:23 fulfilled in AD 70? Should Matthew's command to φεύγετε ("fleeing") in 10:23 do with the description of desolation and typology from Daniel (§290) or the fate of the disciples and

---

36. A few introductory observations are in order. There are important contextual connections between Mark 13:24–27 and 13:14–20 (§290 Desolating Sacrilege). The elect are mentioned three times in Mark 13 so clearly a new discussion emerges. Kubo notes three out of eleven occurrences of the term in the NT appear in Mark here. Kubo, *Reader's Greek-English Lexicon*. The contrast in v. 19 is of the elect suffering in great tribulation compared to the resolution through restoration out of it in v. 27. Verse 27 (the third scene of Mark 13:24–27) describes the gathering of the righteous people by the angels.

Hermeneutics and Exegesis

persecutions foretold (§100 and §289). This is not an easy problem to solve hermeneutically or literarily since its related themes are associated Luke 21:12 with both (Matt 10:17-22 / Mark 13:9-13 / Luke 21:12-19 and Matt 24:15 and 16 / Mark 13:14 / Luke 21:20-21).

Even when the texts are analyzed for their relationships the pattern is "seen" but not observed. The reason is because the literary and historical features of the texts in their present context and the context of the source text (i.e., Matthew) are not taken into account. Luke's gospel tends to take a short-term view on the crisis. Added to this the prevalent notion of an imminence framework and that apocalyptic is a reapplication of the OT and it is clear why fresh meaning in the text is not considered.

Table 4. Sequence in Persecution

Matthew 10:18, 23	Luke 21:12
καὶ ἐπὶ ἡγεμόνας δὲ	καὶ διώξουσιν ὑμᾶς, παραδιδόντες εἰς τὰς συναγωγὰς καὶ φυλακάς, ἀπαγομένους ἐπὶ
καὶ βασιλεῖς ἀχθήσεσθε ἕνεκεν ἐμοῦ εἰς μαρτύριον αὐτοῖς καὶ τοῖς ἔθνεσιν v. 23 Ὅταν δὲ διώκωσιν ὑμᾶς ἐν τῇ πόλει ταύτῃ, φεύγετε εἰς τὴν ἑτέραν· ἀμὴν γὰρ λέγω ὑμῖν, οὐ μὴ τελέσητε τὰς πόλεις τοῦ Ἰσραὴλ ἕως ἂν ἔλθῃ ὁ υἱὸς τοῦ ἀνθρώπου	βασιλεῖς καὶ ἡγεμόνας, ἕνεκεν τοῦ ὀνόματός μου

Matthew 10:23 is a prophetic text relocated by Matthew from the OD and contains teaching about a future mission from Jesus' viewpoint. It is placed by Matthew in its new literary context and addresses the disciples' mission to Israel (Matt 10:1-42). In this saying, Jesus teaches the twelve disciples and sends them out to preach the good news of the kingdom with this warning: "When they persecute you in one city in which the people of Israel live, flee to another. I tell you the truth, you will not finish going through all the towns of Israel before the Son of Man comes."

Matthew 10:23 seems at first to fit as a direct parallel to Luke 21 as the disciples will be brought before governors and kings in both accounts. And both texts are close at a historical level in *this relocated* context but in a limited way. The kingdom message will be preached by the disciples with the expectation that the righteous will believe the message and be vindicated. A lengthy time is envisaged by Jesus as the saying mentions coming before governors and kings (cf. Acts 4:24–25). So in this way, Matthew follows the short-term mission of the disciples both the immediate future and a time after Jesus' resurrection. But the passage also functions at a literary level as historical pattern since it originally takes its context from the OD which focuses on the end time. The original saying of Jesus in Matthew 10:23 retains its original end point—the eschaton, even though extracted from the OD and placed in a fresh context. In other words Matthew's account presents a collapsed eschatology.[37] So what does its meaning become? Matthew, who understands the pattern in Jesus' teaching and the end point of the discourse, recognizes that Jesus points to the end also when followers will go through the towns of Israel with the message of salvation. They will not complete this task before the Son of Man comes. Matthew moves it by pattern to relate it to the historical situation relevant to the twelve disciples and adduces the needs of the church while retaining the original end point which is familiar to Jewish readers, namely the final fulfillment of Daniel's prophecies. So a "coming" in Matthew 10:23 is not fulfilled in AD 70 because it does not function historically here—only literarily as the final fulfillment of Jesus' future prophetic scenario. Historical realization of the Day of the Son of Man theme is indicated in its original source text, namely Matthew 24, which has its own literary context.

What does Matthew's treatment of the pattern and his differences from Mark's account imply both theologically and culturally? Or alternatively, what constraints did each inspired author potentially face? The redaction changes in Matthew and differences in content on the themes associated with Jesus' teaching highlights two potential constraints. First, the Synoptic Gospels show that in terms of developing the message of Jesus about the future there are no solo performances. In other words, no one evangelist can tell the whole story, or nuance all the themes which Jesus taught in his future teaching. Second, in his sovereignty and wisdom, God has chosen not to reveal everything in his plan at once. PD recognizes, and critical realism affirms, that the biblical authors did not have final understanding of what terms like vindication ultimately meant. Furthermore, the differences between Matthew and Mark and between Luke and Mark show that the biblical authors adopted different literary and historical perspectives

---

37. See appendix 1.2 §100 Fate of the Disciples.

in their writing. Capturing both a short-term theme (the fate of the disciples) and the final Day of the Lord theme within a biblical typological reading, Matthew's text can be viewed as prophetic and apocalyptic or PA.[38] Juxtaposing two different settings or sequences is entirely fitting for how apocalyptic operates. Tracing the sequence is paramount. Viewed within a synoptic framework, Mark 13:14 matches Matt 24:16 and can be a continuing antetype to Daniel's prophecy which is forward moving to the final time of desecration. And Matthew 10:23 serves as a historical pattern to flee the coming time of vengeance (appendix 1, no. 2 and 3). This category for Matthew 10:23 is better called typological-HISTORIC because the pattern can be anticipated by the language in Mark and it is related in some sense to OT prophecy. Thus, awareness of how a biblical text operates at a variety of levels, and how such readings are complementary to each other, is essential. Taking a step back further still, biblical readers need to read not only historically, and literarily but also canonically.

Third, the evangelists faced the potential constraint of the readers understanding Jesus' teaching, in primarily grasping the presence of a pattern and then its various themes. These themes reach back into Judaism and have their antecedents in the OT and the history of Israel in the period of Second Temple Judaism. Pedagogical understanding of the pattern was therefore primary. Secondary, it seems was the level of detail associated with certain themes, which in theme or detail may not have belonged to the audience's *Sitz im Leben*. The example of Matthew telescoping the day of the Son of Man in relation to the short-term mission of the twelve disciples (cf. Matt 28:19–20) is a detailed and complex reading that Mark avoids. It is possible that Matthew is able to develop this theme in Jesus' teaching because he senses his audience, to whom he writes, has either implicit knowledge (or forgotten knowledge) in their tradition. It may be fair to assume Mark's audience lacked such a detailed knowledge and understanding of eschatology. In any case, the presence of the pattern in Jesus' teaching is primary as is the disclosure, whether in code or more clear speech that Jesus will return one day.

---

38. See appendix 2, "Sequence and Literary Relationships in the Synoptic Gospels."

Eschatological Relationships and Jesus

Exploring the Theme of the Two Ages: A Comparison with Luke's Theme on the "Visitation"

Exploring the different perspective of Matthew's account above compared with that of Mark and Luke is aided by examining how Luke expands a promise made about God's visitation on Israel to show its short-term fulfillment (Luke 1:68, 78–79; 2:28–32; 7:16; 19:44; Acts 15:14).[39] The purpose here is to demonstrate the Matthew intends two periods when he collapses his eschatology in linking the mission of the righteous to the vindication of the eschatological day in Matthew 10:23.

The theme of the salvation of the righteous in the future aspect of the kingdom is like the different perspective between Luke 7:16 and Luke 19:44 in referring to the visitation of God, and shows a difference in two periods. Luke states the people of Nain recognized God had visited his people in Jesus, "a great prophet."[40] In contrast, Luke 19:44 reveals that Israel had missed the time of her "visitation." The "visit" continues, however, in spite of Israel's rejection of her Messiah and thus failure to believe. Matthew's expansion of the mission theme to the righteous with the final vindication overlaps with Jesus' teaching to the twelve disciples, and shows that the mission continues. He does not need to create a short-term fulfillment. He only needs to connect the two events by the pattern that he recognized in Jesus' teaching. Matthew's development of Jesus' teaching to the disciples is in connecting it by a long trajectory to the final day because he recognizes the short-term mission is a pattern for the salvation of Israel. This salvation is thus different to ways which Judaism presently understands because she has rejected her messiah. Matthew's perspective is possible because of Jesus' teaching and because of progressive revelation. The connection of the final vindication to the mission of the disciples (in the short-term fulfillment) is also for the benefit of the church to point to where God's plan is ultimately leading. The church is another term unique to Matthew as distinct from Israel. The two terms thus related show that somehow, there is a distinction between Israel and the church, and that salvation is linked to what God is currently doing through Christ. Israel does not recognize her Messiah currently. But from the perspective of the eschaton (Matt 24) God will give Israel another opportunity when the righteous will be reached; that somehow from their perspective, in the future, Israel will look in a

---

39. See Bock, "Son of David and the Saints' Task," 447.
40. Ibid.

typological-prophetic way to the past to see what God has done in the mission and is being done for them.

The two periods are further delineated by comparing the OD with Matthew 10:31. In the OD signs occur "immediately after" the tribulation and the Son of Man comes "at that time." Associated with this time is an announcement that "all the nations will mourn" (Matt 24:30). Matthew 10:18 makes the point the disciples will be God's persecuted messengers. Matthew 10:23, which holds to the ultimate vindication of the righteous, takes its reference point in time as the OD. So by application of the pattern, Matthew's "coming" in 10:23 does not function historically in the short-term context of AD 70, but only in its original context in the OD.

Summary

This section has demonstrated that the gospel writers understood that a pattern existed in Jesus' teaching. For Jesus, AD 70 is like the end. It has also demonstrated that the Synoptic Gospels distinguish between the short term, and long-term fulfillment of certain events in Jesus' discourse according to the pattern and always with its ultimate scope in mind. Finally, that the redactional theme of the final vindication in Matthew's gospels is based on Jesus' teaching but links together additional material outside the OD to further highlight synoptic differences and provide proof that such moves are evidence of understanding a pattern that is original with Jesus. PD emphasizes that a correct reading of these texts requires careful identification of five worlds: (1) the historical event, (2) the writing of the event, (3) subsequent response to the written work, (4) the present reader—who can take a canonical perspective, and (5) the scope of the text or where it is leading. Understanding Matthew's account of the disciples' mission in light of the restoration of righteous Israel then requires familiarity with all five worlds. Furthermore, these differences, in general, are a result of wider reflection on Jesus' career and teaching as a whole according to the pattern he held; and specifically in relation to cultural differences which nuance finer points of Jesus' sermon for readers in particular. The basis of this second claim is derived from making observations of the similarities and differences in the Synoptic Gospels with consideration given to readers' level of familiarity and understanding (or potential ignorance) of the JAT in relation to Jesus' teaching.

The pattern is not retrospective in all areas. This means that Jesus' coming does not require a short-term referent. Only the historical crisis prediction, realized in AD 70, is like the end. How Mark's teaching correlates to other NT texts is now explored.

Correlation to Other New Testament Texts

There are several NT passages outside the Synoptic Gospels that correlate with Mark 13:24-27. Some specifics of the comparison are as follows:

Mark 13:26 correlates well with Acts 2:19-20 and 3:19, and even more clearly with Acts 1:11. The first passage calls for Israel to repent so that times of refreshing may come: "Turn to God, so that your sins may be wiped out, that times of refreshing may come from the Lord, and that he may send the Christ, who has been appointed for you." Peter continues: "This one heaven must receive until the time all things are restored, which God declared from times long ago through his holy prophets" (Acts 3:20 NET). For Peter, the restoration of Israel is still future and it is historical. The phraseology in Luke's account of the ascension includes "looking intently up in the sky," "a cloud," and "sight" (Luke 1:9-11). The bodily return of Jesus is something Acts 1:9 predicts.

The combined synoptic accounts of the coming of the Son of Man, with its fuller explanation of signs, divine judgment, and fear of humanity correlate very clearly with 1 Thessalonians 5:1-3. Here Paul expounds the coming Day of the Lord. Destruction will come upon people suddenly, "as in labor pains on a pregnant woman and they will not escape." The apocalyptic signs in 1 Thessalonians 4:16 appear to fit well with our text. The concepts of divine "payback" to Gentiles fit with 2 Thessalonians 1:6-10. However, 1 Thessalonians 4:16 and 1 Corinthians 15:52 strikingly parallel each other more obviously than with Mark 13:26 because in these passages the trumpet sounds awaken the dead at the Parousia. Considering Galatians as an independent tradition, its similarities with Mark are minimal. Galatians has an apocalyptic shift in the sense of a climactic turning point in the divine purpose.[41] However the sharp contrast in the two-worlds in Galatians 1:4; 5:1 (cf. 1 Cor 2:6-8; 2 Cor 4:4) represent a significant theological development in the light of the cross and a "coming to faith" in Christ which is described using traditional apocalyptic terminology (Gal

---

41. Martyn, "Apocalyptic Antinomies," 50.

1:12, 15; 3:25; cf. Rom 8:1).⁴² Mark has clearer parallels with other themes in Galatians such as life in the Spirit and the "spiritual powers" which restrain humanity.⁴³ This reflects the fact that AE in Galatians is in realized form.

The book of James, generally, has the lowest level of correlation but focuses a great deal on enduring present trials and temptations. James has no traditional apocalyptic signs. Instead, "the judge is standing at the door" (Jam 5:9). The scene fits with the "historical" apocalypses (cf. *Pss. Sol.* 8:28–32; 17:26–27). James does fit well with Mark 13:9–12 on the theme of difficulties in faithful living, but not with Mark 13:24–27. Similarly, the restoration of the "fallen tent of David" in Acts 15:16 appear to parallel present salvation more obviously than with a gathering in Mark 13:27.

The concept of apocalyptic eschatology having spacial and temporal perspectives has striking parallels with 1 Peter and Jude. Jesus is exalted in heaven and "angels, authorities and powers are subject to him" (1 Pet 3:22). Similarly, in terms of positive and negative apocalyptic, the final judgment is one aspect of apocalyptic events; salvation is the other (1 Pet 1:3–9; 5:10–11). The "messianic woes" in 1 Peter 4:12–19 has the lowest level of correlation with Mark 13 because Peter describes the believer's trials in terms of Christ's sufferings prior to his "revelation" or return.⁴⁴

Mark 13:27 correlates well with Jude 14–15. Jude obviously has a direct quotation from *1 En* 1:9 in vv. 14–15—the only formal quotation from this written source: "Behold, the Lord comes with thousands upon thousands of his holy ones to judge everyone and to convict all the ungodly of all the ungodly acts they have done in the ungodly way, and of all the harsh words ungodly sinners have spoken against him." We may view Jude as a tradition independent from Mark (but perhaps close to Matthew's tradition). Like 1 Peter, the present persecutions are viewed by Jude as an eschatological crisis.

The spatial realm of Mark 13:24–27 is equivalent to 2 Peter 3 which also depicts the Day of the Lord: "the present heavens and earth are reserved for fire being kept for the day of judgment and destruction of ungodly men" (v. 7). Mark 13:24–27 has few parallels with 2 Peter 3's temporal elements. Large divergences in temporal events are observable in 2 Peter 3, which correlates better with Revelation 21:1 than Mark 13. Mark 13:26

---

42. See n2.
43. Gal 5:16–22 and 3:21–4; 4:3–4; 8–10.
44. See Davids, *First Epistle of Peter*, 15.

does correlate well with 2 Peter 1:16 because of the theme of the power and return of Jesus Christ.

Considering the book of Revelation as an independent tradition source, its correlation with some subjects in Mark is still high. The sun turns black (Rev 6:12). The stars in the sky fall to the earth (Rev 6:13; Isa 34:4 LXX). However, its correlation with other subjects in Revelation is lower. The moon turns blood red (Rev 6:12). The sky recedes like a scroll and every mountain and island is removed (Rev 6:14). The pattern of additional revelation and variation in referents is observable. The first of the seven angels sounds his trumpet and hail and fire is hurled upon the earth (Rev 8:7). The fourth angel sounds his trumpet and a third of the sun, moon and stars are darkened (Rev 8:12). Correlation is absent, however, in the fallen star allegorically described as an angel (Rev 9:1). Revelation 19:11 has a striking parallel with Mark 13:26 regarding the heavenly realm. "Heaven is opened" and a descent is described. Correlation decreases, however, in that the descending individual rides a white horse; he "judges" and "goes to war." This image is more graphic than the cryptic saying depicting war in Matt 24:28 / Luke17:37. Thus, as in Mark, both kinds of metaphorical expressions are employed in the passage and context determines the meaning.

Similarities and Differences in the Constructs

The three constructs by Meyer, Wright and Bock, differ significantly in their hermeneutical presuppositions regarding a perceived relationship between Mark 13:1–2 and Mark 13:24–27. This is not just a matter of a better reading. In Meyer's approach the texts are read in parallel and reflect the events of Jesus' death and the formation of the messianic building after the temple is destroyed early, while in Wright's view, the destruction of Jerusalem is the vindication of believers after church persecutions, while in PD, the texts describe separate events and show that patterns are at work in prophecy.

The strict categorization of Jesus' teaching into public and private ministry and the lack of distinction between Jesus' resurrection and Parousia are common to Meyer and to some extent Wright. The idea that the Olivet Discourse only explains what Jesus taught cryptically in public is a major presupposition in their interpretations. This model fails to distinguish between a historical and literary reading. In short, it overlooks Matthew's redactional concerns to develop the typological-prophetic pattern in Jesus' teaching. So, while critiquing Schweitzer on his interpretation of Matthew

Hermeneutics and Exegesis

10:23, Meyer's reading evidences a hermeneutical blind spot. Thus, he interprets the text entirely within a short-term framework. PD recognizes that a biblical text can be read at a variety of levels. PD also advocates that a text placed in a new literary context requires fresh assessment.

Thus, differences exist, between the constructs in their emphasis on their "global" perspective or worldview. For Meyer, Jesus' temple saying dominates. Meyer takes Jesus' prediction to "destroy this temple" literally (John 2:19).Wright stresses the ongoing exile in the land. He views suffering as an extended part of negative apocalyptic scenario in Second Temple Judaism. PD recognizes overlap in Jesus' teaching on suffering between his private and public ministry. However, a significant difference is a pattern of suffering that escalates in the final end-time period. Thus, the subject of the unprecedented historical crisis is neither Jesus' ministry and passion nor the ordeal of AD 70, but eschatology. The constructs correlate least on this point.

Mark 13:24–27 represents the signs at the end-time suffering subsequent to the coming of the Son of Man to restore his elect. The meaning that Meyer and Wright give to the text is that power is transferred to the church when the temple is destroyed. The "newly gathered" people of God live under the authority of the enthroned Son of Man. The problem with this view is that it does not correspond with the context of the Day of the Lord or the sequence of events in the early church. Furthermore, the first two views do not reflect a cosmic resolution narrative or the contrast in power and environment associated with AE with any consistency.

Conclusion

The historical base in the discourse is seen in Mark 13:1–2 though the temple "buildings" and in Mark 13:24–27 through human "participants." The AE of the discourse functions as a complex whole in regard to multiple subjects therein and in the presence of language describing cosmic reordering. The account begins with the temple and progresses to further remote scenes that involve other subjects related to the cosmic, spiritual and human realms and divine activity. Somehow a future temple desecration and the experience of distress by the elect results in their restoration. Mark does not elaborate on associated events as Paul and the other Synoptic Gospels do. The deployment of a cosmic description is assumed in the figurative language and ER. The basic pattern of two categories, chaos and order, and the triumph of order over chaos, is demonstrated. Some of the figurative language is direct and refers to the actual conflict of the day; namely a demolition of the temple and an experience of a remote temple desecration that triggers a cosmic collapse. Some is indirect such as "powers" (which are spiritual forces) and "four winds" (which are remote boundaries). Interpreting the details in the cosmic themes would be difficult for some first-century readers to grasp. The basic theme of redemption, however, is clear (Luke 21:28).

Two separate time periods are envisaged by Mark through distinct groups of events. The overall subject is eschatology, and not the destruction of the temple. The apocalyptic signs have roots in Isaiah 13 and Joel 2 in the Day of the Lord and in Daniel 7 in the eschatological Judge. In Mark's Christology and the presentation of Jesus as suffering servant, the passage alludes to the promised restoration of order under Messiah.

The unrestricted form of activity involves the disciples and the repeated warnings to "watch." Restricted forms signal non-cyclical, one-off events like the destruction of the temple, the participating in time of cosmic signs and seeing the coming of the Son of Man. The passages reviewed highlight that the cosmic apocalyptic perspective dominates in the NT until the book of Revelation. Both perspectives are found in the church as the book of James attests. The writer of Hebrews holds in dynamic tension the elements of both cosmic and historical perspectives (Heb 1:2–8; 12:26–29).

The last chapter will summarize the constructs and draw final conclusions.

7

Summary and Conclusion

THIS STUDY HAS EXAMINED three theological constructs focusing on eschatological relationships and Jesus. It was stated that critical scholars and traditional dispensationalism have viewed Jesus' future teaching differently: the former are in favor of finding fulfillment in the events of AD 70; the latter a future fulfillment. PD advocates a complementary hermeneutic in which AD 70 is like the end. PD offers some typological pattern options for explaining Jesus' prophetic teaching. In addition, some nondispensationalists, like D. A. Carson, also hold to a pattern reading of Matthew's OD.

The study supports that a compromise of the past and future views is important because as the thesis states, a pattern exists in Jesus' teaching which must be observed before close exegetical study is fruitful. The acceptable part of any compromise is in recognition that a pattern exists in Jesus' teaching that affirms both short and long-term perspectives in regards to specific "earth-bound" historical events. Thus, the persecution for Israel and desecration predicted for the temple are necessary elements to the pattern which sees AD 70 as like the end. This historical crisis points to a greater eschatological crisis in which the future restoration of Israel is depicted as part of the revealing and return of Jesus (the descent of the Son of Man according to Mark).

Identifying the pattern in Jesus' teaching allows the reader of the Synoptic Gospels to observe the development of many themes in Jesus' future teaching. As part of the compromise, treatment of these themes is seen as complimentary not antithetical. Development goes in both directions in the Synoptic Gospels. For Luke, a predominant focus on Jerusalem and the predicted events realized in AD 70 is in view. For Matthew, a predominantly time-of-the-end period is in view. Both Matthew and Luke can develop their perspectives because the pattern originates with Jesus. Such a reading of the OT and apocalyptic literature is not uncharacteristic of Judaism, but its definitiveness in term of two periods, in Jesus, is. Matthew also links Jesus' teaching on the disciples with Jesus' OD to show that the future restoration of Israel will require, faith, reflection and *typological-prophetic* understanding of Scripture because by looking to the past Israel will recognize the disciples' mission is itself a pattern for their future salvation in the tribulation prior to the arrival of the Son of Man.

The purpose of this final section is to present a summary description of apocalyptic eschatology, and the three constructs. Final conclusions identify the key form, hermeneutical, and historical background issues related to eschatology and to Jesus' teaching on the premonitory signs before the coming of the Son of Man. It is hoped this will clarify the relationships between the destruction of the temple and cosmic events in Jesus' eschatology. Then it is possible to explain the discrepancies in Mark with the JAT conceptions, and thus ascertain what is unique to Jesus in this regard. This section will help to clarify the purpose of Mark 13:24–27 and whether or not pattern prophecy and a separate time of suffering for Israel from the destruction of the temple is legitimate.

Meyer assumed apocalyptic adopts the symbolism of prophecy and he does not ask the question about the relationship between the imminent crisis and the eschatological ordeal. His construct fails to recognize that Jesus taught new material in private in addition to his public ministry. He avoids the place of wisdom in apocalyptic or that apocalyptic reveals secrets that require reflection. Wright follows Caird. The framework for their construct is AD 70. PD recognizes Jesus reveals teaching content different from Mark 14 and that Jesus differentiates between events in his career and future teaching. Caird acknowledged the question of whether or not a relationship exists between the historical crisis and the eschatological day. He chose AD 70. Caird believes that the "resolution" of the nature of apocalyptic and the temporal tension within eschatology in Mark 13 is seen in parataxis.

Summary and Conclusion
Summary Views on Apocalyptic

Apocalyptic is the disclosure of secrets otherwise unknown. It has been viewed in five distinct ways in the history of NT interpretation. Apocalyptic was considered unimportant to classic liberalism (Reimarus, Paulus, Schleiermacher, Baur, Strauss). A solution to conflicting viewpoints in NT theology was found by formulating an antithesis between Peter and Paul. Miracles were denied and NT documents were considered second-century works. In contrast to liberalism, apocalyptic was central for Weiss and Schweitzer and meant the catastrophic end of the world. In Jesus' teaching, the kingdom of God was future. Jesus was an apocalyptist who was wrong about the imminent end of the world. A third position viewed apocalyptic as a reinterpretation of the OT by the church and that AE was not part of Jesus' teaching (Bultmann, Käsemann, Dodd, Perrin, Borg). A fourth position viewed apocalyptic as a metaphor for renewal (Caird, Wright). Apocalyptic language has a direct referent. For example, the "Son of Man" is Israel. AE describes Jewish themes such as "immortality" but no others. This scheme views eschatological teaching about the individual (e.g., resurrection) as separate to historical eschatology. The final view on apocalyptic is that apocalyptic was central for Jesus and the church (Beker, Allison). Jesus adapted much of the language and teaching of apocalyptic eschatology.

The scholarly consensus has been that PE and AE are not opposed to each other but that a distinction must be maintained: (1) PE sometimes expects fulfillment in the prophets' own age (Jer 25:8–11), while AE points to a future period, (2) AE presents a cosmic worldview where divine deliverance comes "from above" to real people in a time of crisis. Mythical language is deployed to bring a sense of cosmic power in a way that literal language cannot. PE reflects deliverance through human agents (Zech 14; Mal 3:1).

The move to see eschatology as a subset of apocalyptic is not helpful. Furthermore, the approach of Rowland, Grabbe, Caird, and Wright to view this kind of eschatology as less relevant than discussions of worldview diminishes the capacity for retrieving meaning. It elevates the centrality of certain metaphors, regards symbolism as more important than history, and fails to consider critical links with real world history. Aune has described apocalyptic as a subset of eschatology. This is more in line with the perspective in Jewish apocalyptic writings which exhibit a consistent eschatology. Israel's history relates to suffering (Dan 9:27) not just her restoration (Dan 7:27). Josephus also recognized a pattern in history as do rewritten texts in the JAT. Daniel has been read as relating to two periods—one a destruction and the other a desecration.

Conclusion

Mark 13 presents a sermon of Jesus. Jesus teaches about God's plan. This is a key function of his role as the Son of Man. Mark retains the ambiguity in the sermon regarding the use of sources and figurative language. The other Synoptic Gospels follow Mark to a certain degree. The rearranged eschatological signs draw on allusions from the LXX to form a composite saying which connects the Signs and descent of the Son of Man (LXX Isa 13:10; Joel 2:10; 3:4; 4:15; Isa 34:4). This describes the return of Jesus, the Messiah which Matthew calls the *Parousia*. The paratactic structure is retained. This is very Jewish, and it would not be surprising if it comes from the Jesus tradition. Matthew and Luke follow Mark's use of the OT. The mixing of figurative and direct references in these gospels is also Jewish. Luke makes his version more descriptive in places. The meaning of the Son of Man, however, is clearly established and central in all Synoptic Gospels. This is because the referent is shared in the communities. The "Son of Man" is Jesus. If this had been uncertain to the authors, it would surely have been omitted just as some other material from Mark was deleted. The Son of Man text has direct prophetic fulfillment in Jesus. He is the eschatological judge. The same connotations in Daniel's Son of Man are seen in Mark's text.

Mark's themes do not fit neatly into set or formal standards. Identifying his inconsistencies and his disparate material is fundamental for interpreting his themes. Exploring relationships is more productive rather than speculating on alternative sources. The source question invites the answer that Jesus' sermon is reported differently by three synoptic evangelists. Different points of view emerge. These versions of Jesus' sermon are not disparate sources. PD makes an *a priori case* in explanation of the apparent textual discrepancies and this is based, not on the synoptic writers' failure to integrate separate sources, but on intentional differences in emphasis related to the pattern in the original sermon. The Synoptic Gospels represent condensed and selective reporting of a long unified sermon delivered by Jesus. This selective reporting is in terms which the first church readers would understand. It varies between highlighting short-term realizations (Luke 21:20) and final fulfillment (Matthew 24:15 / Mark 13:14[1]).

---

1. The ambiguities in Mark's passage must be retained because they indicate a pattern.

Summary and Conclusion

The principles of critical realism, such as embracing an external reality and the avoidance of naive assumptions, are fundamental to interpreting Mark's discourse. It is useful for the examination of questions of form, consistency, the author's purpose, interconnection with historical material, Jewish hermeneutics, the function of the text regarding cultural issues, and crucially the meaning of figurative expressions (determining between literal and figurative meanings). In saying that the language of metaphor is not literal, it must be emphasized that it is still used to refer to reality. Metaphorical language, used in the comparison, suggests layers of meaning that a literal language cannot convey.

Allegories are freely constructed figurative descriptions of real events and persons. In Judaism, allegories were usually based on actual conflicts of the day. Cosmic and physical realms are referred to pictorially in Mark as indirect symbols, but they are used in the discourse to describe future history nonetheless, such as the gathering of the elect from the "four winds." In Mark 13 "powers" are a metonymy for all evil angels in the cosmos. Equally important, the impulse behind AE is cosmic thinking. In Mark 13, the basic patterns of myth exist: order triumphs over chaos. Some claim that the world of prophets is real history, while the world of apocalyptic is cosmic conflict but this dichotomy is unfounded. AE tends to be more mythical in its language than PE but no less about real people nor is it ahistorical. PE is more historical in its mode of deliverance while apocalyptic is "from above." Such clarifications are essential to grasp. The question is how the various realms (heavenly, spiritual, earthly) are related.

In exploring the background to Mark 13, allowance must be made for a broader definition of AE in Second Temple Judaism and in the NT. AE, in contrast to PE is found in *1 Enoch*. The ideas put forward in these documents are: (1) that there is comfort for individuals beyond the grave (*1 En* 102, 103, 108), and (2) that when circumstances are dire, heavenly deliverance is expected (*1 En* 90:13–17; 91:7–8; 94:11; 102:3; cf. *Pss. Sol.* 2:1,19; 5:5–7; 17:21–23; *Jub* 23:24). Therefore, Judaism expected a heavenly, ontologically separate, reality to interrupt actual history to bring about deliverance and judgment. Mark 13 evidences this AE but it is not about the afterlife at all. Such data fits within historical hopes of deliverance more than is recognized.[1]

---

[1] As such the recognition of a literary tension regarding imminence and delay should not be dismissed.

Eschatological Relationships and Jesus

The pattern prophecy of AD 70 and time of the end is consistent with Mark's presentation and the forward moving characteristic of apocalyptic. A feature of rewritten history observed in the JAT is that it focuses on events. Writers identified patterns in "prophecy" for their times and historical events were viewed as types awaiting future fulfillment. *1 Enoch* 91:6 cast the picture that "oppression will reoccur" (cf. 93:4, 9; 94:5). Jubilees focuses on a time of future trouble if the nation did not obey (*Jub* 23:11–25). Thus, the JAT apocalypses and wisdom literature view recent past or current events allegorically but typologically for their implications for future judgment. The use of the OT by Jesus in Mark 13 shows continuity and development. Themes are not merely repeated or left unchanged. Short-term events in the environs of the temple illustrate events are still yet to be fulfilled.

In light of this, suggestions on future direction for study of this kind include the following themes: First, how does the author seemingly answer his reader's questions about eschatology? Assessment of eschatological relationships in the context of Mark's gospel is essential to understanding his eschatology. Mark is writing with eschatological questions in mind. His gospel addresses new circumstances facing the early church. The original meaning of the OT is read in the context of Jesus as Messiah, Son of Man. Further fulfillment of prophecy is awaited. How the Synoptic Gospels relate to their audience's cultural understanding of eschatology would be a useful study. How the Gospels balance the related themes of "cosmic" and "historical" apocalyptic theology would also be beneficial. Second, since the theme of judgment is still present in Mark's version, how the other Gospels develop the theme of vengeance on the Gentiles (Matt 11:5 / Luke 4:22)? How does this relate to the theme of restoration and judgment for Israel (Matt 23:34–35 / Luke 11:49–59)?

In determining a purpose for Mark's signs passage, it is important to bear in mind that the coming of the Son of Man is in line with the conceptual framework of negative and positive apocalyptic and is part of an interactive metaphor. The arrival of Jesus the Son of Man in Mark's gospel functions to bridge the gap in Judaism between the heavenly and earthly realms. Other texts in Mark show a link between history and heaven (e.g., Jesus' exaltation, Mark 14:26). The function of the Son of Man in Mark is to bring two realms together: "the heavenly" and "the earthly" as the outworking of OT prophecy. Daniel 7:13–14 preludes restoration and Daniel 9:26–27 preludes the end of Israel's troubles. The connotation of the One

Summary and Conclusion

who "rides the clouds" is one of heavenly authority to exercise restoration. This is distinct from "coming in clouds," which is Mark's perspective. Jesus' claim that he will be seen by many people is an event not envisaged in Jewish apocalyptic. *1 Enoch* only contemplates the category of the individual, but does not conceptually bring earthly and heavenly realms together. Mark's typical style works from "the ground up." He also understands apocalyptic as the disclosure of secrets otherwise unknown. The Messiah has come. At his second advent, Jesus will come again.

Appendix 1

Establishing a Synoptic Framework

APPENDIX 1 SETS OUT to sketch a synoptic framework within which verbal actions may be used in interpreting patterns in eschatology. Identification of patterns is not a given. In order to clarify the relationship between texts, there follows a list of six groups of narrative sayings from the discourses. The titles of each group derive from the 10th print edition of the Aland Synopsis which also gives a verse-by-verse alignment of the parallel passages. Here the text is laid out in a way that makes it easier to recognize at which points the parallel passages have word-by-word alignment. Exact words in the text that are aligned are bolded. Furthermore, each group, except group 1, show two settings side-by-side in a pattern, i.e., the various components of the pattern. Group 1 sets the context near the temple. Groups 4 and 5 introduce Luke's second discourse, which express a connection to the Day of the Lord imagery but without the Temple—the first basic part of the narrative arc. Groups 2 and 6 reflect a historical pattern in Jesus' utterance. Groups, 3, 4 and 5 reflect a biblical typology contained in Jesus' utterance closely connected to the OT and not anticipated elsewhere. These "hinge" or reflect development in the synoptic parallels from Mark's uncertain setting. Groups, 2, 4, and 6 appear in all three parts of Mark's story: beginning, middle, and end, but also align outside Mark's narrative arc. The synoptic framework helps indicate how the traditioning process changed the direction of earlier material and how the social impact in these eschatological patterns is spread across Matthew and Luke's discourses.

Appendix 1

1.1 §287 Prediction of the Destruction of the Temple

Matt 24:1 and 2	Mark 13:1 and 2	Luke 21:5 and 6
Καὶ ἐξελθὼν ὁ Ἰησοῦς ἀπὸ τοῦ ἱεροῦ (Matt 24:1) ἀμὴν λέγω ὑμῖν, οὐ μὴ ἀφεθῇ ὧδε **λίθος ἐπὶ** λίθον ὃς οὐ καταλυθήσεται. (Matt 24:2)	Καὶ ἐκπορευομένου αὐτοῦ ἐκ τοῦ ἱεροῦ (Mark 13:1) οὐ μὴ ἀφεθῇ ὧδε **λίθος ἐπὶ** λίθον ὃς οὐ μὴ καταλυθῇ. (Mark 13:2)	Καί τινων λεγόντων περὶ τοῦ ἱεροῦ (Luke 21:5) Ταῦτα ἃ θεωρεῖτε ἐλεύσονται ἡμέραι ἐν αἷς οὐκ ἀφεθήσεται **λίθος ἐπὶ** λίθῳ ὃς οὐ καταλυθήσεται. (Luke 21:6)
Context – Temple	Source text Note: No real description of how destruction happens.	Context – Temple

1.2 §289 Persecutions Foretold in a Historical Pattern and §100 Fate of the Disciples

Matt 10:17-25	Mark 13:9-13	Luke 21:12-19
ⁱ⁹ ὅταν δὲ παραδῶσιν ὑμᾶς, **μὴ μεριμνήσητε πῶς ἢ τί** λαλήσητε· δοθήσεται **γάρ** ὑμῖν ἐν ἐκείνῃ τῇ ὥρᾳ τί λαλήσητε· ²⁰ οὐ **γὰρ** ὑμεῖς ἐστε οἱ λαλοῦντες ἀλλὰ τὸ πνεῦμα τοῦ πατρὸς ὑμῶν τὸ λαλοῦν ἐν ὑμῖν. Ὅταν δὲ διώκωσιν ὑμᾶς ἐν τῇ πόλει ταύτῃ, φεύγετε εἰς τὴν ἑτέραν· ἀμὴν **γὰρ** λέγω ὑμῖν, οὐ μὴ τελέσητε τὰς πόλεις τοῦ Ἰσραὴλ ἕως ἂν ἔλθῃ ὁ υἱὸς τοῦ ἀνθρώπου (Matt 10:23)	¹¹ καὶ **ὅταν** ἄγωσιν **ὑμᾶς** παραδιδόντες, μὴ προμεριμνᾶτε τί λαλήσητε, ἀλλ' ὃ ἐὰν δοθῇ ὑμῖν ἐν ἐκείνῃ τῇ ὥρᾳ τοῦτο λαλεῖτε· οὐ **γάρ** ἐστε <u>ὑμεῖς</u> οἱ λαλοῦντες ἀλλὰ τὸ πνεῦμα τὸ ἅγιον.	¹⁴ θέτε οὖν ἐν ταῖς καρδίαις ὑμῶν **μὴ** προμελετᾶν ἀπολογηθῆναι· ¹⁵ ἐγὼ **γὰρ** δώσω **ὑμῖν** στόμα καὶ σοφίαν ᾗ οὐ δυνήσονται ἀντιστῆναι ἢ ἀντειπεῖν ἅπαντες οἱ ἀντικείμενοι ὑμῖν. Ὅταν δὲ εἰσφέρωσιν **ὑμᾶς** ἐπὶ τὰς συναγωγὰς καὶ τὰς ἀρχὰς καὶ τὰς ἐξουσίας, **μὴ μεριμνήσητε πῶς ἢ τί** ἀπολογήσησθε ἢ τί εἴπητε· ¹² τὸ **γὰρ** ἅγιον πνεῦμα διδάξει ὑμᾶς ἐν αὐτῇ τῇ ὥρᾳ ἃ δεῖ εἰπεῖν. (Luke 12:11-12)
¹⁹ historical pattern to the time of vengeance; (vv. 19-23a) historical pattern to time of vengeance (23a) and the eschaton or Day of the Lord , found in M (23b)	The gospel writers do not stop with saying that persecution is anticipated in the future. They earlier claim that it was a short term event in the disciples ministry. The sources texts are Mark 13:11 and Q sayings tradition. The scope of the these texts are vast, reaching beyond the ministry of Jesus' first disciples. First, they precedes Mark's narrative arc in chapter 13. Second they extend beyond the placement in Mark's narrative arc here. It is both a historical pattern and a typological-HISTORIC category as a sort term fulfillment mirrors the anticipated end time. This highlights the importance of reading these texts canonically.	The Lukan and Matthaean traditions stress the fate of the disciples as a short-term historical pattern of persecution (Luke 12:11-12 // Matt 10:19). This is another place where language is transferred from one situation to another as Luke goes on to claim that it was the anticipation of events to come in the future which will have implications for disciples and even Israel as a nation (Luke 21:12, 14-15, 20). Note the rare use of the first person subject in Luke 21:15 ("I-here-now" language) which could bring a note of finality to Luke's short-term historical pattern here. Luke does not reinterpret the national in terms of the individual as both appear in his narrative.

Appendix 1

1.3 §290 Desolations and Daniel 9:27 (LXX) and Typological Prophetic Patterns

Matt 24:15, 16 and 10:23	Mark 13:14	Luke 21:20 and 21
Ὅταν οὖν ἴδητε τὸ βδέλυγμα τῆς ἐρημώσεως τὸ ῥηθὲν διὰ Δανιὴλ τοῦ προφήτου ἑστὸς ἐν τόπῳ ἁγίῳ, ὁ ἀναγινώσκων νοείτω (Matt 24:15)	Ὅταν δὲ ἴδητε τὸ βδέλυγμα τῆς ἐρημώσεως ἑστηκότα ὅπου οὐ δεῖ, ὁ ἀναγινώσκων νοείτω,	Ὅταν δὲ ἴδητε κυκλουμένην ὑπὸ στρατοπέδων Ἰερουσαλήμ, τότε γνῶτε ὅτι ἤγγικεν ἡ ἐρήμωσις αὐτῆς (Luke 21:20)
τότε οἱ ἐν τῇ Ἰουδαίᾳ φευγέτωσαν εἰς τὰ ὄρη (Matt 24:16)	τότε οἱ ἐν τῇ Ἰουδαίᾳ φευγέτωσαν εἰς τὰ ὄρη (Mark 13:14)	τότε οἱ ἐν τῇ Ἰουδαίᾳ φευγέτωσαν εἰς τὰ ὄρη (Luke 21:21)
Ὅταν δὲ διώκωσιν ὑμᾶς ἐν τῇ πόλει ταύτῃ, φεύγετε εἰς τὴν ἑτέραν· ἀμὴν γὰρ λέγω ὑμῖν, οὐ μὴ τελέσητε τὰς πόλεις τοῦ Ἰσραὴλ ἕως ἂν ἔλθῃ ὁ υἱὸς τοῦ ἀνθρώπου (Matt 10:23)	[καὶ ἐπὶ τὸ ἱερὸν βδέλυγμα τῶν ἐρημώσεων ἔσται ἕως συντελείας καὶ συντέλεια δοθήσεται ἐπὶ τὴν ἐρήμωσιν Dan 9:27 LXT]	
οὐαὶ δὲ ταῖς ἐν γαστρὶ ἐχούσαις καὶ ταῖς θηλαζούσαις ἐν ἐκείναις ταῖς ἡμέραις. (Matt 24:19)	οὐαὶ δὲ ταῖς ἐν γαστρὶ ἐχούσαις καὶ ταῖς θηλαζούσαις ἐν ἐκείναις ταῖς ἡμέραις. (Mark 13:17)	οὐαὶ ταῖς ἐν γαστρὶ ἐχούσαις καὶ ταῖς θηλαζούσαις ἐν ἐκείναις ταῖς ἡμέραις. (Luke 21:23)
Type v. 16 "flee" in the short term. Matt 10:23 fulfillment to Mark "flee" in the *eschton*	Based on the antecedent in Dan 9:2; 27 (ἐρημώσεων) is Mark's event an antetype or type, where there could be a final fulfillment in v. 14 "flee. It is possible for language which is typical of one situation (ie. in Daniel LXX) to be transferred other situations in such a way that the details of the events can be described either directly or indirectly. "	Type = "Jerusalem" short term in Luke. The category here is typological-HISTORIC. This pattern is can be anticipated in Mark based on knowledge of the historical background. v.20, v.22 "to fulfil" time of vengeance v. 24 "are fulfilled"

Establishing a Synoptic Framework

1.4 §291 False Christ's and §235
Day of the Son of Man (Luke's Order) and Typological Prophetic Pattern

Matt 24:23-27	Mark 13:21 and 23	Luke 17:23-24
τότε ἐάν τις ὑμῖν εἴπῃ, Ἰδοὺ ὧδε ὁ Χριστός, ἤ, Ὧδε, μὴ πιστεύσητε. (Matt 24:23) ἰδοὺ **προείρηκα ὑμῖν** (Matt 24:25) **ὥσπερ γὰρ ἡ ἀστραπὴ ἐξέρχεται ἀπὸ ἀνατολῶν καὶ φαίνεται ἕως δυσμῶν, οὕτως ἔσται** ἡ παρουσία τοῦ υἱοῦ **τοῦ ἀνθρώπου** (Matt 24:27)	καὶ τότε ἐάν τις ὑμῖν εἴπῃ, Ἴδε ὧδε ὁ Χριστός, Ἴδε ἐκεῖ, μὴ πιστεύετε. (Mark13:21) **προείρηκα ὑμῖν** πάντα (Mark 13:23)	καὶ ἐροῦσιν ὑμῖν, Ἰδοὺ ἐκεῖ, ἤ, Ἰδοὺ ὧδε· μὴ ἀπέλθητε μηδὲ διώξητε. Luke 17:23) ²⁴ **ὥσπερ γὰρ ἡ ἀστραπὴ** ἀστράπτουσα ἐκ τῆς ὑπὸ τὸν οὐρανὸν εἰς τὴν ὑπ' οὐρανὸν λάμπει, **οὕτως ἔσται** ὁ υἱὸς **τοῦ ἀνθρώπου** ἐν τῇ ἡμέρᾳ αὐτοῦ (Luke 17:24)
Pattern v. 23 "then if anyone"	Source v. 21 "and if anyone"	The pattern for the future consummation in Luke's account emerges in verse 24. It is possible for Luke to take language which is typical of one situation (namely the OT Day of the Lord) and combine what is transferred from Mark's ambiguous event so that it intended as typological in both. v. 23 "and they will say." These Sayings continue the description of the future judgment and are based on the Day of the Lord imagery (Joel 2:1; Obad 15; Hab 2:3).

Appendix 1

1.4.1. §235 Continued:
Day of the Son of Man and Gen 6 (Noah's Day) a Biblical Historical Pattern

Matt 24:37		Luke 17:26
Ὥσπερ γὰρ αἱ ἡμέραι τοῦ Νῶε, οὕτως ἔσται ἡ παρουσία τοῦ υἱοῦ τοῦ ἀνθρώπου		καὶ καθὼς ἐγένετο ἐν ταῖς ἡμέραις Νῶε, οὕτως ἔσται καὶ ἐν ταῖς ἡμέραις τοῦ υἱοῦ τοῦ ἀνθρώπου
Type from the historical Jesus	Historical pattern from Jesus' use of Genesis 6 (antetype). What Jesus expects is judgement preceding the restoration.	Type from the historical Jesus showing Jesus' authority and based on the Day of the Lord imagery.

1.5 §235 The House Desertion (Luke's order)
and the Day of Son of Man and Typological-Prophetic Pattern

Matt 24:17–18	Mark 13:15–16	Luke 17:31
ὁ ἐπὶ τοῦ δώματος μὴ καταβάτω ἆραι τὰ ἐκ τῆς οἰκίας αὐτοῦ, καὶ ὁ ἐν τῷ ἀγρῷ μὴ ἐπιστρεψάτω ὀπίσω ἆραι τὸ ἱμάτιον αὐτοῦ (Matt 24:17–18)	ὁ δὲ ἐπὶ τοῦ δώματος μὴ καταβάτω μηδὲ εἰσελθάτω ἆραί τι ἐκ τῆς οἰκίας αὐτοῦ, καὶ ὁ εἰς τὸν ἀγρὸν μὴ ἐπιστρεψάτω εἰς τὰ ὀπίσω ἆραι τὸ ἱμάτιον αὐτοῦ. (Luke 13:15–16)	ἐν ἐκείνῃ τῇ ἡμέρᾳ ὃς ἔσται ἐπὶ τοῦ δώματος καὶ τὰ σκεύη αὐτοῦ ἐν τῇ οἰκίᾳ, μὴ καταβάτω ἆραι αὐτά, καὶ ὁ ἐν ἀγρῷ ὁμοίως μὴ ἐπιστρεψάτω εἰς τὰ ὀπίσω. (Luke 17:31)
type "the one who is on the roof"	antetype text "the one who is on the roof"	type "anyone who is on the roof"

1.6 §103 Conditions of Discipleship and §235 The Day of the Son of Man as Historical Pattern (which Foreshadows the Day of the Lord)

Matt 10:39		Luke 17:33
ὁ εὑρὼν τὴν ψυχὴν αὐτοῦ ἀπολέσει αὐτήν, καὶ ὁ ἀπολέσας τὴν ψυχὴν αὐτοῦ ἕνεκεν ἐμοῦ εὑρήσει αὐτήν.		ὃς ἐὰν ζητήσῃ τὴν ψυχὴν αὐτοῦ περιποιήσασθαι ἀπολέσει αὐτήν, ὃς δ' ἂν ἀπολέσῃ ζῳογονήσει αὐτήν.
Matt 10:39 Short-term historical pattern "he who finds his life"	The sayings from Jesus in Luke describes how final judgment take place and is Typological-HISTORIC in its fulfillment. It's placement in Mark's story is prior to the end (vv. 24–27) and prior to Luke 17:24. Luke's discourse is not in chronological order. In Matthew the saying aligns as a historical pattern.	Luke 17:33 long-term historical pattern "he who seeks his life" Here is another occasion where language is transferred from one literary convention to another. The two passages show it is possible for language which is relevant to the disciples story to be used in connection with the future eschatological crisis of national survival.

Appendix 2

Sequence and Literary Relationships in the Synoptic Gospels for Prophetic and Apocalyptic Sayings with Priority Given to Mark's Content and Order

Passage in Aland's Synopsis	Mood	Literary Convention	Relationship	Receivers and Transfer in Matthew	in Mark	in Luke
BEGINNING IN MARK						
§287 Destruction of the Temple Predicted	Voc	P		disciples S 24:1–2	disciples S 13:1–2	disciples S 21:5–6
§289 Persecutions Foretold	Imp	P	PA (Matt)	disciples S 10:17–22 disciples (elect) R/I 10:23 (M)	disciples S 13:9–13	disciples S 21:12–19
§100 The Fate of the Disciples φεύγετε (Matt 10:23)	Sub Sub	P A				
MIDDLE IN MARK §290 The Desolating Sacrilege "Ὅταν δὲ ἴδητε (Mark 13:14) "Ὅταν οὖν ἴδητε (Matt24:15) ὁ δὲ ἐπὶ τοῦ δώματος (Mark 13:15) ὁ ἐπὶ τοῦ. (Matt 24:17)	Sub Imp	I-A I-A T and J	TI-A (Mark) JI-A (Luke)	disciples R T those I 24:15–16 the one I 24:17	disciples R T those I 13:14 the one I 13:15	disciples R J those I 21:20–22
Εἶπεν δὲ πρὸς τοὺς μαθητάς (Luke 17:22) §235 The Day of the Son of Man according to Luke τότε ἐάν Ἰδού..ὧδε (Matt 24:23) καὶ ἐροῦσιν ὑμῖν (Luke 17:23)	Ind Sub/ Ind	P I-A/A	TI-A (Mark) PA (Luke) I-AA (Luke)	anyone I; disciples R/I 24:23 nature I 24:27 (Q)	anyone I / disciples R 13:21	disciples S 17:22 they I / disciples (elect) R A 17:23 nature I 17:24 (Q)
§291 False Christs / Prophets ὥσπερ γάρ (Luke 17:24)	Sub	A				

			Matt	Mark	Luke
§235 continued and Gen 6 οὕτως ἔσται (Lk 17:26) and deserting the house ὃς ἔσται (Lk 17:31) μὴ καταβάτω (Mk 13:15//Mt 24:17// Lk 17:31) §103 Conditions of Discipleship according to Matt ἀπολέσει αὐτήν (Lk 17:33)	Ind Ind/ Imp	A I-A A P	I-AA (Luke) P (Matt)	days of Noah I Matt 24:37–39 (Q) the one I 24:17–18 (§296) 10:39 (Q)	the one I 13:15–16 §290	days of Noah I 17:26–29 (Q) anyone I 17:31 17:33 Q
and §291 False Christs continued . . . ἐκεῖ καὶ οἱ ἀετοὶ ἐπισυναχθήσονται (Lk 17:37)	Ind	A	PA	wherever R 24:28 (Q)		Lord S 17:37b (Q)
END IN MARK §292 The coming of the Son of Man (§288 and §293 are omitted for simplicity)	Ind Ind	A A		they I 24:30 Cosmic elect) I 24:31	they I 13:26 cosmic (elect) I 13:27	they I 21:27
Προσέχετε δὲ ἑαυτοῖς (Lk 21:34) §294 Conclusion "Take Heed, Watch" ἵνα κατισχύσητε ἐκφυγεῖν (Lk 21:36)	Imp	P A	PA (Luke)	disciples S 25:13	disciples S 13:33	disciples S 21:34–35 disciples R 21:36

Sequence and Literary Relationships

Key

Context	Place	Transfer
P = Prophetic	T = Temple	S = Shared transfer
IA = Introductory Apocalyptic	J = Jerusalem	R = Referential transfer
A = Apocalyptic/ypse		I = Indefinite transfer

Eschatolgical Relationships

PA = Prophetic-Apocalyptic Historical Relationships
I-AA= Introductory Apocalyptic-Apocalyptic/ypse Historical Relationships
TI-A= Temple Introductory-Apocalyptic Historical Relationship
JI-A= Jerusalem Introductory-Apocalyptic Historical Relationship

Q = 'Q' tradition stream or sayings commonly recognized for this material

Note

Appendix 2 sets out to sketch the sequence of Mark's account within which verbal actions may be used when exploring synoptic parallels. At a glance, the effective use of the verbal actions and the transfer to different recipients is seen. As a part of this exercise judgments have to be made upon complex sets of data rather than a narrow range of parameters for discussing eschatological relationships. Moving from beginning to end, we find a difference of recipients, literary convention and theological content. Through the juxtaposition of themes such as false Christs to the Days of Noah, deserting the house, conditions of discipleship, and OT Day of the Lord imagery, the awareness emerges that here is a reference to the terrible Day of the Lord, which is now related also to the return of the Son of Man. The prominence given to "The Day of the Lord" and the desecration of the temple is in order; from least to greatest: Luke, Mark and Matthew.

Appendix 3

Biblical Historical Pattern

Description of Biblical Historical Pattern

THE HISTORICAL PATTERN, INVOLVING apocalyptic themes, in the gospels, is distinctly different from JAT typology. The latter present their historical surveys as predictions of an ancient sage to give the impression that all history conforms to God's predetermined plan, and that the imminent climax of history has been revealed to them. On the other hand, by presenting a historical survey as prediction of the historical Jesus, the gospel writer is able to affirm that end time history conforms generally to a sequence in the plan of God, that it conforms with the same OT prophetic base, and matches forms in the Jesus tradition, but that the imminent turning point of history has been revealed to him.[1] A prime example of historical pattern in the Gospels derived from the Day of the Lord theme which works with Jesus' predictions is Luke 17:26–29, §235 "The Day of the Son of Man according to Luke." It is part of Luke's description of judgment before the final restoration. It begins with a connection (*kai*) which matches Luke's account here with the middle section of Mark's story. Genesis 6 describes the antediluvian period but the language as such is not directly anticipated in the OT as a pattern prophecy and has no short term fulfillment. Mark

---

1. Note, the actual point in time of such events is not part of the revelation only the sequence of salvation history in terms of exile and restoration, according to the gospel writer.

does not use this language either. The authority of the prophecy is Jesus and it is remembered as such. *1 Enoch* 1–36 is an example of typological presentation of history in the JAT.

Use of Situation and Heilsgeschichte

In the Gospels the situation of the historical author is clear and open, as is the situation of the original event described. For example the Gospels distinguish between the "righteous" and "unrighteous" in primeval era / days of Noah, the righteous in Jesus' day, the writer's own readers, and the elect in end time. In the JAT literature, the situation of the historical author is concealed, effected in part through use of pseudonym Enoch. The author may or may not refer specifically to actual wars, etc.

Use of Pattern

The Gospel author writes so that the original OT setting and the historical Jesus are retained and compared with the future context. For example, the image of chaos and judgment from Genesis 6 is transferred relatively to the *eschaton* (ἀλλ' οὔπω τὸ τέλος Mark 13:7). Luke's discourse goes further and unpacks the time of judgment before restoration with reference to people and circumstances (Luke 17:23, 26–30, 31, 33–37) and then the end (Luke 17:24). Luke's sequencing of predicted future events does not follow a strict chronological order. Furthermore, even though Jesus reveals God's future, the time of the eschaton has not been revealed to him or the Gospel writers (οὐδὲ ὁ υἱός, εἰ μὴ ὁ πατήρ Mark 13:32). Pseudonym Enoch imposes the setting of the fictive author on his historical situation, often in absolute terms. Emphasis on reoccurring patterns is frequently at the expense of the uniqueness of history.

Suggestions for Understanding Themes

Judgment. Within a biblical historical pattern, history is presented as a warning of certain future judgment at the end time and a specific comparison of two key world events is offered and realized when the pattern occurs. In the JAT typological view, history is implied as a paradigm for explaining the origin and influence of sin and evil.

Appendix 3

Myth. There is a difference between biblical typology / historical patterns and Hellenistic typology. In the Gospels, the author draws on myth and history in a combined form. With the historical situation specified, the problem at hand is integrated with cosmic realities. In the JAT, with no historical situation specified the crisis/problem is transferred to a mythical plane.

Bibliography

Achtemeier, Paul J. *An Introduction to the New Hermeneutic.* Philadelphia: Westminster, 1969.
Achtemeier, Paul J., et al., eds. *Introducing the New Testament: Its Literature and Theology.* Grand Rapids: Eerdmans, 2001.
Aland, Kurt, ed. *Synopsis of the Four Gospels: Greek-English Edition of the Synopsis Quattuor Evangeliorum.* 10th ed. Stuttgart: German Bible Society, 1993.
Aland, Kurt, et al., eds. *Studia Evangelica: Papers Presented to the International Congress on "The Four Gospels in 1957."* Berlin: Akademie, 1959.
Allison, Dale C. "Apocalyptic." In *Dictionary of Jesus and the Gospels*, edited by Joel B. Green et al., 17–20. Downers Grove: InterVarsity, 1992.
―――. *The End of the Ages Has Come: An Early Interpretation of the Passion and Resurrection of Jesus.* Philadelphia: Fortress, 1985.
―――. "The Eschatology of Jesus." In *The Encyclopedia of Apocalypticism*, edited by John J. Collins, 1:267–302. New York: Continuum, 1998.
―――. "Jesus and the Victory of Apocalyptic." In *Jesus and the Restoration of Israel: A Critical Assessment of N. T. Wright's Jesus and the Victory of God*, edited by Carey C. Newman, 126–41. Downers Grove: InterVarsity, 1999.
―――. *Jesus of Nazareth: Millenarian Prophet.* Minneapolis: Fortress, 1998.
―――. "A Plea for Thoroughgoing Eschatology." *Journal of Biblical Literature* 113 (1994) 651–68.
Aune, D. E. "Apocalypticism." In *Dictionary of Paul and His Letters*, edited by Gerald F. Hawthorne et al., 25–35. Downers Grove: InterVarsity, 1993.
―――. "The Eschatology of Jesus." In *The Anchor Bible Dictionary*, edited by David Noel Freedman, 2:599–600. New York: Doubleday, 1992.
―――. *Prophecy in Early Christianity and the Ancient Mediterranean World.* Grand Rapids: Eerdmans, 1983.
―――. *Revelation 1–5.* Word Biblical Commentary 52. Dallas: Word, 1997.
―――. "The Significance of the Delay of the Parousia for Early Christianity." In *Current Issues in Biblical and Patristic Interpretation*, edited by G. F. Hawthorne, 87–109. Grand Rapids: Eerdmans, 1975.
―――. "Transformations of Apocalypticism in Early Christianity." In *Knowing the End from the Beginning: The Prophetic, the Apocalyptic and Their Relationships*, edited by Lester L. Grabbe and Robert D. Haak, 54–64. London: T. & T. Clark, 2003.

Bibliography

Avis, Paul D. L. *God and the Creative Imagination: Metaphor, Symbol, and Myth in Religion and Theology*. New York: Routledge, 1999.

Baker, David L. "Typology and the Christian Use of the Old Testament." *Scottish Journal of Theology* 29 (1976) 127–57.

Bakhos, Carol. *Ancient Judaism in Its Hellenistic Context*. Journal for the Study of Judaism in the Persian, Hellenistic, and Roman Periods 95. Leiden: Brill, 2005.

Barr, David L., ed. *The Reality of Apocalypse: Rhetoric and Politics in the Book of Revelation*. Atlanta: SBL, 2006.

Barr, James. "Jewish Apocalyptic in Recent Scholarly Research." *Bulletin of the John Rylands University Library of Manchester* 58 (1975) 9–35.

———. *The Semantics of Biblical Language*. London: Oxford University Press, 1961.

Barrett, C. K. "The Interpretation of the Old Testament in the New." In *The Cambridge History of the Bible: From the Beginning to Jerome*, edited by P. R. Ackroyd and C. F. Evans, 1:377–411. Cambridge: Cambridge University Press, 1970.

Bateman, Herbert W., ed. *Three Central Issues in Contemporary Dispensationalism: A Comparison of Traditional and Progressive Views*. Grand Rapids: Kregel, 1999.

Bauckham, Richard. "Apocalypses." In *Justification and Variegated Nomism*, edited by D. A. Carson et al., 1:135–87. Grand Rapids: Baker Academic, 2001.

———. *The Jewish World around the New Testament: Collected Essays I*. Tübingen: Mohr Siebeck, 2008.

Bautch, Kelley Coblentz. *A Study of the Geography of 1 Enoch 17–19: "No One Has Seen What I Have Seen."* Boston: Brill, 2003.

Beasley-Murray, G. R. *A Commentary on Mark Thirteen*. New York: Macmillan, 1957.

———. "The Interpretation of Daniel 7." *Catholic Biblical Quarterly* 45 (1983) 44–58.

———. *Jesus and the Future: An Examination of the Criticism of the Eschatological Discourse, Mark 13 with Special Reference to the Little Apocalypse Theory*. New York: Macmillan, 1954.

———. *Jesus and the Last Days: The Interpretation of the Olivet Discourse*. Peabody: Hendrickson, 1993.

———. "The Rise and Fall of the Little Apocalypse Theory." *Expository Times* 64 (1952–53) 346–49.

———. "So That Your Faith May also Be Your Hope in God (1 Peter 1:21)." In *Reconciliation and Hope: New Testament Essays on Atonement and Eschatology*, edited by Robert J. Banks, 262–74. Grand Rapids: Eerdmans, 1974.

———. "The Two Messiahs in the Testaments of the Twelve Patriarchs." *Journal of Theological Studies* 48 (1947) 1–12.

Beker, Johan Christiaan. *Paul the Apostle: The Triumph of God in Life and Thought*. Philadelphia: Fortress, 1980.

Blaising, Craig A. "Dispensationalism: The Search for Definitions." In *Dispensationalism, Israel and the Church: The Search for Definition*, edited by Craig A. Blaising and Darrell L. Bock, 13–34. Grand Rapids: Zondervan, 1992.

———. "Premillennialism." In *Three Views on the Millennium and Beyond*, edited by Darrell L. Bock, 157–227. Grand Rapids: Zondervan, 1999.

Blaising, Craig A., and Darrell L. Bock, eds. *Dispensationalism, Israel and the Church: The Search for Definition*. Grand Rapids: Zondervan, 1992.

———. *Progressive Dispensationalism*. Grand Rapids: Baker, 1993.

Bibliography

Bock, Darrell L. *Blasphemy and Exaltation in Judaism and the Final Examination of Jesus: A Philological-Historical Study of the Key Jewish Themes Impacting Mark 14:61-64*. Tübingen: Mohr Siebeck, 1998.

———. "Blasphemy and the Jewish Examination of Jesus." *Bulletin Biblical Review* 17 (2007) 53–114.

———. "Hermeneutics of Progressive Dispensationalism." In *Three Central Issues in Contemporary Dispensationalism: A Comparison of Traditional and Progressive Views*, edited by Herbert W. Bateman, 85–101. Grand Rapids: Kregel, 1999.

———. "The Kingdom of God in New Testament Theology." In *Looking into the Future: Evangelical Studies in Eschatology*, edited by David L. Baker, 28–60. Grand Rapids: Baker, 2001.

———. *Luke: 9:51—24:53*. Vol. 2. Baker Exegetical Commentary on the New Testament 3B. Grand Rapids: Baker, 1994.

———. "Luke-Acts." In *A Biblical Theology of the New Testament*, edited by Roy B. Zuck and Darrell L. Bock. Chicago: Moody, 1994.

———. *Proclamation from Prophecy and Pattern: Lucan Old Testament Christology*. JSNT Supplement Series 12. Sheffield: JSOT Press, 1987.

———. "The Reign of the Lord Christ." In *Dispensationalism, Israel and the Church: The Search for Definition*, edited by Craig A. Blaising, 37–67. Grand Rapids: Zondervan, 1992.

———. "Scripture Citing Scripture: Use of the Old Testament in the New." In *Interpreting the New Testament Text: Introduction to the Art and Science of Exegesis*, edited by Darrell L. Bock and Buist M. Fanning, 255–76. Wheaton, IL: Crossway, 2006.

———. "The Son of David and the Saints' Task: The Hermeneutics of Initial Fulfillment." *Bibliotheca sacra* 150 (1993) 440–57.

———. *Studying the Historical Jesus: A Guide to Sources and Methods*. Grand Rapids: Baker, 2002.

———. "Summary Essay." In *Three Views on the Millennium and Beyond*, edited by Darrell L. Bock, 279–309. Grand Rapids: Zondervan, 1999.

———. "The Trial and Death of Jesus in N. T. Wright's Jesus and the Victory of God." In *Jesus and the Restoration of Israel: A Critical Assessment of N. T. Wright's Jesus and the Victory of God*, edited by Carey C. Newman, 101–25. Downers Grove: InterVarsity, 1999.

———. "Use of the Old Testament in the New." In *Foundations for Biblical Interpretation: A Complete Library of Tools and Resources*, edited by David S. Dockery, 97–114. Nashville: Broadman, 1994.

———. "The Words of Jesus in the Gospels: Live, Jive or Memorex." In *Jesus Under Fire*, edited by Michael J. Wilkins and J. P. Moreland, 73–99. Grand Rapids: Zondervan, 1995.

Bock, Darrell L., and Gregory J. Herrick, eds. *Jesus in Context: Background Readings for Gospel Study*. Grand Rapids: Baker, 2005.

Bockmuehl, Markus. "The New Testament Resistance and Redemption in the Jesus Tradition." Chapter 5 in *Redemption and Resistance: The Messianic Hopes of Jews and Christians in Antiquity*, edited by William Horbury et al. London: T. & T. Clark, 2007.

Borg, Marcus J. *Conflict, Holiness and Politics in the Teaching of Jesus*. Studies in the Bible and Early Christianity 5. New York: Mellen, 1984.

———. *Jesus, a New Vision*. San Francisco: Harper & Row, 1988.

Bibliography

———. "Jesus Was Not an Apocalyptic Prophet." In *The Apocalyptic Jesus: A Debate*, edited by Robert J. Miller, 31–48. Santa Rosa, CA: Polebridge, 2001.

———. "An Orthodoxy Reconsidered: The 'End-of-the-World Jesus.'" In *The Glory of Christ in the New Testament*, edited by L. D. Hurst and N. T. Wright, 207–17. Oxford: Clarendon, 1987.

———. "A Temperate Case for a Non-Eschatological Jesus." *Foundations and Facets Forum* 2 (1986) 81–102.

Borg, Marcus J., and N. T. Wright. *The Meaning of Jesus: Two Visions*. San Francisco: HarperSanFrancisco, 1999.

Bornkamm, Günther. *Jesus of Nazareth*. Translated by I. and F. McLuskey. New York: Harper & Row, 1960.

———. "μυστήριον." In *Theological Dictionary of the New Testament*, edited by Gerhard Friedrich, translated and edited by Geoffrey W. Bromiley, 4:802–28. Grand Rapids: Eerdmans, 1967.

Bousset, Wilhelm. *Kyrios Christos: A History of the Belief in Christ from the Beginnings of Christianity to Irenaeus*. Translated by John E. Steely. Nashville: Abingdon, 1970.

Bowman, Alan K. et al. *The Cambridge Ancient History*. 2nd ed. Vol. 11, *The High Empire A.D. 70–192*. 13 vols. Cambridge: Cambridge University Press, 2000.

Braaten, Carl E. *Christ and Counter-Christ: Apocalyptic Themes in Theology and Culture*. Philadelphia: Fortress, 1972.

———. "The Significance of Apocalypticism for Systematic Theology." *Interpretation* 25 (1971) 480–99.

Breisach, Ernst. *On the Future of History: The Postmodernist Challenge and Its Aftermath*. Chicago: University of Chicago Press, 2003.

Brown, C. "Prophet." In *The New International Dictionary of New Testament Theology*, edited by Colin Brown, 3:84–89. Grand Rapids: Zondervan, 1986.

Brown, Raymond E. "How Much Did Jesus Know?" In *The Historical Jesus: Critical Concepts in Religious Studies*, edited by Craig A. Evans, 3:50–82. New York: Routledge, 2004.

Buchanan, George Wesley. "Meyer's Support for Weiss's Eschatology." *Downside Review* 110 (1992) 83–96.

Bultmann, Rudolf. "The Concept of Revelation in the New Testament (1929)." In *Existence and Faith*, translated by Schubert M. Ogden, 58–91. New York: Meridian, 1960.

———. *History and Eschatology: The Gifford Lectures 1955*. Edinburgh: Edinburgh University Press, 1957.

———. *The History of the Synoptic Tradition*. Translated by J. Marsh. New York: Harper & Row, 1963.

———. *Jesus Christ and Mythology*. New York: Scribner, 1958. Reprint, London: SCM, 1960.

———. "New Testament and Mythology." In *Kerygma and Myth*, 1–44. London: SPCK, 1953; German original, 1941.

———. *Primitive Christianity in Its Contemporary Setting*. New York: Meridian, 1956.

Burkitt, F. C. *Jewish and Christian Apocalypses*. Schweich Lectures 1913. London: Oxford University Press, 1914.

———. "Mark 8.12 and εἰ in Hellenistic Greek." *Journal of Theological Studies* 28 (1926) 274–76.

———. "Robert Henry Charles, 1855–1931." In *Proceedings of the British Academy*, 17:437–45. London: Milford, 1931.

Bibliography

Bury, J. B., et al. *The Cambridge Ancient History*. Vol. 1, *Egypt and Babylonia to 1580 B.C.* 12 vols. Cambridge: Cambridge University Press, 1923.

Caird, G. B. *Jesus and the Jewish Nation*. London: Athlone, 1965.

———. *The Language and Imagery of the Bible*. Philadelphia: Westminster, 1980.

———. *New Testament Theology*. With L. D. Hurst. Oxford: Clarendon, 1994.

———. *The Revelation of St. John the Divine*. Harper's New Testament Commentaries. New York: Harper & Row, 1966.

———. *Saint Luke*. Edited by D. E. Nineham. Philadelphia: Westminster, 1977.

Cancik, Hubert. "The End of the Worlds of History and of the Individual in Greek and Roman Antiquity." In *The Encyclopedia of Apocalypticism*, edited by John J. Collins, 1:84–125. New York: Continuum, 1998.

Caragounis, C. C. "Kingdom of God." In *Dictionary of Jesus and the Gospels*, edited by Joel B. Green et al., 417–30. Downers Grove: InterVarsity, 1992.

Carroll, John T. *Response to the End of History: Eschatology and Situation in Luke-Acts*. SBL Dissertation Series 92. Atlanta: Scholars, 1988.

Carson, D. A. "Matthew." In *Expositor's Bible Commentary*, edited by Frank E. Gaebelein, vol. 8. Grand Rapids: Zondervan, 1984.

Case, Shirley J. *The Evolution of Early Christianity: A Genetic Study of First-Century Christianity in Relation to Its Religious Environment*. Chicago: University of Chicago Press, 1914.

Casey, P. M. *Son of Man: The Interpretation and Influence of Daniel 7*. London: SPCK, 1979.

Charles, R. H. *The Assumption of Moses: Translated from the Latin Sixth Century MS., the Unemended Text of Which Is Published Herewith....* London: Black, 1897.

———. *The Book of Enoch*. Rev. ed. Oxford: Clarendon, 1912.

———. "The Book of Jubilees: Introduction." In *The Apocrypha and Pseudepigrapha of the Old Testament in English*, 2:1–10. Oxford: Clarendon, 1913.

———. *A Critical History of the Doctrine of a Future Life in Israel, in Judaism, and in Christianity*. Rev. 2nd ed. London: Black, 1913.

———. "An Early Source of the Testaments of the Twelve Patriarchs." *Jewish Quarterly Review* 19 (1907) 566–80.

———. *Eschatology: The Doctrine of a Future Life in Israel, Judaism and Christianity*. New York: Schocken, 1963.

———. *Religious Development between the Old and New Testaments*. London: Williams & Norgate, 1914. Reprint, 1921.

———. *The Revelation of St. John*. International Critical Commentary 2. Edinburgh: T. & T. Clark, 1920.

———. *The Rise and Development of the Belief in a Future Life in Judaism and Christianity: Drew Lecture on Immortality*. Oxford: Clarendon, 1912.

Charles, R. H., and W. R. Morfill. *The Book of the Secrets of Enoch*. Oxford: Clarendon, 1896.

Chilton, Bruce, and Craig A. Evans. *Jesus in Context: Temple, Purity, and Restoration*. Leiden: Brill, 1997.

———. *Studying the Historical Jesus: Evaluations of the State of Current Research*. Leiden: Brill, 1994.

Chilton, Bruce, et al. *The Missing Jesus: Rabbinic Judaism and the New Testament*. Boston: Brill, 2002.

Bibliography

Clifford, Richard J. "The Roots of Apocalypticism in the Near East Myth." In *The Encyclopedia of Apocalypticism*, edited by John J. Collins, 1:3–38. New York: Continuum, 1998.

Coelho, Ivo. *Hermeneutics and Method: The Universal Viewpoint in Bernard Lonergan.* Toronto: University of Toronto Press, 2001.

Colani, T. *Jésus Christ et les croyances messianiques de son temps.* 2nd ed. Strasbourg: Treuttel & Wurtz, 1864.

Collins, John J. "Apocalypse and Apocalypticism: Early Jewish Apocalypticism." In *Anchor Bible Dictionary*, edited by David Noel Freedman, 1:282–88. New York: Doubleday, 1992.

———, ed. *Apocalypse: The Morphology of a Genre.* Semeia 14. Missoula, MT: Scholars, 1979.

———. "Apocalyptic Eschatology as the Transcendence of Death." *Catholic Biblical Quarterly* 36 (1974) 21–43.

———. *The Apocalyptic Imagination: An Introduction to Jewish Apocalyptic Literature.* 2nd ed. Grand Rapids: Eerdmans, 1998.

———. *Apocalypticism in the Dead Sea Scrolls.* New York: Routledge, 1997.

———. "Eschatologies of Late Antiquity." In *Dictionary of New Testament Background*, edited by Craig A. Evans and Stanley E. Porter, 330–37. Downers Grove: InterVarsity, 2000.

———. "From Prophecy to Apocalypticism: The Expectation of the End." In *The Encyclopedia of Apocalypticism*, edited by John J. Collins, 1:129–61. New York: Continuum, 1998.

———. Introduction to volume 1. In *The Encyclopedia of Apocalypticism*, edited by John J. Collins, 1:xiii–xvii. New York: Continuum, 1998.

———. "Prophecy, Apocalypse and Eschatology: Reflections on the Proposals of Lester Grabbe." In *Knowing the End from the Beginning: The Prophetic, the Apocalyptic and Their Relationships*, edited by Lester L. Grabbe and Robert D. Haak, 44–52. London: T. & T. Clark, 2003.

———. Review of *The Language and Imagery of the Bible*, by G. B. Caird. *Journal of Religion* 63 (1983) 183–84.

———. *Seers, Sybils, and Sages in Hellenistic-Roman Judaism.* Journal for the Study of Judaism in the Persian, Hellenistic, and Roman Periods Supplement 54. Leiden: Brill, 1997.

Cook, Stephen L. "Mythological Discourse in Ezekiel and Daniel and the Rise of Apocalypticism in Israel." In *Knowing the End from the Beginning: The Prophetic, the Apocalyptic and Their Relationships*, edited by Lester L. Grabbe and Robert D. Haak, 85–106. London: T. & T. Clark, 2003.

———. *Prophecy and Apocalypticism: The Postexilic Social Setting.* Minneapolis: Fortress, 1995.

Cotterell, Peter, and Max Turner. *Linguistics and Biblical Interpretation.* Downers Grove: InterVarsity, 1989.

Cranfield, C. E. B. *The Gospel according to Saint Mark: An Introduction and Commentary.* Cambridge Greek Testament Commentary. Cambridge: Cambridge University Press, 1959.

Crossan, John Dominic. *The Birth of Christianity: Discovering What Happened in the Years Immediately after the Execution of Jesus.* San Francisco: HarperSanFrancisco, 1998.

Bibliography

Daniélou, Jean. *From Shadows to Reality: Studies in the Biblical Typology of the Fathers.* Translated by Wulstan Hibberd. Westminster: Newman, 1960.

———. "The New Testament and the Theology of History." In *Studia Evangelica: Papers Presented to the International Congress on "The Four Gospels in 1957" Held at Christ Church, Oxford 1957*, edited by Kurt Aland et al., 25–34. Berlin: Akademie, 1959.

Davids, Peter H. *The First Epistle of Peter.* Grand Rapids: Eerdmans, 1990.

Davidson, Richard M. *Typology in Scripture: A Study of Hermeneutical τύπος Structures.* Berrien Springs, MI: Andrews University Press, 1981.

Davies, W. D. *Christian Origins and Judaism.* Philadelphia: Westminster, 1962.

———. *The Territorial Dimension of Judaism.* Berkeley: University of California Press, 1974.

Denton, Donald L. *Historiography and Hermeneutics in Jesus Studies: An Examination of the Work of John Dominic Crossan and Ben F. Meyer.* Journal for the Study of Historical Jesus Supplement Series 262. London: T. & T. Clark, 2004.

Dodd, C. H. *The Apostolic Preaching and Its Developments, with an Appendix on Eschatology and History.* New York: Harper, 1936.

———. "Jesus as Teacher and Prophet." In *Mysterium Christi: Christological Studies by British and German Theologians*, edited by G. K. A. Bell and D. Adolf Deissmann, 53–66. London: Longmans, 1930.

———. *New Testament Studies.* Manchester: Manchester University Press, 1953.

———. *The Parables of the Kingdom.* London: Nisbet, 1935.

———. *The Parables of the Kingdom.* Rev. ed. New York: Scribner, 1961.

Driver, R. H. *The Book of Daniel.* Cambridge: Cambridge University Press, 1900.

———. *Studies in the Apocalypse.* Edinburgh: T. & T. Clark, 1913.

Duhm, Bernhard. *Das buch Jesaia.* 4th ed. Göttingen: Vandenhoeck & Ruprecht, 1892.

Dunn, J. D. G. "Can the Third Quest Hope to Succeed?" In *Authenticating the Activities of Jesus*, edited by Bruce Chilton and Craig Evans, 31–38. New Testament Tools and Studies 28.2. Leiden: Brill, 1999.

———. "He Will Come Again." *Interpretation* 51 (1997) 42–56.

———. *Jesus Remembered.* Cambridge and Grand Rapids: Eerdmans, 2003.

———. *The Partings of the Ways: Between Christianity and Judaism and Their Significance for the Character of Christianity.* London and Philadelphia: SCM and Trinity, 1991.

———. Review of *The Aims of Jesus*, by Ben F. Meyer. *Scottish Journal of Theology* 34 (1981) 474–76.

———. *Unity and Diversity in the New Testament: An Inquiry into the Character of Earliest Christianity.* London: SCM, 1977.

Dunn, J. D. G., and Scot McKnight, eds. *The Historical Jesus in Recent Research.* Winona Lake, IN: Eisenbrauns, 2005.

Ebeling, Gerhard. *Die Geschichtlichkeit der Kirche und ihre Verkündigung als theologisches Problem.* Tübingen: Mohr, 1954.

Eddy, Paul Rhodes. "Jesus as Diogenes? Reflections on the Cynic Jesus Thesis." *Journal of Biblical Literature* 115 (1996) 449–69.

Ehrman, Bart D. *The New Testament: A Historical Introduction to the Early Christian Writings.* 3rd ed. New York: Oxford University Press, 2004.

Ellis, E. Earle. *The Making of the New Testament Documents.* Leiden: Brill, 2002.

Evans, Craig A. *Ancient Texts for New Testament Studies: A Guide to the Background Literature.* Peabody: Hendrickson, 2005.

Bibliography

———. "The Function of the Old Testament in the New." In *Introducing New Testament interpretation*, edited by Scot McKnight, 163–93. Grand Rapids: Baker, 1989.

———. "Jesus of Nazareth: Who Do Scholars Say that He is?" *Crux* 23 (1987) 15–19.

———. *Mark 8:27—16:20*. Word Biblical Commentary 34B. Nashville: Nelson, 2001.

———. *Noncanonical Writings and New Testament Interpretation*. Peabody: Hendrickson, 1992.

Farmer, William R., ed. *Crisis in Christology: Essays in Quest of Resolution*. Great Modern Debates 3. Livonia, MI: Dove, 1995.

———. "Reflections upon 'The Historical Perimeters for Understanding *The Aims of Jesus*': A paper presented for discussion." In *A Symposium Honoring Professor Ben F. Meyer*. McMaster University, 1989.

Feinberg, John S. *Continuity and Discontinuity: Perspectives on the Relationship Between the Old and New Testaments*. Westchester, IL: Crossway, 1988.

Feinberg, Paul D. "Hermeneutics of Discontinuity." In *Continuity and Discontinuity*, edited by John S. Feinberg, 109–27. Westchester, IL: Crossway, 1988.

Fitzmyer, J. Review of *An Aramaic Approach to the Gospels and Acts*, by Matthew Black, with an Appendix on the Son on Man, by Geza Vermes. *Catholic Biblical Quarterly* 30 (1968) 417–28.

Floyd, Michael H., and Robert D. Haak, eds. *Prophets, Prophecy and Prophetic Texts in Second Temple Judaism*. London: T. & T. Clark, 2006.

Foulkes, Francis. *The Acts of God: A Study of the Basis of Typology in the Old Testament*. London: Tyndale, 1958.

France, R. T. *The Gospel of Mark: A Commentary on the Greek Text*. Grand Rapids: Eerdmans, 2002.

———. *Jesus and the Old Testament: His Application of Old Testament Passages to Himself and His Mission*. Downers Grove: InterVarsity, 1971.

Frost, Stanley B. "Apocalyptic and History." In *The Bible in Modern Scholarship*, edited by J. Philip Hyatt, 98–113. Nashville: Abingdon, 1965.

———. "Eschatology and Myth." *Vestus Testamentum* 2 (1952) 70–80.

———. *Old Testament Apocalyptic: Its Origins and Growth*. London: Epworth, 1952.

Fuchs, Ernst. *Hermeneutik*. 3rd ed. Bad Cannstatt: Mullerschön, 1963.

———. "On the Task of a Christian Theology." In *Apocalypticism*, edited by Robert W. Funk, 69–98. Journal for Theology and the Church 6. New York: Herder & Herder, 1969.

Funk, Robert W. "Apocalyptic as an Historical and Theological Problem in Current New Testament Scholarship." In *Apocalypticism*, edited by R. W. Funk, 175–91. Journal for Theology and the Church 6. New York: Herder & Herder, 1969.

Funk, Robert W., and Roy W. Hoover. *The Five Gospels: The Search for the Authentic Words of Jesus*. San Francisco: HarperSanFrancisco, 1997.

Gadamer, Hans Georg. *Truth and Method*. New York: Continuum, 1975.

Gadamer, Hans-Georg, et al. *Truth and Method*. 2nd ed. New York: Continuum, 2004.

García, Martínez F. "Encore l'apocalyptique." *Journal for the Study of Judaism in the Persian, Hellenistic and Roman Periods* 17 (1986) 224–32.

Garrett, Duane A. "Type, Typology." In *Evangelical Dictionary of Biblical Theology*, edited by Walter A. Elwell, 785–87. Grand Rapids: Baker, 1996.

Gathercole, Simon J. *Where Is Boasting? Early Jewish Soteriology and Paul's Response in Romans 1–5*. Grand Rapids: Eerdmans, 2002.

Bibliography

Geddert, T. J. "Apocalyptic Teaching." In *Dictionary of Jesus and the Gospels*, edited by Joel B. Green et al., 20–27. Downers Grove: InterVarsity, 1992.

Gnilka, Joachim. *Jesus of Nazareth: Message and History*. Peabody: Hendrickson, 1997.

Goguel, Maurice. "Eschatologie et apocalyptique dans le christianisme primitif." *Revue de l'histoire des religions* 106 (1932) 381–424.

Goppelt, Leonhard. *Theology of the New Testament*. Translated by John E. Alsup. Vol. 2. Edited by Jürgen Roloff. Grand Rapids: Eerdmans, 1982.

———. *Typos: The Typological Interpretation of the Old Testament in the New*. Translated by Donald H. Madvig. Grand Rapids: Eerdmans, 1982.

Grabbe, Lester L. "Introduction and Overview." In *Knowing the End from the Beginning: The Prophetic, the Apocalyptic and Their Relationships*, edited by Lester L. Grabbe and Robert D. Haak, 2–43. London: T. & T. Clark, 2003.

———. "Prophecy and Apocalyptic: Time for New Definitions—and New Thinking." In *Knowing the End from the Beginning*, edited by Lester L. Grabbe and Robert D. Haak, 46:107–33. London: T. & T. Clark, 2003.

Grabbe, Lester L., and Robert D. Haak, eds. *Knowing the End from the Beginning: The Prophetic, the Apocalyptic and Their Relationships*. Journal for the Study of the Pseudepigrapha Supplement Series 46. London: T. & T. Clark, 2003.

Gray, John A. "The Day of Yahweh in Cultic Experience and Eschatological Prospect." *Svensk exegetisk årsbok* 39 (1974) 5–37.

Gressmann, Hugo. *Der Ursprung der israelitisch-jüdischer Eschatolgie*. Göttingen: Vandenhoeck und Ruprecht, 1905.

Gunkel, Hermann. *Schöpfung und Chaos in Urzeit und Endzeit*. Göttingen: Vandenhoeck & Ruprecht, 1895.

Guthrie, Donald. *A Shorter Life of Christ*. Grand Rapids: Zondervan, 1970.

Halpern-Amaru, Betsy. *Rewriting the Bible: Land and Covenant in Postbiblical Jewish Literature*. Valley Forge, PA: Trinity, 1994.

Hanhart, Robert. *Septuaginta*. Rev. ed. Stuttgart: Deutsche Bibelgesellschaft, 2006.

Hanson, Paul D. *The Dawn of Apocalyptic*. Philadelphia: Fortress, 1975.

———. "Jewish Apocalyptic against Its Near Eastern Environment." *Biblical Research* 78 (1971) 31–58.

———. *Old Testament Apocalyptic*. Nashville: Abingdon, 1987.

———. "Old Testament Apocalyptic Reexamined." *Interpretation* 25 (1971) 454–79.

———. "Zechariah 9 and the Recapitulation of an Ancient Ritual Pattern." *Journal Biblical Literature* 92 (1973) 37–59.

Harris, Murray J. *The Second Epistle to the Corinthians: A Commentary on the Greek Text*. Grand Rapids: Eerdmans 2005.

Harris, W. Hall. "Apocalyptic Genre: Visions and Symbols." In *Interpreting the New Testament Text: Introduction to the Art and Science of Exegesis*, edited by Darrell L. Bock and Buist M. Fanning, 241–54. Wheaton, IL: Crossway, 2006.

Hawkin, David. "The Markan Horizon of Meaning." In *Self-Definition and Self-Discovery in Early Christianity: A Study in Changing Horizons*, edited by David J. Hawkin and Tom Robinson, 1–30. Studies in Bible and Early Christianity 26. Lewiston, NY: Mellen, 1990.

Heater, Homer. "Destruction Genre in the Prophets." Paper presented to the Eastern Regional Meeting of the Evangelical Theological Society, Lanham, MD, March, 1996.

———. "Do the Prophets Teach That Babylonia Will Be Rebuilt in the Eschaton?" *Journal of the Evangelical Theological Society* 41 (1998) 23–43.

Bibliography

Heidegger, Martin. *On Time and Being*. New York: Harper & Row, 1972.
Hendriksen, William. *The Gospel according to Luke*. New Testament Commentary. Grand Rapids: Baker, 1978.
Hengel, Martin. *Judaism and Hellenism: Studies in Their Encounter in Palestine during the Early Hellenistic Period*. Translated by John Bowden. 2 vols. Philadelphia: Fortress, 1974.
———. *Studies in Early Christology*. Edinburgh: T. & T. Clark, 1995.
———. *Was Jesus a Revolutionist?* Philadelphia: Fortress, 1971.
Hölscher, Gustav. "Die Entstehug des Buches Daniel." *Theologische Studien und Kritiken* 92 (1919) 113–38.
Holtzmann, H. J. "Lebensbild Jesu nach der Quelle A." In *Die synoptischen Evangelien: Ihr Ursprung und geschichtlicher Charakter*, 468–96. Leipzig: Engelmann, 1863.
Horsley, Richard A. *Hearing the Whole Story: The Politics of Plot in Mark's Gospel*. Louisville: Westminster John Knox, 2001.
———. "The Kingdom of God and the Renewal of Israel: Synoptic Gospels, Jesus Movements, and Apocalypticism." In *The Encyclopedia of Apocalypticism*, edited by John J. Collins, 1:303–44. New York: Continuum, 1998.
———. *Revolt of the Scribes: Resistance and Apocalyptic Origins*. Minneapolis: Fortress, 2010.
———. "Wisdom and Apocalypticism in Mark." In *In Search of Wisdom: Essays in Memory of John G. Gammie*, edited by Leo G. Perdue, 223–44. Louisville: Westminster John Knox, 1993.
Hyde, Michael J., and Craig R. Smith. "Hermeneutics and Rhetoric: A Seen but Unobserved Relationship." *Quarterly Journal of Speech* 65.4 (1979): 347–63.
Instone-Brewer, David. *Traditions of the Rabbis from the Era of the New Testament*. Vol. 1, *Prayer and Agriculture*. Grand Rapids: Eerdmans, 2004.
Jeremias, J. *Abba: Studien zur neutestamentlichen Theologie und Zeitgeschichte*. Göttingen: Vandenhoeck & Ruprecht, 1966.
———. "Das Lösegeld für Viele (Mk.10:45)." *Judacia* 3 (1947) 249–64.
———. *Die Abendmahlsworte Jesu*. Göttingen: Vandenhoeck & Ruprecht, 1935.
———. "Eine neue Schau der zukunftsaussagen Jesu." *Theologische Blätter* 20 (1941) 216–22.
———. *The Eucharistic Words of Jesus*. Translated by Arnold Ehrhardt. New York: Macmillan, 1955.
———. "Jesus als Weltvollender." *Beiträge zur Förderung christlicher Theologie* (1930) 35–44.
———. *Jesus' Promise to the Nations*. Translated by S. H. Hooke. Studies in Biblical Theology 24. London: SCM, 1958.
———. *New Testament Theology: The Proclamation of Jesus*. Translated by John Bowden. New York: Scribner, 1971.
———. *The Parables of Jesus*. Translated by S. H. Hooke. 2nd ed. New York: Scribner, 1954.
———. *The Parables of Jesus*. Translated by S. H. Hooke. 3rd ed. New York: SCM, 1972.
———. *The Prayers of Jesus*. Naperville, IL: Allenson, 1967.
———. *The Problem of the Historical Jesus*. Translated by N. Perrin. Philadelphia: Fortress, 1964.
Jindo, Job Y. "On Myth and History in Prophetic and Apocalyptic Eschatology." *Vetus Testamentum* 55 (2005) 412–15.

BIBLIOGRAPHY

Johnson, Elliot E. "Apocalyptic Genre in Literal Interpretation." In *Essays in Honor of J. Dwight Pentecost*, edited by Stanley D. Toussaint and Charles H. Dyer, 197–210. Chicago: Moody, 1986.

———. *Expository Hermeneutics: An Introduction*. Grand Rapids: Zondervan, 1990.

Johnston, Christopher C. "Jesus and the Climax of Israel's Story: An Exploration of the Hermeneutic of 'Story' with Reference to Matthew 24-25, Mark 13 and Luke 21." PhD thesis, Murdoch University, 2012.

Josephus, Flavius. *The Works of Josephus: Complete and Unabridged*. Translated by William Whiston. New updated ed. Peabody: Hendrickson, 1987.

Just, Arthur A. *The Ongoing Feast: Table Fellowship and Eschatology at Emmaus*. Collegeville: Liturgical, 1993.

Kähler, Martin. *The So-Called Historical Jesus and the Historic, Biblical Christ*. Translated by Carl E. Braaten. Philadelphia: Fortress, 1964.

Käsemann, Ernst. "The Beginnings of Christian Theology." In *New Testament Questions of Today*, edited by C. F. D. Moule, 82–107. London: SCM, 1969.

———. "Die Anfänge christlicher Theologie." *Zeitschrift für Theologie und Kirche* 57 (1960) 162–85.

———. "On the Subject of Primitive Christian Apocalyptic." In *New Testament Questions of Today*, edited by C. F. D. Moule, 108–37. London: SCM, 1969.

———. "The Problem of the Historical Jesus." In *Essays on New Testament Themes*, translated by W. J. Montague, 15–47. London: SCM, 1954. Reprint, 1964.

Keel, Othmar. *The Symbolism of the Biblical World: Ancient Near Eastern Iconography and the Book of Psalms*. Translated by Timothy J. Hallett. New York: Crossroad, 1985.

Koch, Klaus. *Ratlos vor der Apokalyptik*. Gütersloh, Germany: Gütersloher Verlagshaus, 1970.

———. *The Rediscovery of Apocalyptic: A Polemical Work on a Neglected Area of Biblical Studies and Its Damaging Effects on Theology and Philosophy*. Translated by Margaret Kohl. Naperville, IL: Allenson, 1970.

Körtner, Ulrich H. J. *The End of the World: A Theological Interpretation*. Translated by Douglas W. Scott. Louisville: Westminster John Knox, 1995.

———. *Weltangst und Weltende: Eine theologische Interpretation der Apokalyptic*. Göttingen: Vandenhoeck & Ruprecht, 1988.

Kubo, Sakae. *A Reader's Greek-English Lexicon of the New Testament: And a Beginner's Guide for the Translation of New Testament Greek*. Grand Rapids: Zondervan, 1975.

Kulik, Alexander. *Retroverting Slavonic Pseudepigrapha: Toward the Original of the Apocalypse of Abraham*. Text-Critical Studies 3. Atlanta: SBL, 2004.

Ladd, George E. "Apocalyptic and New Testament Theology." In *Reconciliation and Hope*, edited by Robert J. Banks, 285–96. Grand Rapids: Eerdmans, 1974.

———. "Historic Premillennialism." In *The Meaning of the Millennium: Four Views*, edited by Robert G. Clouse, 17–40. Downers Grove: InterVarsity, 1977.

———. *Jesus and the Kingdom: The Eschatology of Biblical Realism*. New York: Harper & Row, 1964.

———. "The Kingdom of God in the Jewish Apocryphal Literature." *Bibliotheca sacra* 109 (1952) 55–62.

———. *The New Testament and Criticism*. Grand Rapids: Eerdmans, 1967.

———. *The Presence of the Future: The Eschatology of Biblical Realism*. Rev. ed. Grand Rapids: Eerdmans, 1974.

Bibliography

———. "Why Not Prophetic-Apocalyptic." *Journal of Biblical Literature* 76 (1957) 192–200.

Lane, William L. *The Gospel according to Mark*. New International Commentary of the New Testament. Grand Rapids: Eerdmans, 1974.

Lawrence, Irene. *Linguistics and Theology: The Significance of Noam Chomsky for Theological Construction*. ATLA Monograph Series 16. Metuchen, NJ: Scarecrow, 1980.

Lewis, Scott M. *What Are They Saying about New Testament Apocalyptic?* New York: Paulist Press, 2004.

Lietaert Peerbolte, L. J. *The Antecedents of Antichrist: A Traditio-Historical Study of the Earliest Christian Views on Eschatological Opponents*. Leiden: Brill, 1996.

Lindblom, Johannes. *Die jesaja-apocalypse Jes. 24–27*. Lunds Universitets Årsskrift, Lund: Gleerup, 1938.

———. *Prophecy in Ancient Israel*. Philadelphia: Muhlenberg, 1962.

———. *The Servant Songs in Deutero-Isaiah: A New Attempt to Solve an Old Problem*. Lund: Gleerup, 1951.

———. *A Study on the Immanuel Section in Isaiah: Isa. 7:1—9:6*. Scripta Minora Regiae Societatis Humaniorum Litterarum Lundensis 1957-1958. Lund: Gleerup, 1958.

Lonergan, Bernard J. F. *Insight: A Study of Human Understanding*. Rev. ed. New York: Harper & Row, 1978.

———. "Metaphysics as Horizon." *Gregoriarum* 44 (1963) 307–18.

———. *Method in Theology*. London: Darton, Longman and Todd, 1973.

Lonergan, Bernard J. F., and Frederick E. Crowe. *A Third Collection: Papers*. New York: Paulist, 1985.

Lonergan, Bernard J. F., et al. *Collected Works of Bernard Lonergan*. Toronto: Published by University of Toronto Press for Lonergan Research Institute of Regis College, 1988.

Lonergan, Bernard J. F. et al. *A Second Collection: Papers*. Toronto: Published by University of Toronto Press for Lonergan Research Institute of Regis College, Toronto, 1996.

Lubac, Henrie de. "'Typologie' et 'allégorisme.'" *Recherches de science religieuse* 34 (1947) 180–226.

Lücke, F. *Versuch einer vollständigen Einleitung in die Offenbarung Johannis in die gesamte apokalyptische Literature*. Bonn: Webber, 1832.

Manson, T. W. *The Old Testament in the Teaching of Jesus*. Manchester: Manchester University Press, 1952.

———. *The Teaching of Jesus: Studies of Its Form and Content*. Cambridge: Cambridge University Press, 1931.

———. *The Teaching of Jesus: Studies of Its Form and Content*. 2nd ed. Cambridge: Cambridge University Press, 1935. Reprint, 1955.

Margolis, Joseph. *Philosophy Looks at the Arts: Contemporary Readings in Aesthetics*. New York: Scribner, 1962.

Mason, Rex, et al. *After the Exile: Essays in Honour of Rex Mason*. Macon, GA: Mercer University Press, 1996.

Marshall, I. Howard. "Historical Criticism." In *New Testament Interpretation: Essays on Principles and Methods*, edited by I. Howard Marshall, 126–38. Grand Rapids: Eerdmans, 1977.

———. "Is Apocalyptic the Mother of Christian Theology?" In *Tradition and Interpretation in the New Testament*, edited by Gerald F. Hawthorne and Otto Betz, 33–42. Grand Rapids: Eerdmans, 1987.

Bibliography

———. Review of *The Aims of Jesus*, by Ben F. Meyer. *Journal for the Study of the New Testament* 7 (1980) 67–69.

———. "The Son of Man Debate: A History and Evaluation." *Evangelical Quarterly* 73 (2001) 348–49.

———. "The Synoptic Son of Man Sayings in Recent Discussion." *New Testament Studies* 12 (1966) 327–51.

Martínez, García F. "Encore l'apocalyptique." *Journal for the Study of Judaism in the Persian, Hellenistic, and Roman Periods* 17 (1986) 224–32.

Martyn, J. Louis. "Apocalyptic Antinomies in Paul's Letters to the Galatians." *New Testament Studies* 31 (1985) 410–24.

McGinn, Bernard. "Early Apocalypticism: the Ongoing Debate." In *The Apocalypse in English Renaissance Thought and Literature*, edited by C. A. Patrides and J. Wittreich, 23–29. Manchester: Manchester University Press, 1984.

McKnight, Scot. "Jesus and Prophetic Actions." *Bulletin for Biblical Research* 10 (2000) 197–232.

———. "Source Criticism." In *Interpreting the New Testament: Essays on Methods and Issues*, edited by David Alan Black and David S. Dockery, 74–105. Nashville: Broadman & Holman, 2001.

McKnight, Scot, and Grant R. Osborne. *The Face of New Testament Studies: A Survey of Recent Research*. Grand Rapids: Baker, 2004.

McKnight, Scot, and Matthew C. Williams. *The Synoptic Gospels: An Annotated Bibliography*. Institute of Biblical Research Bibliographies 6. Grand Rapids: Baker, 2000.

McNicol, Allan J. "The Composition of the Synoptic Eschatological Discourse." In *The Interrelations of the Gospels*, edited by David L. Dungan, 157–200. Leuven: Leuven University Press, 1990.

Meier, John P. *A Marginal Jew: Rethinking the Historical Jesus*. Vol. 1. Anchor Bible Reference Library. New York: Doubleday, 1991.

Metzger, Bruce M. *Oxford Annotated Apocrypha: The Apocrypha of the Old Testament Revised Standard Version*. New York: Oxford University Press, 1977.

Meyer, Ben F. *The Aims of Jesus*. London: SCM, 1979. Reprint, San Jose, CA: Pickwick, 2002.

———. "Appointed Deed, Appointed Doer: Jesus and the Scriptures." In *Crisis in Christology: Essays in Quest of Resolution*, edited by William R. Farmer, 311–32. Livonia, MI: Dove, 1995.

———. *Christus Faber: The Master Builder and the House of God*. Princeton Theological Monograph Series 29. Allison Park, PA: Pickwick, 1992.

———. *Critical Realism and the New Testament*. Allison Park, PA: Pickwick, 1989.

———. "The Expiation Motif in the Eucharistic Words: A Key to the History of Jesus?" *Gregorianum* 69 (1988) 461–87.

———. "Jesus and the Remnant of Israel." *Journal of Biblical Literature* 84 (1965) 123–30.

———. "Jesus's Scenario of the Future." *Downside Review* 109 (1991) 1–15.

———. "Many (= All) Are Called, but Few (= Not All) Are Chosen." *New Testament Studies* 36 (1990) 89–97.

———. *Reality and Illusion in New Testament Scholarship: A Primer in Critical Realist Hermeneutics*. Collegeville, MN: Michael Glazier, 1994.

———. "The Relevance of 'Horizon.'" *Downside Review* 112 (1994) 1–14.

Bibliography

Meyer, Marvin W., and Charles Hughes. "The Jesus Seminar and the Quest: Robert Funk." In *Jesus Then and Now: Images of Jesus in History and Christology*, 130–40. Harrisburg, PA: Trinity, 2001.

Millar, William R. *Isaiah 24–27 and the Origin of Apocalyptic*. Harvard Semitic Monograph Series 11. Missoula, MT: Scholars, 1976.

Miller, Robert J., ed. *The Apocalyptic Jesus: A Debate*. Santa Rosa, CA: Polebridge, 2001.

Morris, Leon. *Apocalyptic*. Grand Rapids: Eerdmans, 1972.

Moule, C. F. D. *An Idiom Book of New Testament Greek*. Cambridge: Cambridge University Press, 1953.

Mounce, William D. *Basics of Biblical Greek Grammar*. 2nd ed. Grand Rapids: Zondervan, 2003.

Murphy, Frederick James. *The Structure and Meaning of Second Baruch*. SBL Dissertation Series 78. Atlanta: Scholars, 1985.

Murphy, J. F. *The Religious World of Jesus*. Nashville: Abingdon, 1991.

Nestle, E., and K. Aland, eds. *Novum Testamentum Graece*. 27th ed. Stuttgart: Deutsche Bibelgesellschaft, 1998.

Neusner, Jacob. *The Mishnah: A New Translation*. New Haven: Yale University Press, 1988.

Newman, Carey C., ed. *Jesus and the Restoration of Israel: A Critical Assessment of N. T. Wright's Jesus and the Victory of God*. Downers Grove: InterVarsity, 1999.

Nir, Rivkah. *The Destruction of Jerusalem and the Idea of Redemption in the Syriac Apocalypse of Baruch*. SBL Early Judaism and Its Literature 20. Atlanta: SBL, 2003.

O'Callaghan, Paul. *The Christological Assimilation of the Apocalypse: An Essay on Fundamental Eschatology*. Portland, OR: Four Courts, 2004.

Orchard, Bernard, and Harold Riley. *The Order of the Synoptics: Why Three Synoptic Gospels?* Macon, GA: Mercer University Press, 1987.

Osborne, Grant. *The Hermeneutical Spiral: A Comprehensive Introduction to Biblical Interpretation*. Downers Grove: InterVarsity, 1991.

Pearson, Brook W. R. Review of *The Language and Imagery of the Bible*, by G. B. Caird. *Journal for the Study of the New Testament* 75 (1999) 116.

Perrin, N. "Eschatology and Hermeneutic: Reflections on Method in the Interpretation of the New Testament." *Journal of Biblical Literature* 93 (1974) 1–13.

———. *The Kingdom of God in the Teaching of Jesus*. Philadelphia: Westminster, 1963.

———. *The New Testament: An Introduction*. New York: Harcourt, Brace, 1974.

Piper, Ronald A. *Wisdom in the Q-Tradition: The Aphoristic Teaching of Jesus*. Society for New Testament Studies Monograph Series 61. Cambridge: Cambridge University Press, 1989.

Plöger, Otto. *Theocracy and Eschatology*. Translated by S. Rudman. Richmond, VA: John Knox, 1968.

Polaski, Donald C. *Authorizing an End: The Isaiah Apocalypse and Intertextuality*. Leiden: Brill, 2001.

Powell, Mark A. *Introducing the New Testament: A Historical, Literary, and Theological Survey*. Grand Rapids: Baker, 2009.

Pym, Anthony. *Translation and Text Transfer: An Essay on the Principles of Intercultural Communication*. New York: Lang, 1992.

Rad, Gerhard von. *Old Testament Theology*. Translated by D. M. G. Stalker. Vol. 2, *The Theology of Israel's Prophetic Traditions*. New York: Harper & Row, 1962.

Bibliography

———. "Οὐρανός." In *Theological Dictionary of the New Testament*, edited by Gerhard Friedrich and Geoffrey W. Bromiley, translated by Geoffrey W. Bromiley, 5:497–543. Grand Rapids: Eerdmans, 1967.

Ramm, Bernard. *Protestant Biblical Interpretation: A Textbook of Hermeneutics*. 3rd ed. Grand Rapids: Baker, 1975.

Reader, William W., and Anthony J. Chvala-Smith. *The Severed Hand and the Upright Corpse: The Declamations of Marcus Antonius Polemo*. SBL 42. Atlanta: Scholars, 1996.

Reddish, Mitchell G., ed. *Apocalyptic Literature: A Reader*. Peabody: Hendrickson, 1995.

Reese, Alexander. *The Approaching Advent of Christ*. London: Marshall, Morgan & Scott, 1937. Reprint, Grand Rapids: Grand Rapids International, 1975.

Reumann, John. Review of *The Aims of Jesus*, by Ben F. Meyer. *Journal of Biblical Literature* 100 (1981) 296–300.

Rhodes, David M. Review of *The Language and Imagery of the Bible*, by G. B. Caird. *Currents in Theology and Mission* 26 (1999) 136.

Roberts, J. J. M. "Myth Versus History." *Catholic Biblical Quarterly* 38 (1976) 1–13.

Rollins, Wayne G. "The New Testament and Apocalyptic." *New Testament Studies* 17 (1971) 454–76.

Rowland, Christopher. "Apocalyptic." In *A New Dictionary of Christian Theology*, edited by Alan Richardson and John Bowden, 28–29. London: SCM, 1983.

———. *The Open Heaven: A Study of Apocalyptic in Judaism and Early Christianity*. New York: Crossroads, 1982.

Rowland, Christopher, and John Barton, eds. *Apocalyptic in History and Tradition*. Journal for the Study of the Pseudepigrapha Supplement 43. London: Sheffield Academic, 2002.

Rowley, H. H. *The Relevance of Apocalyptic: A Study of Jewish and Christian Apocalypses from Daniel to the Revelation*. 3rd ed. London: Lutterworth, 1944. Reprint, London: Attic, 1963.

———. *The Relevance of Apocalyptic: A Study of Jewish and Christian Apocalypses from Daniel to the Revelation*. Rev. ed. New York: Harper & Row, 1946.

Russell, D. S. *Apocalyptic, Ancient and Modern*. Philadelphia: Fortress, 1978.

———. *Divine Disclosure: An Introduction to Jewish Apocalyptic*. Minneapolis: Fortress, 1992.

———. *The Method and Message of Jewish Apocalyptic 200 BC–AD 100*. Philadelphia: Westminster, 1964.

———. *Prophecy and the Apocalyptic Dream: Protest and Promise*. Peabody: Hendrickson, 1994.

Ryrie, Charles C. *Dispensationalism*. Rev. ed. Chicago: Moody, 2007.

———. *Dispensationalism Today*. Chicago: Moody, 1965.

Saldarini, Anthony J. *The Fathers according to Rabbi Nathan (Abot de Rabbi Nathan) Version B: A Translation and Commentary*. Leiden: Brill, 1975.

Sanders, E. P. "Defending the Indefensible." *Journal of Biblical Literature* 110 (1991) 463–77.

———. *Jesus and Judaism*. Philadelphia: Fortress, 1985.

———. "Jesus and the Kingdom: The Restoration of Israel and the New People of God." In *Jesus, the Gospels, and the Church: Essays in Honor of William R. Farmer*, edited by E. P. Sanders, 463–77. Macon, GA: Mercer University Press, 1987.

Bibliography

Saucy, Mark. *The Kingdom of God in the Teaching of Jesus in 20th Century Theology*. Dallas: Word, 1997.

Saucy, Robert L. *The Case for Progressive Dispensationalism: The Interface Between Dispensational and Non-Dispensational Theology*. Grand Rapids: Zondervan, 1993.

———. "A Rationale for the Future of Israel." Paper presented to Far-West Regional Meeting of the Evangelical Theological Society, El Cajon, CA, April, 1983.

———. "The Time of the Fulfillment of the Messianic Prophecies." Paper presented to the Annual Meeting of the Evangelical Theological Society, Dallas, December, 1983.

Sauter, Gerhard. *What Dare We Hope? Reconsidering Eschatology*. Harrisburg, PA: Trinity, 1999.

Schnackenburg, Rudolf. *God's Rule and Kingdom*. Translated by John Murray. New York: Herder & Herder, 1963.

Scholes, Robert. *Textual Power: Literary Theory and the Teaching of English*. New Haven: Yale University Press, 1985.

Schürmann, H. "Zur Traditions-und Redaktionsgeschichte von Mt. 10:23." *Biblische Zeitschrift* 3 (1959) 82–88.

Schweitzer, Albert. *The Quest of the Historical Jesus: A Critical Study of Its Progress from Reimarus to Wrede*. Translated by W. Montgomery. London: Black, 1910.

———. *Von Reimarus zu Wrede: Eine Geschichte der Leben Jesu Forschung*. Tübingen: Mohr, 1906.

Scott, James M. *Exile: Old Testament, Jewish, and Christian Conceptions*. Leiden: Brill, 1997.

———. *Restoration: Old Testament, Jewish, and Christian Perspectives*. Leiden: Brill, 2001.

Soskice, Janet Martin. *Metaphor and Religious Language*. London: Oxford University Press, 1985.

Sproul, R. C. *The Last Days according to Jesus*. Grand Rapids: Baker, 1998.

Stein, Robert H. *Studying the Synoptic Gospels: Origin and Interpretation*. 2nd ed. Grand Rapids: Baker, 2001.

———. "Synoptic Problem." In *Dictionary of Jesus and the Gospels*, edited by Joel B. Green et al., 784–92. Downers Grove: InterVarsity, 1992.

Stone, Michael E. "Lists of Revealed Things in Apocalyptic Literature." In *Magnalia Dei: The Mighty Acts of God*, edited by F. M. Cross et al., 414–52. New York, 1976.

———. "Three Transformations in Judaism: Scripture, History and Redemption." In *Selected Studies in Pseudepigrapha and Apocrypha: With Special Reference to Armenian Tradition*. Leiden: Brill, 1991.

Strauss, David Friedrich. *The Life of Jesus: A Critical Examination of His History*. Vol. 4. London: Hetherington, 1844.

———. *The Life of Jesus Critically Examined*. Philadelphia: Fortress, 1972.

Streeter, B. H. "Synoptic Criticism and the Eschatological Problem." In *Studies in the Synoptic Problem*, edited by W. Sanday, 425–36. Oxford: Clarendon, 1911.

Swing, Albert T. *The Theology of Albrecht Ritschl*. New York: Longmans Green, 1901.

Telford, W. R. *The Theology of the Gospel of Mark*. New Testament Theology. Cambridge: Cambridge University Press, 1999.

Thames, James. "Doctrinal Statement." In *Dallas Theological Seminary 2006–2007 Catalog*, 182–86. Dallas: Dallas Theological Seminary, 2006.

Theissen, Gerd. "Historical Skepticism and the Criteria of Jesus Research." *Scottish Journal of Theology* 49 (1996) 147–76.

Bibliography

Theissen, Gerd, and Annette Merz. *The Historical Jesus: A Comprehensive Guide.* Translated by John Bowden. Minneapolis: Fortress, 1998.
Thiselton, Anthony C. *Thiselton on Hermeneutics: Collected Works with New Essays.* Grand Rapids: Eerdmans, 2006.
Thomas, Robert L. "The Hermeneutics of Progressive Dispensationalism." *The Master's Seminary Journal* 6 (1995) 79–95.
Throckmorton, Burton H., Jr. *The New Testament and Mythology.* Philadelphia: Westminster, 1959.
Tigchelaar, E. J. C. "More on Apocalyptic and Apocalypses." *Journal for the Study of Judaism in the Persian, Hellenistic and Roman Periods* 18 (1987) 137–44
Travis, Stephen H. "The Value of Apocalyptic." In *Tyndale Bulletin* 30 (1978) 53–75.
Troeltsch, E. "Historiography." In *Encyclopædia of Religion and Ethics*, edited by James Hastings, 6:716–23. New York: Scribner, 1908.
———. *Was heisst "Wesen des Christentums"?* Gesammelte Schriften 2. Tübingen: Mohr, 1922.
Turner, David L., and Darrell L. Bock. *The Gospel of Matthew, the Gospel of Mark.* Cornerstone Biblical Commentary. Carol Stream, IL: Tyndale, 2005.
Vawter, Bruce. "Apocalyptic: Its Relation to Prophecy." *Catholic Biblical Quarterly* 22 (1960) 33–46.
Vermes, Geza. *Jesus the Jew: A Historical Reading of the Gospels.* New York: Macmillan, 1973.
Vielhauer, Philipp, and Georg Strecker. "Apocalypses and Related Subjects: Introduction." In *New Testament Apocrypha*, edited by Edgar Hennecke et al., 2:542–68. Philadelphia: Westminster, 1963. Reprint, Louisville: Westminster John Knox, 1991.
Wacholder, Ben Zion. *The New Damascus Document: The Midrash on the Eschatological Torah of the Dead Sea Scrolls: Reconstruction, Translation and Commentary.* Studies on the Texts of the Desert of Judah 56. Leiden: Brill, 2007.
Wallace, Daniel B. *Greek Grammar beyond the Basics: An Exegetical Syntax of the New Testament.* Grand Rapids: Zondervan, 1996.
Warnke, Georgia. *Gadamer: Hermeneutics, Tradition and Reason.* Stanford: Stanford University Press, 1987.
Watts, Rikki E. "Consolation or Confrontation: Isaiah 40–55 and the Delay of the New Exodus." *Tyndale Bulletin* 41 (1990) 31–59.
———. *Isaiah's New Exodus and Mark.* Tübingen: Mohr Siebeck, 1997.
Weiffenbach, W. *Der Weiderkunftsgedanke Jesu nach den Synoptikern kritisch untersucht und dargestellt.* Leipzig: Breitkopf und Härtel, 1873.
Weiss, Johannes. *Die Nachfolge Christi und die Predigt der Gegenwart.* Göttingen: Vandenhoeck & Ruprecht, 1895.
———. *Die Schriften des Neuen Testaments.* 2 vols. Göttingen: Vandenhoeck & Ruprecht, 1907.
———. *Jesus' Proclamation of the Kingdom of God.* Translated and edited by R. H. Hiers and D. L. Holland. *Die Predigt Jesu vom Reiche Gottes,* Göttingen: Vandenhoeck & Ruprecht, 1892. Reprint, Fortress, Philadelphia, 1971.
Wellhausen, Julius. *Israelitische und jüdische Geschichte.* Berlin: Reimer, 1894.
Wenham, David. *Paul: Follower of Jesus or Founder of Christianity?* Grand Rapids: Eerdmans, 1995.
———. *The Rediscovery of Jesus' Eschatological Discourse.* Gospel Perspectives 4. Sheffield: JSOT, 1984.

———. "The Synoptic Problem Revisited." *Tyndale Bulletin* 23 (1972) 3–38.
Whitman, Jon. "From the Textual to the Temporal: Early Christian 'Allegory' and Early Romantic 'Symbol.'" *New Literary History* 22 (1991) 161–76.
Wilder, Amos N. "Norman Perrin and the Relation of Historical Knowledge to Faith." *Harvard Theological Review* 82 (1989) 201–11.
———. "The Rhetoric of Ancient and Modern Apocalyptic." *Interpretation* 25 (1971) 436–53.
Wills, Lawrence M., and Benjamin G. Wright, eds. *Conflicted Boundaries in Wisdom and Apocalypticism*. SBL Symposium Series 35. Atlanta: SBL, 2005.
Witherington, Ben *The Christology of Jesus*. Minneapolis: Fortress, 1990.
———. *Jesus, Paul and the End of the World: A Comparative Study in New Testament Eschatology*. Downers Grove: InterVarsity, 1992.
Wright, J. Edward. *The Early History of Heaven*. New York: Oxford University Press, 2000.
Wright, N. T. *The Challenge of Jesus: Rediscovering Who Jesus Was and Is*. Downers Grove: InterVarsity, 1999.
———. *The Contemporary Quest for Jesus*. Minneapolis: Fortress, 2002.
———. *Jesus and the Victory of God*. Vol. 2, *Christian Origins and the Question of God*. Minneapolis: Fortress, 1996.
———. "New Introduction." In *The Aims of Jesus*, by Ben F. Meyer, 9a–9l. London: SCM, 1979. Reprint, San Jose, CA: Pickwick, 2002.
———. *The New Testament and the People of God*. Vol. 1, *Christian Origins and the Question of God*. Minneapolis: Fortress, 1992.
———. *What Saint Paul Really Said: Was Paul of Tarsus the Real Founder of Christianity?* Grand Rapids: Eerdmans, 1997.
———. *Who Was Jesus?* Grand Rapids: Eerdmans, 1992.
Xeravits, Géza G. *King, Priest, Prophet: Positive Eschatological Protagonists of the Qumran Library*. Studies on the Texts of the Desert of Judah 47. Leiden: Brill, 2003.

Index of Scripture and Other Jewish Literature

HEBREW BIBLE

Genesis

2	135
6	214, 220, 221
8:22	127
29:30-31	107
42:17	89
49:10	110, 117

Exodus

14:20	164
19:6	98
19:16	89
34:5	164

Leviticus

11:44	98
19:2	98
20:7	98

Numbers

10:34	164

Deuteronomy

7:25-26	163
30:3-4	161, 179

Joshua

2:16	88, 89

Judges

5:5	161

1 Samuel

15:29	111
25:24	112

1 Kings

14:24	163
19	95

2 Kings

20:5, 8	88
23:13	163

1 Chronicles

9:24	179

2 Chronicles

15:8	163
26:11	177

Index of Scripture and Other Jewish Literature

Ezra
1:2-4	94
3:1-6:22	94
10:2-5	94

Job
28:25	179

Psalms
8	113
17:8	177
18:7	161
25:14	98
50:3-5	161
69:34	112
72:7	127
73:25-26	52
81:5	176
96:5	132
96:11	112
102:21	177
102:25-26	127
104	112
104:3	164
109:1	109
110:1	51, 165
114:7	161
146:6	112
148	112
148:2	177

Isaiah
2:2-3	121, 124
4:3-5	93
6:1-13	93
7	155
7:9	93
7:14	72, 156
7:15-17	157
8:1-4	157
4:3-5	92
6:1-13	98
7:14	156
10:20	93
9:1	71
10:20-23	95
11	22, 28, 71
11:1-2	162
11:1-9	121
11:10	91
11:11	179
11:12	91
11:16	179
13	177, 180, 200
13:6-10	174
13:9-11	114, 176
13:10	119, 139, 161, 176-77, 205,
13:13	175
13:14	174
13:19-20	176
19:1	164
22:22	111, 117
24:4	176
24–27	15, 21, 33, 35
26:17	174
27:1	174
27:12	174, 179, 182
28:16	90
32:1	71
34:1-3	114, 176
34:4	139, 161, 174, 176, 198, 205
35:1-2, 5-6	132
35:10	132
37:31	93
40	156
40–55	126
43:6	161
52:15	92
53:4-6, 10-12	92
56–66	21
56:7	121, 124
56:8	91
57:14	93
57:15	93
58:1	93
60:3	91
60:21	93
61:1	82, 94
61:8	93
62:12	93
63:8	93
65:9, 15, 23	93
65:10-22	93
66:8	160

Index of Scripture and Other Jewish Literature

66:22-24	114, 176

Jeremiah

4:23-26	114, 121, 176
7:26	137
16:18	163
23:3	93
23:18-22	98
25:8-11	204
30:5, 7	97
30:8	93
31:10	93
32:37	161

Ezekiel

5:11	163
11:23	88
14:17	88
32:7	161
34:15	93
37:9	179
38–39	21, 34
39:27	179

Daniel

2	22, 28, 29, 135, 136
2:48	100
3:12	100
4:17, 25, 32	121
7	55, 57, 113, 119, 135, 136, 174, 200
7:2	179
7:7-8	35
7:9-27	121
7:13	13, 57, 96, 99, 114, 119, 164, 181
7:13-14	3, 51, 97, 121, 126, 138, 179, 207
7:21	29, 140
7:24	35
7:25	113, 118
7:27	97, 113, 204
8:3-5, 9	35
8:13	160
8:13-14	9
9	62, 135, 136, 184, 189
9:2	14, 101, 184
9:13	29
9:17	173
9:20-27	173, 174
9:21, 22	31
9:24-27	108, 138, 167, 168, 204, 212
9:27	9, 64, 160, 184, 204
9:26-27	29, 64, 108, 138, 182, 207
11:30-32	138
11:31	9, 29, 64, 160, 163
11:40–12:3	4
12:1	97, 160, 187
12:1-4	174
12:2	73
12:7	121
12:11-12	9, 64, 137, 159

Hosea

6:2	89

Joel

2	200
2:1	213
2:1-11	21, 34
2:10	161, 176, 205
2:28-29	162
2:31	161
3–4	21, 34
3:4	205
3:15	161
4:15	205

Amos

3:1	93, 98
3:7	99
3:11, 12	98
8:9	161
9:5	161

Jonah

1:17	89

Micah

1:4	161
2:12	93

Index of Scripture and Other Jewish Literature

Micah (cont.)

3:12	137
4:6	93, 98
7:18, 20	93, 98
5:1-5	72
5:4	121

Nahum

1:5	161

Habakkuk

2:3	213
3:6	161

Zephaniah

2:3	93, 98

Zechariah

1–8	21, 34
2:6	161
2:10	161, 179
1:13-16	35
1:18-21	35
3:11-13	93, 98
8:21-23	121
9	32, 33
9:9-10	121, 124
9:14	182
12–14	174
14	175, 204
14:21	158

Malachi

3:1	204
3:24	100

NEW TESTAMENT

Matthew

1:17	109
2:13	109
3:7-10, 19	119, 123
3:13-17	123
5:3-48	87
5:17, 21-47	131
6:11	96
6:9-13	92
7:5	107
8:11	45, 87, 90
10	74, 79, 186, 192
10:1-16	81
10:5-6	9, 121, 124
10:15	81
10:19	6
10:22	74, 111
10:23	6, 9, 46, 74, 7, 96, 103, 109, 121, 123, 125, 171, 189-95
10:17-25	6, 75, 186, 191
10:32	88
10:34-36	83
10:41-42	47
11:4-6	132
11:5	71, 87, 92, 207
11:10	86
11:12	82
11:13	109
11:19	82
11:20-24	55, 81
11:23	48
11:25	82
12:4, 13	47
12:22	50
12:27	58, 82
12:32	48
12:40	96
12:41-42	81, 91
13:12	48
13:24-30	77, 124, 190
13:44-46	77
14:24, 30	179
15:21-47	131
15:24	91
16	95
16:4	96
16:17-19	87
16:18	82, 91, 93
18:17	82
19:2	59
19:3-9	132
19:28-30	83
21:12-13	129
22:1-14	58

Index of Scripture and Other Jewish Literature

22:44	109	1:24-26	87
23	88	1:27	86
23:37	88, 89, 90, 123	2:16	82
23:9	82	3:13-19	81
23:24	107	3:26	101
23:34-36	88, 97, 207	3:20-27	55
23:37-39	86, 188	3:31-35	132
23:38	153	4	90
24	74, 186, 195	4:10	127
24–25	4	4:30-32	91
24:1-2	86, 172, 173, 210	4:39	87, 179
24:3	109, 134, 186	5:13	87
24:4-5	170	6:4	86
24:6, 8	107	6:1-13	46
24:13	75, 162	6:10	109
24:14-22	6, 187	6:15	85
24:15, 16	6, 163, 169, 186, 191, 193, 205, 212	6:7-11	81
		6:12-16	80
24:15-28	75	6:41	54
24:16-27	74, 75	6:48	179
24:20	6	7:1-28	132
24:21	109, 122, 187	7:6	86
24:22	73	7:17	127
24:14-22,23	6	8:12	96, 111
24:23-28	170, 187, 213	8:31	46, 50, 182
24:29-31	7, 175	8:34-37	107
24:30	75, 187, 195	8:38	3, 165
24:31	110	9:1	10, 51, 96, 109, 121
24:36	103	9:1-5	80
24:37-39	81, 187	9:12	3, 46
24:38-39	44	9:31	50
24:45	100	9:43-47	50
25:15	108	10	21
25:21	100	10:3	80
25:31-46	55, 91	10:17	50
25:40	82	10:23	127
25:31-46	83, 109	10:24	50
26:26-29	83, 109	10:25	107
26:41	92	10:29	82
26:61	90	10:31	50
27:40	90	10:33	46
28:19-20	194	10:37	106
		10:39	86
Mark		10:45	74, 84
1:1	138, 169	11	142
1:2, 3	3, 86	11:17	121, 124, 128
1:2-11	9	11:18	90
1:9-11	123	11:15-19	9, 121, 123, 129, 175

Index of Scripture and Other Jewish Literature

Mark (cont.)

12:9	175
12:10-11	3
12:16	97
12:18-27	55
12:25	50
12:36	109
13	2, 4, 6-9, 13, 14, 16, 21, 24, 40-41, 54, 57, 59, 60, 64, 71, 76, 78, 89, 99, 101, 104, 106, 107, 110, 111, 114-117, 125, 127, 130, 137, 139, 146, 157-58, 162-63, 172-73, 205-06
13:1-2	9, 14, 121, 123, 124, 134, 137, 138, 171, 180, 182, 186, 199, 210
13:1-7	157
13:2	5, 9, 12, 13, 43, 49, 51, 60, 63, 82, 86, 101, 104, 118, 120, 142, 182
13:3	182
13:4	109, 134, 139
13:3-13	53
13:5-6	170
13:5-13	134
13:7-8	108, 159, 162, 168, 185
13:9-13	75, 161, 191, 197, 211
13:10	3
13:13	159
13:14	62, 108, 153, 159, 167-69, 182, 184-86, 193, 205, 212
13:14-20	6, 60, 82, 100, 133, 134, 180, 187
13:16	75, 214
13:19	109, 122, 160, 162, 187
13:20	168, 180
13:21-23	170, 213
13:23-27	101
13:24	9, 91, 160, 182
13:25	9, 91, 114, 118, 161
13:26	3, 76, 77, 90, 91, 110, 114, 118, 119, 127, 164, 165, 179, 187, 196, 197
13:27	10, 109, 124, 160, 190, 197
13:24-27	3, 5, 7, 11-14, 54, 56, 61, 63, 77, 78, 82, 84, 102, 109, 115, 116, 119-22, 124-26, 129, 134, 137, 139, 142-44, 160, 168, 171, 172, 175-83, 190, 191, 196-200, 203
13:25-28	49, 51
13:29	9
13:30	96
13:32	3, 5, 59, 60, 61, 76, 77, 91, 97, 103
13:33	115, 125
14	57, 77, 99, 101
14:9	3
14:21-25	3, 83
14:25	10, 45, 83, 109
14:26	207
14:28	50
14:38	92
14:49, 14:53-65	3, 50, 86, 187
14:58	84, 88, 90-93, 96, 175
14:62	3, 54, 77, 142, 165
14:65	86
15:29	90, 93, 96, 175

Luke

1-19	187
1-24	155
1:1-4	61
1:9-11	196
1:68, 78-79	194
2:28-32	194
2:40	61
3:21-22	123
3:7-9	121, 123
4:9-13	92, 188
4:18-19	82
4:22	92, 207
6:12-16	81
7:16	194
7:22-23	86, 132
7:31	121
7:34	51
7:39	86
8:13	92
9:1-5	51, 81
10:3,12,13-15	81
10:18	55, 86
10:25-37	92
11:2-4	92
11:19	82
11:20	50, 58
11:30	51

Index of Scripture and Other Jewish Literature

11:31-32	81
11:49-57	88, 97, 207
12:8-9, 40	51
12:10	51
12:49-53	55, 83
13:3	90
13:28	45
13:32	96
13:33-35	86, 123, 187, 188
14:26	107
15:1	82
15:11-32	140
17	7, 188, 189
17:11-19	92
17:20-21	2, 73, 78, 91
17:22-37	53, 81, 87, 126, 221
17:23-24	161, 187, 213, 215, 221
17:26	48, 51, 214
17:26-30	44, 187, 218, 220
17:30-31	51, 121, 122, 125, 214
17:35	215
17:37	198
18:7-8	121, 122
19:1-10	83
19:5	82
19:44	188, 194
19:45-46	129
19:47	90
20:43	109
21	188, 192
21:5-6, 7	86, 172, 186, 210
21:9	108
21:12-19	75, 186, 191, 211, 217
21:20	169, 186-88, 191, 205, 212
21:20-24	6, 9, 121, 123, 187
21:24	153, 182, 212
21:25-28	7, 174, 187, 188, 200
22:15-20	83, 84
22:28	92
22:28-30	83
22:30	59
22:40, 46	92
22:54-71	187
23:30	153
23:27-32	93, 97, 123
23:43	151
26:26-27	81

John

1:1-2	61
1:11	188
1:29-34	123
2	95
2:13-17	129
2:19	88, 91, 93, 141, 199
3:18	151
4	76
14:17	62
14:21-22	121
14:26	62, 75
15:21	75
16:2	75
16:12	61

Acts

1:1-9	162, 164, 165
1:6-11	179, 196
1:8	61, 95
1:9	164, 196
1:22	109
1:29-34	122
2-5, 7-13	155
2:14-36	70
2:19-20	196
2:36	73
3:19-21	95, 121, 124, 155, 165, 196
4:24-25	192
6:14	175
10:42	165
11:18	121
15:11, 40	111
15:14	194
15:16	197
16:2, 5	111
17:31	165
24:15	52

Romans

1:3-4	73
1:5, 8	162
5:12-21	152
6:10	151
8:1	197
8:16-17	151

Index of Scripture and Other Jewish Literature

Romans (cont).

8:34	70
9–11	94, 95
10:18	162
11:1, 5	95
11:25-32	95
15:18-24	162
16:8	95

1 Corinthians

1:8	146
2:6-8	113, 197
3	71
5:5	53
7	70
12–14	36
3:16, 6:19	36
11:22-25	69, 83
15	85
15:3-5	70
15:20-28, 45-9	152, 165
15:52	197
16:22	146

2 Corinthians

4:4	197
5:6-8	52
5:16	70, 71

Galatians

1:4, 12, 15	197
3:25	197
4:3-10	197
5:1, 16-22	197
6:16	95

Ephesians

2:15	145
5:8-14	4

Philippians

1:23	53
2:5-8	61
2:6-11	70
3:20	146

Colossians

1:5-6, 23	162
1:16	111, 113

1 Thessalonians

	184
1:10	116, 146
4	21
4:14	179
4:16	197
5:1-9	146, 197
5:2-8	4

2 Thessalonians

1:6-10	197
2	21
2:1-3	116, 122

Titus

2:13	146

Hebrews

1:2-8	201
1:4	111
2:7	100
9:12	151
12:23	53
12:26-29	201

James

	201
5:9	197

1 Peter

1:3-9	197
1:13	146
3:18	53
3:22	197
4:6	53
4:12-19	197
5:10-11	197

Index of Scripture and Other Jewish Literature

2 Peter

1:16	198
2:9	146
3	198
3:7-12	146

1 John

1:15	107
2:18	170

2 John

1:7	170

Jude

14-15	197, 198

Revelation

	22, 54, 200
1:1	8, 173
1:7	146
1-5	25
1:9	160
2:7, 11, 17, 26	162
3:5, 12, 21	162
3:7	111
6:9-11	53
6:10	53
6:12, 13, 14	177, 198
6:17	146
7:14	160
8:7, 12	198
9:1	198
13:1	35
16:14	146
17:12-13	35
19:11	198
19–22	165
21:1	198
21:7	162
22:12, 20	146

OTHER JEWISH LITERATURE

Apocrypha

Song of the Three Young

29-68	112

Epistle of Jeremiah

1:6	110

1 Maccabees

1:54	160
1:54-64	64
2	140
2:42	98
3:42	177
3:52	140
4:13	183
7:2	177
7:12-14	98

2 Maccabees

6:2	160

Sirach

16:18	177
24:3-4	112
43:1-33	112
43:26	110
48:10	100
48:19	177

Tobit

5:4	110
14:10	161
12:22	110

Wisdom of Solomon

3:7	137

Apocalypse of Abraham

19, 20	140
27	137

Index of Scripture and Other Jewish Literature

Assumption of Moses
9:6	19

2 Baruch
	15, 20, 140
	137
1-8	137
25:4	12
35-40	135

4 Baruch
1-4	137

1 Enoch
	2, 20, 26, 39 139, 207
1–36	221
1:1	180
1:1-2	174, 178
1:9	198
4:10	177
5:2-3	178
5:7-8	173
14:8-16:3	179
17–19	178
18:2-3	179
37–71	139
40:1	37
40:9	177
47:3	100
53:2	100
57:2	161
62:13-14	161
65:6	178
76:1-12	179
81:1	100
82:7-8	178
83:3-10, 84:5	12
86–87	178
89:20	178
90:13-17	206
91:6	173, 207
91:7-8	206
91:16	178
92:19	178
93:4, 9	207
94:5, 11	206
96:1-3	173
102:1-3	174, 178, 206
103:14-15	174
108	206

2 Enoch (Slav.)
	20, 55
39:2	36
65.5	36

3 Enoch
	21

4 Ezra
	32, 111, 140
4:33, 37	96
11-12	135
13:3	118

Jubilees
	20, 26, 100, 140
1:29	178
3:2	99
3:10	100
23:11-25	207
23:22-25	139, 206, 207
49:2	178

Martyrdom and Ascension of Isaiah
	20
2:2	178

Psalms of Solomon
2:1	173, 206
5:5-7	206
8:1	183
8:28	161, 197
11:1-4	161
17:21-23	206
17:26, 28	161, 197

Index of Scripture and Other Jewish Literature

Sibling Oracles
3:265-81 — 137
4:115-8 — 137

Testament of Twelve Patriarchs
— 19, 26

Testament of Asher
2:10 — 100
7:2 — 100

Testament of Levi
5:5 — 100
14:4 — 19
19:1 — 19

Testament of Reuben
3:11 — 37

Testament of Moses
4:2 — 179
10:1-5 — 160

10:1-10 — 137, 161
12:12-13 — 179

Qumran

4Qp (pesharim on Psalms)
Psalm 37 — 82

Josephus

Jewish Antiquities
8:80 — 179
10:276 — 168
12:321-24 — 168
12:322 — 130, 136
18:37 — 10
18:257-60 — 168
18:261-88 — 168

Jewish War
6:248-274 — 161
6:271-309 — 188
6:288-90 — 188
6:290-296 — 136
6:310 — 136
6:312-15 — 130, 136, 137

www.ingramcontent.com/pod-product-compliance
Lightning Source LLC
Chambersburg PA
CBHW050437240426
43661CB00055B/2411